Andy and Don

Center Point
Large Print

Also by Daniel de Visé and available from
Center Point Large Print:

I Forgot to Remember
(with Su Meck)

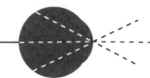

**This Large Print Book carries the
Seal of Approval of N.A.V.H.**

Andy and Don

THE MAKING OF A FRIENDSHIP AND A CLASSIC AMERICAN TV SHOW

Daniel de Visé

CENTER POINT LARGE PRINT
THORNDIKE, MAINE

This Center Point Large Print edition is published in the year 2015 by arrangement with Simon & Schuster, Inc.

The text of this Large Print edition is unabridged. In other aspects, this book may vary from the original edition. Printed in the United States of America on permanent paper. Set in 16-point Times New Roman type.

ISBN: 978-1-62899-789-7

Library of Congress Cataloging-in-Publication Data

De Visé, Daniel.
Andy and Don : the making of a friendship and a classic American TV show / Daniel de Visé. —
 Center Point Large Print edition.
pages cm
ISBN 978-1-62899-789-7 (hardcover : alk. paper)
1. Andy Griffith show (Television program)
 2. Griffith, Andy, 1926–2012. 3. Knotts, Don, 1924–2006.
 4. Actors—United States—Biography. 5. Large type books. I. Title.
PN1992.77.A573D43 2015b
791.45′72—dc23
                                                        2015032950

To Sophie, Madeleine, and Donovan,
my beautiful family.

Contents

Introduction

Andy Taylor and Barney Fife could make the world stand still. Stretching out on the front porch of Andy's Mayberry home, Andy and Barney would reel off hypnotic meditations on the mundanities of life. Their conversations defied the frenetic pulse of their medium, network television. For millions of viewers, *The Andy Griffith Show* was a sanctuary in a nervous world, with two friends at its center, reclining on a porch.

"Ya know what I think I'm gonna do?" Barney tells Andy in one moment of Mayberry Zen, as Andy strums a guitar. "I'm gonna go home, have me a little nap, then go over to Thelma Lou's and watch a little TV." Several seconds pass in silence. "Yeah, I believe that's what I'll do: go home, have a nap, head over to Thelma Lou's for TV." More silence. "Yep, that's the plan: ride home, a little nap . . ."

The Andy Griffith Show endures like no other artifact of television's golden era. In the fifty-five years since its October 1960 debut, *Andy Griffith* has never left the airwaves. At the dawn of 2015, *Griffith* episodes air several times a day, watched by a fan club with more than one thousand chapters and celebrated in an annual festival that draws thirty thousand fans to a real-life Mayberry. To fully appreciate this program's staying power, even by comparison to other television classics, try to find a *Honeymooners* convention.

The *Griffith Show* tapped the talents of its era's finest television producers, writers, and directors —along with an unparalleled ensemble of actors, a cast that included not only Don and Andy but also future Hollywood powerbroker Ron Howard and the multitalented Jim Nabors. But the program's undeniable quality does not fully explain its longevity.

There is something iconic, something quintessentially American, about *The Andy Griffith Show.* The program appeared at a moment of dramatic flux in American society. People were leaving farms for factories and towns for cities. The civil rights movement was waxing, and antiwar protests were brewing. It was a time of assassinations, electrified music, and slackening standards on sex and drugs. Yet, the *Griffith Show* refused to embrace those changes, or even to acknowledge them. Instead, the program trained its gaze backward, revisiting and reviving the rural Americana of the 1930s, the time of Andy's childhood in North Carolina and Don's in West Virginia. The *Griffith Show* helped viewers recall a simpler time, helped them reconnect with their own past, at a moment when Americans desperately needed the reminder. As Technicolor chaos swirled around them, millions of viewers embraced the black-and-white tranquility of the *Griffith Show* and held on tight.

The *Griffith Show* would showcase television's most tender friendship: "Ange," affable sheriff of the rural hamlet called Mayberry, and "Barn," his jumpy deputy. Andy was a gentle parody of a country lawman, fighting crime in a town that had none, protecting a citizenry that was palpably safe. Barney was a parody of Andy, bug-eyed, childlike, and diminutive. Andy protected Barney from the outside world, holding its bitter realities at bay, just as he protected Mayberry itself, its denizens and its homespun traditions.

Sheriff Taylor's fatherly bond with Deputy Fife emanated from real life; it was the foundation of their friendship. Their personalities meshed. Andy was dominant; Don was submissive. Andy was big and loud, ribald and wild, quite the opposite of the sage sheriff. Don was gaunt and quiet, restrained and reserved, a sharp contrast to the manic deputy. They shared a past. Both had known stark poverty: Andy's first bed was a bureau drawer, Don's a cot in the kitchen. They grew up on the same diet of radio—Jack Benny, Edgar Bergen, *The Lone Ranger*—and amid cinema's golden age. Both men embraced entertainment as an identity as they approached manhood. Both rode their talents as far as their local arts scene would take them. Both men came to New York and bombed, retreated to the South, then returned to take Manhattan by sheer force of talent and will.

Above all, Andy and Don shared a transcendent sense of whimsy, a particular way of looking at the world. The same Southern peccadilloes cracked them up: Old men ruminating for hours about buying a bottle of pop. Daddy asking the tailor to throw in an extra pair of socks with that new suit. An uncle slapping a "five spot" into your palm with great fanfare. Old ladies fussing about the pickle contest at the county fair. Families dressing up to dine at the *Eye-talian* restaurant with the fancy checkered tablecloths.

Like any friendship worthy of study, theirs was complicated. Andy sacrificed his own comedic talent to play Don's straight man. This selfless act would reap enormous profits for Andy as half owner of the *Griffith Show*. Don, by contrast, left *Griffith* after five years with far less money in his pocket and little financial stake in its future.

Both men recognized the strength of their pairing. Neither would reach the same comedic heights alone. Yet, Andy refused Don's offer of partnership beyond the *Griffith Show*. Andy wanted to stand on his own feet. Years later, when Andy finally found success again with the courtroom drama *Matlock* and his ego recovered, he finally, magnanimously, offered a part to Don, who was himself struggling for work, and the partnership was briefly rekindled.

Neither man's story can be told alone. Andy was a master entertainer and an occasionally brilliant dramatic actor. Don was a comedic great, his oeuvre a sort of missing link between the celebrated eras of Jerry Lewis and Woody Allen. Yet, like all the best comedy teams, Andy and Don were better together than apart. Their best work invokes Abbott and Costello, Laurel and Hardy. Every time they sat down to write, the results were timeless.

Prologue: The Call

Don Knotts and his wife, Kay, spent the evening of February 15, 1960, playing bridge in the beige-carpeted living room of Pat and Marjorie Harrington. The Harringtons lived in a rented Spanish colonial on Le Conte Avenue in Westwood, not far from the historic Fox Theater and UCLA. The room was large but sparsely furnished: a baby-grand piano, butterfly chairs, and a coffee table, around which the two couples sat. Pat was a young actor, yet to hit his peak as the mustachioed handyman Schneider in the urban sitcom *One Day at a Time*. He and Don had struck up a casual friendship on the set of *The Steve Allen Show*, an irreverent sketch-comedy affair that had just migrated from New York to Hollywood. The cast had moved west with the show, and the shared journey had fortified the friendship between Don and Pat. This night was bridge night; Don took his bridge seriously.

Steve Allen would air at ten o'clock; yet, that Monday evening was a night off for Don and Pat, whose show had passed from live broadcast to prerecorded tape with the move west. The gathering was bittersweet: *Steve Allen* had just been canceled, a victim of diminished energy and dwindling ambitions, maladies Don attributed to the retreat from live broadcast. Both Don and Pat would soon be out of work. But Pat, at least, had a prospective gig on the horizon: a guest spot on *The Danny Thomas Show*, a CBS ratings powerhouse that aired an hour before *Steve Allen*. At nine o'clock, Pat paused the bridge game so he could watch that night's episode. He switched on the set. As the dot of light swelled to life on the screen, Don beheld the face of an old friend.

The program opened with a hand-drawn sketch of Andy Griffith, a young actor from North Carolina with wild eyes and tousled hair, known chiefly for his jubilant portrayal of farm boy Will Stockdale in the Southern military farce *No Time for Sergeants*, first on Broadway and then in the movies. The drawing shortly gave way to a shot of Andy sitting in a Ford Galaxie 500 squad car, escorting Danny Thomas and his family through a town called Mayberry. Andy was its sheriff.

"You picked on the wrong guy this time, Clem," Danny bristled.

"Name ain't Clem," Andy replied, his face cleaving into a broad grin. "It's Andy. Andy Taylor." On that cue, the audience erupted in polite applause.

Andy and Don had lost touch since forging a powerful bond in the Broadway cast of *No Time for Sergeants*, half a decade earlier. Now, they were three thousand miles apart—Don in Hollywood, Andy in New York—and they had allowed their correspondence to fall off. Andy was unaware *Steve Allen* had been canceled. Don had no inkling Andy was working on a television show.

As Don beheld Andy on Pat Harrington's television set, "the wheels in my brain began to whirl," Don recalled. The part of Sheriff Andy Taylor seemed perfect for Andy. A show like that would be honey to the sponsors, with all its homespun charm. And Don wondered if there might be a place for him in Mayberry. A part on Andy's new show just might rekindle Don's career—and revive his old friendship with Andy. Don had always hoped he and Andy might work together again someday.

Don told no one at the bridge table of his plans: He wasn't about to give Pat Harrington a jump on his part. He waited till the next day. Then, he placed a call to New York, where Andy was headlining a halfhearted Broadway musical titled *Destry Rides Again*. Andy was surprised and delighted to receive Don's call. Don told Andy how much he'd enjoyed the pilot. Then he asked, "Listen, don't you think Sheriff Andy Taylor ought to have a deputy?"

1.

Don's Demons

Don's journey to Hollywood began on a broken-down farm outside Morgantown, West Virginia. William Jesse Knotts, Don's father, a man of average build and sky-blue eyes, made a living buying derelict farms, fixing them up, and selling them again. By the close of the 1910s, Jesse and his wife, Elsie, had settled on one farm long enough for Elsie to bear three children, all boys. Jesse raised crops and mined some coal he had found on the land. Theirs was not a prosperous life, but at least it was stable.

One day, probably in 1919, Jesse collapsed in the fields. He was borne home by other men. "I can't see," he cried, although it seemed to others that he could. They called it hysterical blindness. Jesse lay in bed, sightless, for two weeks. His vision returned in time, but his mind did not. Jesse Knotts was said to have suffered a nervous breakdown, though more likely he was an undiagnosed schizophrenic. His physical health, too, fell into rapid decline, and soon he could no longer mind the family farm. Elsie, his wife, was left to tend the family fortunes.

When Elsie lost the farm, she moved the family

into town to occupy a succession of rental homes, sometimes sharing the space with various Knotts kin; Jesse's incapacity had brought the Depression to the Knotts household a decade early.

Into this arrangement Jesse Donald Knotts was born on July 21, 1924. His first home seems to have been a boxy American Foursquare on Jefferson Street in Westover, just across the Monongahela River from central Morgantown. By 1929, the family had crossed the river and settled into a permanent dwelling: a large house on University Avenue, which Elsie rented from the Galusha family, owners of a corner grocery store. Elsie confined her family to the main floor; the upper rooms she rented to students, itinerants, and anyone else who could put a dollar down.

Don was fourteen years younger than his next youngest sibling, William Earl, a boy so slender he was called Shadow. Don was an accident. Elsie, thirty-nine and married to a forty-two-year-old invalid, had not planned to bring another child into the world.

Don's childhood was bleak, even by the sepia-toned standards of the Depression. The house on University Avenue sat in a crowded row of unkempt wooden colonials set against a steep hill. He slept on a cot in the kitchen, next to the stove. Two of his older brothers, Shadow and Sid, shared a bedroom with a boarder. Willis Vincent "Bill" Knotts, the most ambitious sibling, had already decamped to seek his fortune as a manager at Montgomery Ward. Don's mother and father slept in the living room, and Jesse Sr. spent most of his waking hours on the sofa, staring into space. Don's brothers liked to drink and fight; there was little to distinguish them from the vagabonds who paraded in and out of the University Avenue home.

Don emerged from infancy with a ghostly pallor, a skeletal frame, and a predisposition to illness, traits he shared with his older brother Shadow. "I did not come into the world with a great deal of promise," Don recalled. "By the time I started grammar school, I was already stoop-shouldered, painfully thin, and forever throwing up due to a nervous stomach."

Three decades later, Elsie Knotts would ask Don, "Do you remember when you were in nappies, and your father used to hold a knife to your throat?" Don did not. Only in therapy did the memories come flooding back. Don spent his first years living in fear of the monster on the couch. Jesse Knotts harbored a primal jealousy toward Don, the unexpected baby who drew Elsie's attention away from her bedridden husband. From the day Don arrived, he competed with his father for his mother's care.

The only path out of Don's kitchen bedroom led through the living room, where his father lay. Don would try to tiptoe by. Sometimes he would pass unnoticed. Other times, the father would emerge from his fever dreams and train his bloodshot eyes on his youngest son. Don would freeze as he heard the ragged growl of an unpracticed voice: "Come here, you little son of a bitch." Don would slowly retreat from the room. Usually, the summons was an empty threat. But on occasion, Jesse would rise from the couch like a shambling ghoul and stagger into the kitchen to find a blade. Then he would stumble through the house in search of his son; the hunt wouldn't take long, as there was nowhere for Don to go. Jesse would pin Don against the wall, raise the knife to his throat, and terrorize the child with dark oaths: "I'll kill you, you son of a bitch."

Jesse terrorized the rest of his family, as well. He was twice confined in the state mental hospital in Weston after threatening Elsie with a butcher knife. Those stays bought Don moments of relative peace in the family home.

Over years of shrewd observation, Don learned to divine his father's moods, to read his face and voice. In this effort, Don developed a preternatural power to interpret body language and vocal tics. Perhaps Don's hypervigilance was a source of his comedic gifts: What was the Nervous Man, after all, if not an ensemble of twitches and quirks?

Repulsed by his father, Don was drawn to his mother. Elsie Knotts was the angel to Jesse's foul-breathed demon, the sunlight to his darkness. Elsie was "one of the truly good people of the world," Don recalled, "more comfortable with the downtrodden than the high and mighty. Elsie found time to help any soul who needed her."

Elsie was raised a born-again Christian. But as an adult, she hewed to her own code of right and wrong. She was, in a sense, the real-life Aunt Bee. Ever mindful of people's feelings, Elsie couldn't bear the thought of walking home from the A&P past the window of the Galushas' grocery store, lest the Galusha brothers should see her carrying groceries from another market. Instead, she and Don would detour around the block to the back of their house. Elsie also thought it improper for a Knotts boy to walk through the front door of the city jail. When Don's older brother Shadow was locked up on a drunk-and-disorderly charge, she packed a box of sandwiches and tobacco and instructed an Opie-aged Don, "I don't want you going into that jail. I want you to go around to the back and yell up to the window there and get him to come to the window and throw this up to him."

Though she embraced fundamentalist Christianity, Elsie also loved to play cards, and she collected autographs from the stars of screen and stage. "My mother took me to movies from the very beginning," Don recalled. He and his mother probably saw *Steamboat Willie*, the first Disney film with synchronized sound, and

Broadway Melody, the first talking musical, at Morgantown's Metropolitan Theatre. But nothing impressed Don quite like Stan Laurel and Oliver Hardy, the nation's premier comedy duo. Don was transfixed by their choreographed slapstick, just as he was mesmerized by Jack Benny's uncanny comic timing on the radio. Don loved the way those men could make his mother laugh. He dreamed that Elsie might ask for his own autograph one day.

Elsie Knotts had a lovely, infectious, musical laugh, and everyone in the Knotts home wanted to hear it. Laughter brought escape from the pall that threatened to envelop them all. From an early age, Don set about finding the skills to summon that beautiful laugh. His principal instructor was his sickly brother.

Shadow Knotts, born in 1910, had been the baby of the family for more than a decade when Don arrived; thereafter, it seemed as if Elsie Knotts had two youngest children, as their personalities developed along strikingly similar lines. Shadow suffered from asthma so severe that he slept sitting up. Yet, he filled the Knotts home with irrepressible wit. Don would follow Shadow around the house like a pint-size Ed McMahon, encouraging his cracks with peals of delighted laughter. Long before Don's birth, Shadow had fallen into the role of family jester. He was about ten when his father's mind broke, and he discovered, long before Don, that laughter could deliver his family from the darkness of dementia and poverty. Don once recounted the typical scene at the Knotts dinner table, where Shadow would labor to repel the chill that rose from his father, stony and silent at the head of the table.

"The clowning would begin with Shadow buttering his bread as if it were a violin, tucking it under his chin and using the butter knife for a bow," Don recalled, "and it might continue with Shadow commenting to Sid under his breath, but loud enough for all to hear, that poor Tom Helfrick"—a beloved boarder who joined the family at the table—"had helped himself to two helpings of meat already. Sometimes the dinner hour would become complete mayhem, and I would laugh so hard I would have to leave the table, and the tears would run down the cheeks of my dear mother."

Shadow seemed a natural comedian. He would walk past the university clock tower, look up to the man cleaning its face, and yell, "Hey, buddy, you wouldn't happen to have the time?" Once, while Elsie Knotts hosted a bridge party, Shadow walked into the bathroom, left the door ajar, and emptied an entire bucket of water into the toilet in a slow dribble, creating the impression of a ceaseless flow of urine. By the time he was done, the ladies at the bridge table were ashen.

Shadow's humor endured even when he was

bedridden, which was often. During one such spell, Don asked him what was wrong; Shadow replied, "Everything I eat goes to my stomach."

Whenever Shadow opened the door to leave the house, Don would beg him to stay. Once Shadow was gone, the family home would sink into despair. Don would escape the gloom "by filling my space with imaginary characters with whom I would act out some happy drama. This was my first stage and, I suspect, the beginning of my acting career."

Don's other brothers were a mixed bag. Bill, seventeen years older, was off working for Montgomery Ward by the time Don entered adolescence, moving from place to place with the retail chain. By the standards of the Knotts clan, Bill was a staggering success. He would send money home to help keep the family afloat, supplementing his mother's meager income from renting rooms and sewing and cooking for students. Nonetheless, Elsie Knotts was compelled to sell her beloved upright piano one month to pay the rent.

Ralph "Sid" Knotts, the eldest brother, was another story. By the time of Don's birth, eighteen-year-old Sid had already run away from home, married, and fathered a child, who was discreetly dispatched to a grandmother on a family farm upon Sid's return. "Sid was a real hick," recalled Richie Ferrara, Don's childhood friend. "Sid was the decadence of West Virginia. He was a coal miner and he was an alcoholic, and he'd go out and get drunk and come back and get mean. He'd get mean to Don. Sometimes he would attack him, abuse him, hit him."

Between odd jobs, Sid brewed moonshine to survive. Don wondered, later, whether drink had damaged Sid's brain. Sober, he was a gentle soul, joining brother Shadow in high jinks at the dinner table. Drunk, he was a bully. Once, Don stumbled upon Sid in the house, drinking home brew with friends. Don thought of their mother and scolded Sid, "You can't be down here like that." Sid raised the bottle and emptied it over Don's head. "Now I'm gonna tell Mama you've been drinking," he slurred.

Sid would crash into the house after a midnight binge, singing, "Is it true what they say about Sidney?" to the tune of "Is It True What They Say about Dixie?" Then he would storm into the kitchen to clatter around and fry eggs, waking Don on his cot. When Don would protest, Sid would slap him across the face, saying, "Ha ha, get back down, you little brat."

Between her sons' escapades and those of her boarders, Elsie Knotts spent countless hours policing propriety in her home. "I think my mother spent half her time chasing girls out of the rooms she rented to male students," Don recalled, "to say nothing of my brothers' tarts. More than once as a youngster did I see a half-naked woman dive out a bedroom window, and my mother charging through the front door, broom in hand, in an effort to head her off at the pass."

The Depression brought hobos, as well, and a steady parade passed through the Knotts home. Some would try to jump the rent by lowering their suitcases from the window. But some of the male boarders would show a paternal interest in Don, who was essentially fatherless, taking him aside and teaching him small amusements. An itinerant guitarist showed Don how to play the ukulele. A carnival barker revealed how he fleeced his customers.

Don spent many hours in his uncle's barbershop, a welcome escape from the perils of home. Uncle Lawrence, in some ways an antecedent to Mayberry's Floyd, would keep the customers laughing for hours with jokes and tall tales while Don sat and soaked it up. Lawrence would cut Don's hair for free, but only after the last paying customer had left.

Don feared Sunday church just as he feared his father's daily schizophrenic ravings at home. Church was a weekly spectacle of fire and brimstone; overwrought parishioners would work themselves into a froth of faith, speak in tongues, fall to their knees, and roll in the aisles, sweating and twitching and weeping. Don would watch the congregation shake and shudder and babble, plainly enraptured by the Lord, and he would sit and wait for the wave of divinity to wash over him, and it never did. He feared he was doomed to hell.

Finally, Don brought his fears to his mother. Elsie took him to see the preacher.

"It's all right, son," the preacher said.

"But—I'm not feeling that thing that everyone's feeling," Don said.

"Don't worry, son. You're saved."

Jesse Knotts, Don's menacing father, died of pneumonia in spring 1937, at fifty-five. The family mourned; yet, after a time, it seemed to Don as if a bitter chill had lifted from the University Avenue house. His demon father exorcised, twelve-year-old Don began to come into his own, embarking upon that path of socialization and self-promotion that renders someone visible who has previously been invisible.

With Shadow often too sick to jest, bit by bit the role of court jester in the Knotts household passed from him to Don. His first performances reprised scenes from Laurel and Hardy films or Abbott and Costello routines from the Kate Smith radio show. Don would play them for his mother while she baked bread. She would laugh in all the right places and offer rich dollops of praise when he was done. She was his first fan. Years later, when an interviewer asked why a scrawny kid such as him thought he could make it in New York, Don replied, "Because my mother said I could."

It occurred to Don that magic might be his way into show business. Whenever he could gather ten cents, he would send away for a magic trick from Johnson Smith & Company, a mail-order house that advertised on the backs of comic books. He would approach his brothers at the card table with his new tricks, only to be shooed away when Shadow would crack, "How about doing that disappearing trick?"

Around the start of junior high school, Don glimpsed a Johnson Smith ad that beckoned, "Send ten cents and get your Ventrilo." Don was thrilled: He never missed Edgar Bergen's radio show. Sadly, Don opened the Ventrilo package to find a glorified birdcall. But it came with a book explaining the art of throwing one's voice. By happy coincidence, a neighborhood grocer was selling a miniature Charlie McCarthy dummy on a promotion for a somewhat richer sum—fifty cents and three proof-of-purchase seals from Cocomalt drink mix. Once Don had amassed the necessary coin and Cocomalt, he rushed out in a rainstorm to buy the dummy. When Don returned home, Shadow leaped up and ran toward Don excitedly, hands outstretched. "But when he got to me, instead of grabbing the dummy, he grabbed [my] umbrella, sat down, put the umbrella on his knee, and asked it, 'Who was that lady I saw you out with last night?' "

Don practiced and practiced until he could voice the dummy without moving his lips. He went out on the front porch and tried his act on passersby. It worked, and one woman protested, "Have you got a recording in that dummy?" He wrote some material, borrowing heavily from the Bergen-McCarthy act. One day, a neighbor asked him to perform at his party. They passed the hat, and Don returned home with nearly a dollar in change. "I was in show business at last," he recalled. Word spread, and soon Don was performing at other parties. A local handyman crafted Don a professional-quality dummy in his workshop. Elsie sewed him a tiny outfit. Don named him Danny.

Don's professional world was about to expand. One day in the seventh grade, Don found himself in gym class, standing on a wrestling mat opposite a much larger boy. "We were supposed to wrestle each other," Richie Ferrara recalled. "I must've weighed fifty pounds more than him. We looked like Laurel and Hardy. And we laughed at each other. And we walked off and we had a Coke together."

Richie, the son of Italian immigrants (his mother called Don "Donuts"), was bright, effervescent, and talented. He played the violin, the piano, and the banjo. He hosted a live revue at lunchtime every Friday in the school auditorium. At Don's request, Richie put him onstage with Danny. They were a hit, and soon the two boys were talking of a partnership. Don admired Richie for his extroversion. Richie respected Don for his talent and wit. "We blended together," Richie recalled.

Don invited Richie to his home to write material. They would test their ideas on Elsie in the kitchen. "She would sit in her rocking chair and smile," Richie recalled. "When she laughed and approved of it, then we'd go out and have confidence."

Richie often stayed for dinner. "They had a little bit of this, a little bit of that, a cupful of mashed potatoes, a cupful of apple sauce. . . . And then after we'd eat, Don would entertain me. Don used me as an audience. And I would listen to all of his skits, all of his jokes. I love to tell jokes, too, but I don't know of one joke that's good that didn't come from him."

Adolescence brought Don both strength and confidence. One night, probably around his fourteenth year, drunken Sid crashed into the kitchen and commenced slapping Don around. Don picked up a wine bottle, smashed it, and held the jagged edge to Sid's throat. Elsie burst in and separated the brothers, begging Don to stand down. Later, she asked Don, "You weren't really gonna do it, were you?" Yes, Don replied. He was.

To the end of his days, Don would recoil at that memory, and he seldom spoke of Sid. Yet, the moment Don rose up against his brother marked a sort of turning point. Don had been a victim, prey to the demons in his home. Now, he would fight back.

Don entered Morgantown High School as a conquering hero. He had vanquished his fears, and he was bursting with creative energy. The next four years would be "the happiest and most fertile of my life," he recalled, second only to his time on *The Andy Griffith Show*.

This may have been Don's first onstage joke, told at a Morgantown High School assembly when he was fifteen, poking fun at Morgantown's two great passions, church and drink:

"If I had all the whiskey in this town, I would throw it in the river. If I had all the whiskey in this state, I would throw it in the river. If I had all the whiskey in this country, I would throw it in the river. And now, will the congregation please stand and sing 'Shall We Gather at the River?' "

One night, at a roller rink, Don met Jarvis Eldred, a dashing boy from a prominent family who had access to his mother's '29 DeSoto. Don quickly became besotted with Jarvie, who was not only wealthier but smoother with the ladies. "His father employed many of the people in town," Richie recalled. "And he had a car. He was a spoiled kid." Jarvie was musical, as well. Now, he and Don formed their own duo, with Jarvie on the musical saw. "He'd do 'Ave Maria' on the saw, and I'd get a few laughs with Danny, and then we'd harmonize a couple of numbers and do a little soft-shoe," Don recalled.

Richie, who was a year behind, joined the group when he reached high school, singing and playing mandolin. "We called ourselves the Radio Three," Richie recalled. "We started to be popular, and we were hired for a few bucks to play the churches, social events. But we [also] did a lot of stuff for charity, like the Rotary, and we became really known."

Don, the businessman of the group, saw to it that the Radio Three charged for their entertainment, aside from the charity gigs. "We always had some pocket change for fun and dates," Richie recalled, "which usually consisted of a movie or singing or dancing, a Coke, a hot dog, and sometimes the old West Virginia 3.2 beer."

Don took a job as an usher at the art deco Warner Theater on High Street downtown. He sometimes became entranced by the movie while patrons stumbled around for seats. One day in fall 1941, while Don was tearing tickets, his brother Sid entered the lobby and walked up to him, clearly inebriated.

"What's wrong?" Don asked.

"You'd better change your clothes and come

home with me," Sid said. "It's Shadow. Shadow's dead."

Poor, sickly Shadow had perished in his sleep while visiting Bill, his brother, at his home in Illinois. The cause was an unchecked asthma attack. Shadow's death, at thirty-one, was a blow from which Elsie Knotts never fully recovered. "He never should've been left alone," she said, over and over.

Shadow had been Don's inspiration, a beacon of warmth amid the gloom of the Knotts home. His death left less in life for Don to laugh about. The next night, Don went downtown on an errand and passed the old clock tower on the university campus, the spot where Shadow had heckled the cleaner. Now, the light on the clock was out. "I had walked by Woodburn Hall maybe a thousand nights and I had never seen the light out in that clock," Don recalled.

Don had embraced and absorbed his older brother's dry wit, had watched his own comic star rise within the family home as sickly Shadow's had waned. Don had learned everything Shadow could teach him. It was time for Don to come into his own.

By his senior year, Don was class president and writing a humor column for the Morgantown High School newspaper. "I was a terrible president, though, because I took nothing seriously," he recalled. "When I spoke at school assemblies, they usually laughed. I figured they were going to laugh at me anyway, so I always told jokes. I was loose, crazy, and free."

One June morning after graduation, Don set out for New York with a close friend from high school named Ray Gosovich. Don wanted to audition for *Major Bowes Amateur Hour*, a radio show that was the *American Idol* of its day. "We told everyone in our senior class that we were going to New York," Ray recalled, "and when you live in Morgantown, West Virginia, and you tell everyone you're going to New York, you'd better go to New York."

Elsie offered Don this parting wisdom: "Remember, Donald, if things don't work out up there, it might be a good idea to come back home and go to college."

The boys planned to hitchhike, but they soon found themselves stranded two hundred miles out of Morgantown in Harrisburg, Pennsylvania. They took a Greyhound bus the rest of the way, a concession that depleted their travel funds. They arrived at Thirty-Second Street, near the Hotel Pennsylvania, but rented a room at the more affordable Sloan House YMCA on Thirty-Fourth Street, near the Empire State Building, then the largest residential Y in the nation.

His first night in Manhattan, Don walked over to Times Square. He happened upon the theater that was playing *Claudia*, a forgotten Rose Franken production. A sign in the window touted "twofers." Don asked the ticket seller if he could have one ticket at half price and got a withering glare in return. Don stood there until the man barked, "Okay," and sold him a nosebleed seat for twenty-five cents. It was Don's first Broadway play.

Don quickly secured a job as an elevator operator at the Cornish Arms Hotel, next to the Grand Opera House at Eighth Avenue and Twenty-Third Street. One day, he earned five dollars by doing a ventriloquism show with Danny at the Y. That show led to an appearance at an open-mike night at the Village Nut Club, on Seventh Avenue, giving Don a small footnote in the storied history of New York's bohemian district. By day, Don snatched up the free tickets at the Y and watched dozens of radio broadcasts, taking notes on dialogue, delivery, and timing. When he had a dollar, he would buy a balcony seat at a Broadway show.

Don had no contacts and no clout, and he never did make it onto *Major Bowes*. A few weeks into his New York odyssey, he finally landed an audition for *Camel Caravan*, another talent showcase. Don showed up with Danny and did his routine for a matronly woman. When he was finished, she told him, "You seem like a nice boy. Why don't you take your dummy and go home and go back to school?"

Don limped back to Morgantown. "New York City was still standing," Don recalled; "I was the one who'd been brought to his knees." He spent the second half of summer cleaning chickens in the stockroom at Raese's grocery store.

In September, Don attended West Virginia University, where his mother had helpfully enrolled him before the ill-fated trip. He worked at the campus employment office, he lived at home, and he studied. Don felt his theater days were over. He applied for an announcer job at the campus radio station and was told he lacked a radio-quality voice, an ironic rebuff for the future radio star. Don parlayed his ventriloquism act into free entry to the Phi Sigma Kappa fraternity, entertaining at parties and representing the chapter at talent shows.

But the fire had gone from Don's belly; this was not the same boy who had blazed through Morgantown High School. "My ambition evaporated, and I became withdrawn," he recalled. "If it hadn't been for the war, I most probably would have become a teacher of dramatic arts."

The Japanese attack on Pearl Harbor had come midway through Don's senior year of high school. "Most of us in our teens felt obliged to volunteer," Don recalled. But Don did not. Instead, he waited until the draft ensnared him, in summer 1943, at age nineteen.

By this time, Don had already acquired a

healthy respect for his own mortality. He had caught most of the childhood diseases and had nearly died of diphtheria. Friends and loved ones thought him frail. In Don's grammar-school years, a county nurse, alarmed by his emaciated frame, had enrolled him in a government nutrition program. Don was actually in fine health by adulthood, but so many people seemed to think otherwise that he began to believe it. So began Don's lifelong battle with hypochondria.

Don weighed in at one pound below the army's minimum weight requirement for a man of his height, which was probably 125 pounds. He had to sign a waiver to enlist. The waiver gave Don a potential means of escape, and he thought of it often as he slogged through basic training in an antiaircraft artillery unit at Fort Bliss.

Privately, Don began to research which military assignments were the safest and to scheme at how he might maneuver into one of them. But he soon concluded that even a cook or a truck driver could die in a war. At the end of basic training, Don went to his sergeant, produced his waiver, and asked to be released from duty. The sergeant had him step on a scale. Don was horrified to see he'd gained ten pounds. There would be no escape.

Don wasn't a religious man, but this seemed a good time to reconnect. He began to pray, day and night, begging God for a miracle.

Some days later, it arrived. A telegram from the

War Department ordered Don to Fort Meade, outside Washington, to join Detachment X, a mysterious unit of the Special Service. Don felt his prayers had been answered, although he wasn't sure exactly how.

Detachment X was a company of army men drawn from various branches who shared a background in entertainment. Don had been chosen for citing "ventriloquist" as a skill on his enlistment form. The company spent two chilly months in rehearsal, preparing a revue titled *Stars and Gripes*, written by Harold Rome, a Broadway composer who would later score the Andy Griffith musical *Destry Rides Again*. Talented men began to trickle in from around the country: three tap dancers, two singers, one magician, and no fewer than four accordionists. The thirty-five-man roster included no big names but several big talents: Mickey Shaughnessy, a New Jersey nightclub performer who would find fame playing lovable lugs in films; Donald "Red" Blanchard, a radio cowboy in Chicago; Red Ford, a raucous comic from Houston; and Al Checco, a song-and-dance man from Pittsburgh who would become Don's lifelong friend.

Detachment X was the USO with helmets. The army wanted a company it could send to the front lines, just behind the invading force, to put on a show and create an illusion of safety, a veneer of civilization. "It was an experimental thing. All the little islands they hit in the Pacific and the South Pacific, they wanted to have something for the morale, to get the soldiers to relax a little bit," Al Checco recalled. "We were in the forward areas, often only a day or two after they were invaded."

Don dutifully polished his ventriloquism act, but he envied the comedians and yearned to join their skits. He was sitting with the guys one night, having a beer, when he noticed Red Ford, one of the pros, seated at another table, staring at him and laughing. Eventually, Red walked over and said, "You know something? You're a funny little son of a bitch." Red began to teach Don some of his jokes and coached him on the finer points of deadpan comedy. "Before I knew it, I was onstage playing Red Ford's second banana," Don recalled. This would be Don's theatrical boot camp.

In March 1944, the men boarded the troopship *Sea Witch* and zigzagged across the Pacific, ever alert for enemy subs. Forty tense days later, they arrived at Milne Bay, an expanse of hard-won mangrove swamp. The scene that greeted Don there sounds in hindsight like a set from *Apocalypse Now*: "It was raining when we dropped anchor in the harbor. We could see the steam rising from the jungle, and the air was hot and humid. As we looked on from the harbor, the jungle looked beautiful but forbidding."

The performers sat in their ship with nowhere to go, awaiting orders. Finally, the company disembarked. "We were a motley crew as we sloshed through the mud and climbed into two waiting trucks, struggling with duffel bags and drums and horns and props," as well as rifles and gas masks, Don recalled. "We were driven to a desolate-looking camp where we were dropped off at a structure laughingly called a barracks. It was actually no more than a long roof covering two rows of army cots."

For days, the men sat in the barracks beneath ceaseless rain. Finally, a commanding officer arrived with a performance schedule. The men would pile into trucks every night and head out into the swamp to play for groups of soldiers stationed at spots around the bay. "We performed on whatever we could put together to be a stage," Al Checco recalled. "Sometimes it might be just the backs of [the] trucks." There were no seats, so soldiers sat on boxes or crates, often in pouring rain. "If you wonder why they would sit on a box in the rain to watch a show," Don recalled, "bear in mind that there was *nothing* to do in New Guinea, and I mean absolutely nothing."

The shows were meant to distract the men not just from their miserable existence but also from the constant threat of violent death. "The Japanese kept bombing us at about the same time every night during the first act, just before I was supposed to sing a song," Al recalled. When the barrage began, "the sirens would go off, and we'd have to stop the show, jump into our foxholes or whatever, and then come out and finish the show."

One song was called "Pinup Girl," Al recalled, "and Don was always the closing of that number. He'd come out at the end with hardly any clothes on, and he was the pinup girl."

Outrageous then, the routines sound comparatively tame now. In one skit, Don and Mickey Shaughnessy are fishing. Mickey's lips are pursed.

"Whaddaya got in your mouth?" Don asks.

"Worms," Mickey replies.

Don grimaces. "Well, why don't you just hold them?"

"Too nasty."

As much as Don was learning onstage, the long hours offstage proved unbearable. "The constant rain was maddening," Don recalled, "and our clothes never seemed to get quite dry. Malaria was a constant threat, so we had to sleep under mosquito nets, and they fed us atabrine tablets every day." The pills turned Don's skin yellow. "We usually wore leggings, but the mud still slipped into our shoes and slithered down our socks. Some guys grew a fungus on their feet the GIs called jungle rot. Of all things, I began to get it on my hands."

The tour filled Don's head with a View-Master reel of horror. He once watched the capture of a Japanese soldier. "He was frothing at the mouth," Don recalled. "He was so full of rage. He was like an animal. They kept saying, 'Keep back,' like he was a rabid dog." Don watched American soldiers rip the gold teeth from a corpse. And then there was the unsettling performance Detachment X gave for survivors of the Bataan Death March, beaten and starved on a sixty-mile trek through the Philippine jungles. "They filtered in to watch us," Don recalled, "but they didn't laugh once. They barely applauded."

In time, Don began to fear for his sanity. One day, he wandered into the jungle to get away from the miserable barracks. Farther and farther he walked. Suddenly, he was gripped with terror: Don thought someone was chasing him. He began to run, faster and faster. Then he stopped and turned around. No one was there. He thought to himself, "This is it: I'm going crazy, just like my father."

From that day, Don thought he was hiding a terrible secret: he was going insane. That fear made Don reluctant to speak, feeding an essential shyness that would define him for the rest of his life.

Several months into the tour, the company took a five-week leave in Brisbane, Australia. Don's jungle rot cleared up in the hot, dry sunshine, and the dance-hall girls buoyed his spirits. He felt that his sanity was restored.

After the leave, the company moved up the coast to the provincial capital of Hollandia, and then to Los Negros, and thence to Biak and Manus, where the performers gazed upon a vast armada set to invade the Philippines. The men performed on battleships and aircraft carriers. When the Allies invaded, Detachment X followed.

Don's comedic ambitions had outgrown Danny the dummy. He yearned to be a comedian, and he was learning from some of the best, playing second banana to Red Ford and Mickey Shaughnessy. He appealed to the senior officers to let him drop the ventriloquist act and focus on the comedy pairings. They insisted he continue with Danny. When the company sailed from Manus Island, Danny mysteriously vanished. "Out of the clear, blue sky, that suitcase was gone," Al Checco recalled. "When we asked Don about it, he just shuffled back and forth and sheepishly said, 'Well, I don't know. I don't know.' " Don was free to be a comic.

Don was in a Philippine jungle in August 1945 when someone came running up to the troupe and cried, "The war is over!" The performers were speechless, then incredulous. How could the war be over? "No, it's over," the breathless messenger said. Then, a sense of relief and euphoria washed over Don, like nothing he'd felt before. He had thought it distinctly possible he would be out in the jungles, covered in rot, for the rest of his life.

Most of the entertainers from *Stars and Gripes* had endured what amounted to a two-year setback in their professional careers. For Don, the military had the opposite effect, honing his skills and restoring the confidence he'd lost in that first, demoralizing visit to New York.

Don returned to West Virginia University intent on continuing his studies and eager to keep busy—if only to ward off the demons that still haunted him after that delirious run through the jungle and the recurring visions of madness. Don was an extrovert again, performing in university plays and resuming his variety act with faithful friends Jarvie Eldred and Richie Ferrara. The Radio Three could now command fifty dollars a night. Don's solo act, newly polished, electrified fraternity parties. He had returned from Detachment X with dozens of stage-ready characters, some of them prototypes of the Nervous Man. One of the best was a harried football announcer who spewed spoonerisms, deliberate slips of the tongue. "Everybody was in stitches with that," recalled Jim Allen, a fraternity buddy. "Even sober, you had to lay down on the floor and laugh."

When summer break came, Don took to hitchhiking the eighty miles to Pittsburgh and calling on booking agents with his stand-up act.

He struck out again and again. He shared his frustration with Richie. Richie offered to go along the next time. Don and Richie made the rounds together, to no avail. They visited one last agent, climbing the steps to her third-floor office. Richie knocked. A woman answered, "It's five o'clock; we're closed."

Richie cut in, "Wait a minute, it's not for me. I'm a medical student."

Suddenly the agent grew interested. "Do you know anything about irritable bowel syndrome?"

"Sure, I just learned about it."

"Come in."

Richie did, and Don snuck in behind him. Richie listened as the agent bemoaned her irritable bowels, nodding empathetically. Finally, Richie directed the agent's attention to the man sitting quietly in the corner: "He's a great comedian, and he needs a job."

The agent asked, "What can he do?"

"Don, do one of your routines."

Don launched into his spoonerism routine. "And she died laughing," Richie recalled. Don had an agent.

All that summer and the next, Don worked dates across Pennsylvania, playing clubs in Meadville, Oil City, and Wilkes-Barre. His effect on an audience was immediate and electric. "He would just stand up in front of a crowd and he'd say one word, and they would laugh," Richie recalled. "He had something about his nature that was funny. Not for what he said. It was just his expressions, his style, his person, his spirit. There's something in it that's indescribable."

Don earned ten dollars a night, twenty-five dollars on weekends, plus bus fare. "In most cases," Don recalled, "I would pocket the bus fare and hitchhike. Even so, I rarely came out ahead." Once he played a stag show, a realization that dawned only when the first performer turned to Don and said, "Stand by the piano, honey, and I'll hand you my clothes." It was his first glimpse of a naked woman.

Richie Ferrara proved a charming and resourceful friend, and not just with theatrical agents. "When we got back from the army, he was in school and I was in school," Richie recalled. "I didn't have time to arrange a date. . . . So, I'd call up this sorority house that I knew and say, 'Is there anyone available?' I would date one of them, and Don would date the other." One Saturday that spring, Richie brought Don to a campus sorority mixer. When the party ended at five o'clock, they lingered, and soon they found themselves competing with several other young men for the attention of Kay, a petite freshman with arched eyebrows and a delicate beauty. By the time they went home, Don was in love.

Kathryn Metz was a woman of substance, the daughter of a Northern Baptist minister from

Wheeling, a West Virginia city so far north that it was almost Ohio. She was studying speech and English. She knew Don as "the fair-haired boy in the drama department. He was often the lead in the plays that they did." And Kay knew of the vaudeville act Don, Richie, and Jarvie played around town.

The university campus was flooded with returning GIs. Kay had many suitors, and Don immediately found himself vying with another boyfriend named Kent. But Don was relentless, and Kay kept saying yes. Don would keep Richie up past midnight moaning and groaning "about how much he loved her."

Don had many fans at the university. Random people kept approaching Kay, unbidden, and urging her to pair off with him. "He was very charismatic," she recalled. "I recognized that almost immediately. He was funny and outgoing, and we could talk. He had a lot of depth of character, and that was interesting to me."

Given Don's stature on campus, Kay was surprised when, about a year after their first date, he took her home to the threadbare rooming house on University Avenue. They would go there for lunch. Elsie would prepare a full meal, with two desserts, a cake and a pie. Then, the three would sit and watch Elsie's favorite soap operas, and Don would poke fun at the characters and the lines until Kay and Elsie couldn't stop laughing.

Kay had a warm, encouraging laugh, just like Don's mother.

Kay and Don dated for two years. One summer in that span, Don drove Kay to a seasonal job at a hotel in Beach Haven, New Jersey. He intended to drop her there and go off in search of stand-up work. But when they arrived and Don sized up the romantic competition among the employees at the inn, he abandoned his own plans and took a job as a dishwasher. He wanted to keep Kay close.

Don married Kay in December 1947 in a ceremony at her father's church. He graduated from West Virginia University the following spring.

Having finally won the girl, Don struggled mightily to support her. He sold shirts for a time. Then, frustrated by the lack of jobs, he enrolled in a graduate theater program at the University of Arizona. Don's successful older brother, Bill, owned property there. But Don and Kay stayed only a few months because Don's GI Bill records were lost and he wasn't receiving his student aid. They returned to Morgantown in winter. Don took a holiday job selling toys at a department store. In quiet moments there, Don would chat up the man playing Santa Claus in the Christmas display. A theater buff, Santa urged Don to return to New York. "Go for it," Santa would say. "You don't need any more college." In later years, Don would tell nightclub audiences that the man's advice had launched his career: "Don't tell me there's no Santa Claus!"

Santa's urgings surely put New York in Don's mind. But the final straw came one day in the university drama department. Don was sitting with some fellow thespians when a young man walked in and cried, "Guess what? Next week, I'm leaving for New York!" At those words, "something snapped inside of me," Don recalled. " 'Dammit!' I said to myself. 'I'm going to New York!' And just like that, I made the decision." He rushed home and told Kay. She was ready.

Don had twenty dollars to his name, so once more he hit up brother Bill, who loaned him one hundred dollars for the trip. It was the last time Don would have to borrow car fare.

2.

Laugh, Lest Ye Cry

Carl and Geneva Griffith lived on the wrong side of Mount Airy, North Carolina—the south side. The neighborhood was home to the hosiery mills that employed the town's working-class women and the furniture mills that employed many of the men, including Carl. The north side of Mount Airy housed the men who owned those mills, and the children who would inherit them. In north Mount Airy, many of the streets were named for trees. In south Mount Airy, they were named for industries: Factory Street, Depot Street, Granite Street.

The birth registry says Andy Samuel Griffith was born on June 7, 1926. In later life, Andy apparently adopted a new birth date, June 1. He said he learned his parents had stalled in reporting the birth because "Mama wasn't quite ready with a name." When she finally found one, it was a nickname—Andy, not Andrew. A working-class name for a working-class boy.

Young Andy had a shock of blond hair and a strawberry birthmark on the back of his head, traits for which classmates would later tease him. His first home was a converted barn on

South Street shared with Geneva's sister and her husband. Andy's crib was a repurposed bureau drawer. Carl Griffith was a skilled carpenter, but jobs were scarce, so the family hopscotched from one relative's home to another, living with Geneva's mother in Ohio, then rejoining her sister in Mount Airy, before amassing the savings to purchase a three-room house on Haymore Street. The house cost eight hundred dollars. The toilet sat on the back porch. Andy slept on a straw bed in the kitchen, an arrangement upon which he could later compare notes with Don.

Carl Griffith finally landed a steady job with the Mount Airy Chair Company, building dining-room furniture with a band saw. It didn't pay particularly well; then again, the Griffiths didn't need much money. Andy was an only child, and Carl's income was split just three ways. Andy ate well. Geneva pampered him and sewed his clothes. Some of Andy's boyhood friends felt like pups in a litter by comparison.

"It seemed like he had everything," recalled J. B. Childress, a childhood friend. "My family, I was one of eight, and we were extremely poor."

On the playground, Andy's socioeconomic status became a liability. He wasn't like other neighborhood boys. They ran wild, stayed out late, and came home with skinned knees and torn clothes that no one cared to mend. Andy (or Ange, as he was affectionately known, even then) went home early, avoided running in the streets, seldom got dirty, and invariably emerged from his house looking clean. He was too shy to skinny-dip with the other boys at the local swimming hole.

This reflected the influence of Geneva Griffith. "She didn't really care for him being out that late," recalled Garnett Steele, another boyhood friend who was himself the youngest of ten. "He had a certain time he had to be home."

It didn't help that Andy was naturally clumsy. "He was a big boy," Garnett recalled. "He could hit you hard in football, but he wasn't an athlete. He wasn't good with catching a ball. Almost like having all thumbs."

Andy's gawkishness, coupled with his unmistakable aura of mama's boy, made him a target. "He would put himself into positions that made him vulnerable," Garnett recalled.

"We picked on him a little bit," J. B. Childress recalled. "He seemed to be spoiled. Even I—I didn't realize it was wrong to do at the time—I can remember him riding his bicycle, and I stuck out my foot and almost wrecked him."

Time and again, in later life, Andy would frame his childhood as a ceaseless battle against bullies. "The other fellas—and worse, the girls—used to laugh at me," he recalled. "Not *with* me, mind you, but *at* me. My mama made me wear long underwear, and when we had to change in the gym, the other guys would double over in hysterics. It finally got so I'd dress in the shower or toilet where they couldn't see me. . . . I was an awful shy, scraggly, homely kid, and I'd fall over imaginary objects and trip myself up with my own big feet. I wanted to belong like the rest of the kids, but I was too embarrassed to express myself or my needs. I don't even think I knew what my needs were. There were times when I thought I just wanted to die."

Andy would forgive his mother for dressing him funny. He would not so easily forgive his friends and classmates for taking note. "I felt second-class all the time," Andy recalled. "I think I was driven to do the things I did so I could get out of Mount Airy."

Andy's first appearance before an audience, in the third grade, would fade over time into an enigmatic tale, sometimes recounted as an episode of humiliation, other times as a moment of triumph.

Andy's grammar school held regular Friday assemblies and encouraged students to perform. One Friday, Andy had a mind to sing a song. He told a classmate named Albert McKnight, "I'll get up to sing if you will." Albert agreed. When the time came, Andy stood; Albert did not. Andy looked down at his classmate, saw a smirk on his face, and realized he'd been had.

"I don't know why I didn't sit back down," he

recalled years later. "I walked up there on that stage. Center stage. Never said a word. My hair was as white as it is now. And I sang 'Put On Your Old Grey Bonnet,' twice. Once slow, once fast, with my hands behind me swaying around." The audience exploded in cruel laughter.

That Friday afternoon was surely the low point in young Andy Griffith's life. Or was it a turning point? Sometimes, when Andy told the same story, he gave it a happy ending.

"I don't know to this day what made me do it," Andy said in another retelling. "I guess I was just plumb tired of being made a fool of. But I marched up to the stage and started reciting the poem we'd learned." (In this version of the story, the song has become a verse.) "In between the lines, I'd make little comments of my own on what I thought of the poem and the person who wrote it, and they started laughing. I found out I could get them to laugh, or listen, whenever I wanted them to. What an experience, that great sea of laughter. From that time on, no one kidded me because they knew I could whip them verbally. And, most important, I knew it."

This much is certain: Humor delivered Andy from the strictures of his Mount Airy childhood. For a boy who lacked money and athletic prowess—in a community that prized little else— laughter became a currency all its own.

"I did it as a matter of self-protection," he

recalled. "All the time I was training myself, although I didn't know it."

The Griffith home lay half a mile south of the Rockford Street Grammar School. Andy's childhood played out along Rockford Street: He would walk up past Spring Street in the morning for class, then walk back home to Haymore Street for lunch, then back to school. After the final bell, Andy might retreat to Mrs. Allred's cow pasture on Granite Street for an aromatic game of football among the cow pies. Then, perhaps, down to Broad Street to congregate with the other boys on Garnett Steele's front porch, then out into the streets to play kick the can until nightfall.

Andy and his friends were no strangers to high jinks. One Halloween night, Garnett recalled, the boys skated up and down the streets of Mount Airy letting air out of car tires. As they went to work on one vehicle, the owner climbed out, produced a hand pump, and demanded that the boys reinflate the tires. The pumping occupied the rest of the evening. When Garnett retold the story in an episode of *This Is Your Life*, Andy claimed not to remember it. "He was a person who didn't want anything to take away from him, from his prestige, if you know what I mean," Garnett recalled.

On wet days, Andy and Garnett would retreat into Andy's basement. There, the boys had built an entire city in miniature from blocks and scraps, a poor man's model train set. Andy's daughter, Dixie, suspects the work paid homage to Andy's father, the master carpenter.

The household of Carl Lee and Geneva "Nannie" Griffith was "a very pleasant one to be around," Garnett recalled. Carl, thirty-one at Andy's birth, was "much younger than most of the dads back then," Garnett says. Carl and his only child spent a lot of time together. Andy would go to the furniture factory after school to work alongside Carl. Then, they would walk home together. "And we'd be just draggin' along," Andy recalled. "Finally, Dad would say, 'We'd better hurry up. We're gonna miss *The Lone Ranger.*' So we'd sit together by the radio."

When the Lone Ranger called, "Hi-yo, Silver, away!" Carl would cry, "Whoooeee!" That whoop was Carl's signature. "If something really astounded him, or if he saw a really pretty woman, he'd do a whole-body take, go 'Whoooeee!'—and he'd walk out of the room and come back and do it again," Andy recalled.

Andy picked up many of his father's exaggerated Southern mannerisms and his rustic humor. Carl, more than anyone else, was the wellspring of Andy's wit.

"He simply adored his father," recalled Dixie, Andy's daughter. "It feels to me that his work ethic and his perseverance and those things were a result, in a sense, of his father's work ethic and perseverance, and his determination, and getting up and doing the grind. He had a great deal of respect for his father, and what he did, and how he did it. Granddaddy would have these little looks and little nods and little idiosyncrasies. And Daddy, he'd say, 'This is how Granddaddy used to do it.' "

Andy grew up in a deceptively matriarchal society. Half the women seemed to hold jobs in the hosiery mills; the other half ran large households. The fathers of Mount Airy, by contrast, were comparatively shiftless. "A lot of the men, like my daddy, stayed drunk all the time," J. B. Childress recalled. "The ones who were sober worked in furniture mills."

Carl Griffith wasn't a drunk, but he drank, and he may well have been an alcoholic. Later in life, Andy told Don of his heavily inebriated father wobbling into the room one night as the younger Griffith poured a drink and telling his son, "Ah need to have a talk with you about yer drinkin'," before passing out cold on the floor himself.

Yet, Carl was always a hard worker. Andy claimed his father had gone to work at age twelve to offset his own father's gambling.

While Andy adored his father, his relationship with Geneva was more complex. She sometimes seemed to manipulate Andy like a puppet, sewing his clothes, dictating his comings and goings, and locking him indoors at the first sign of dark or chill. She ruled the Griffith home.

"This'll tell you as much about my mother as you need to know," Andy once told an interviewer. Andy and his parents were sitting in a restaurant with the principals of *The Andy Griffith Show*. A waiter spilled something on Geneva's suit. "Oh, she just went crazy," Andy recalled. "Finally she said, 'Carl, why couldn't you have been setting here?' That's my mother."

Geneva Nunn Griffith came from Patrick County, Virginia, twenty miles east of Mount Airy in the Blue Ridge Mountains, a place sparsely populated to this day. To the Griffith home she brought a tradition of spirited mountain jam sessions. "They used to have what they call play parties, dances," Andy recalled. "The Nunns, they all played, fiddle or something."

Andy was veritably surrounded by music. A steady pulse of country-western hits blared from the family's Majestic radio. Sunday mornings were filled with hand-clapping, head-swaying gospel at Haymore Baptist Church, where Andy would take careful note of the fire-and-brimstone sermons. The Griffiths spent many summer evenings swept up in the sweaty delirium of tent revivals, led by a procession of self-styled Elmer Gantrys.

Andy wanted to make music of his own. "I looked at the Spiegel catalog, day after day," he recalled. "And they had two pages of musical instruments, and I was just staring at those instruments every day, every day, every day."

When Geneva had errands to run, she would send Andy down to Main Street with a few coins in his pocket for an afternoon's entertainment. In winter 1941, Andy saw a film called *Birth of the Blues*—a misnomer, as the picture actually chronicles the advent of jazz. Andy was smitten with the stylings of Weldon Leo "Jack" Teagarden, the Big T, a man sometimes cited as father of the jazz trombone. "He took the bell off that trombone and played with a glass on the end of the slide," Andy recalled. Years later, Andy would invite Big T to play a town councilman in an episode of *The Andy Griffith Show*.

Andy took a job sweeping out Mount Airy High School. Though he was only fifteen, he lied and said he was sixteen, the minimum age for employment under Franklin Roosevelt's National Youth Administration. He began putting down six dollars a month toward a thirty-three-dollar trombone. Five and a half months later, the horn was his.

He didn't know quite what to do with it. Mount Airy High School had no band. A foreman at Carl Griffith's furniture factory told Carl to look up Ed Mickey, the minister at the local Moravian church. The Moravians, one of the oldest and smallest Protestant denominations, were known for their brass bands.

One afternoon, Andy pedaled his bicycle to Grace Moravian Church on North Main Street and found Edward T. Mickey Jr., the young pastor, sitting on the steps.

Mickey looked up. "Sitting astride his bicycle was a rawboned boy of sixteen with curly, blond hair," he recalled.

"You the teacher here?" Andy asked.

Yes, the pastor replied.

"You teach horn?"

Yes, Mickey replied guardedly.

"You teach me? I'll pay you."

"I can't take pay for this." Why, Mickey asked, did Andy want to play a horn?

"So I can lead a swing band."

The disdainful pastor could not dissuade the eager boy. "Well, come again next Wednesday and bring your horn. We'll see what we can do."

Mickey was betting the boy wouldn't lug a trombone two miles across Mount Airy on his bicycle. But there he was the next Wednesday, with his bicycle, his trombone, and "enthusiasm for life in quantity enough for half a dozen boys," Mickey recalled.

The pastor sent Andy home with a lesson. Andy brought it back the next week and played it perfectly. So it went, week after week. Finally, Mickey asked Andy where he found time for so much practice. Andy said he was getting up at five in the morning.

Playing and singing with the Moravians, Andy said, "was the turning point in my life. Because, you see, we didn't have money. I was not athletic and I wasn't a good student, so I was kind of nobody. So when I started all this music business . . . I became a little somebody then."

The Griffiths joined the Moravian church. When Andy sang or played his horn, his insecurities dissolved. Mount Airy audiences began to glimpse a jubilant, wild-eyed, larger-than-life Andy Griffith.

North and south Mount Airy, rich and poor, converged on Mount Airy High. Andy arrived there as an anonymous member of the class of 1944. In Andy's sophomore year, a teacher selected him to take the lead in a school production called *Major Nose*, another homage to the ubiquitous radio talent show *Major Bowes*.

It was a breakthrough, and Andy credited his English teacher, Miss Haymore. She "was the kind they used to make movies about," he recalled. "She encouraged me to go all out for music, if that was what I wanted. She got me to understand that I was really doing something pleasurable, not only for other people but for myself."

At Mount Airy High, Andy found his first love: Angie Marshall, captain of the girls' basketball team. For three years, they were an item on campus. "All the younger students loved to watch as he turned on the school water fountain for her," recalled Eleanor Powell, a classmate.

Otherwise, Andy remained largely invisible at Mount Airy High, and not entirely by choice. He held a string of after-school jobs to help support his family. "In the afternoon, when I was going to football practice, Andy was bagging groceries in the Piggly Wiggly," recalled classmate Robert Merritt.

At the very end of his high school career, Andy finally made an impression. For the senior class banquet, the school tapped local talent; the war effort precluded hiring out-of-towners. "So we lined up people to read a poem or play a piano," Robert Merritt recalled. One of them was Andy Griffith, who came to the stage and sang "Long Ago and Far Away," a popular tune in its day.

"And what I remember," Robert recalled, "was a voice at the back of the room: 'Golly, old Ange can sing!' We didn't know."

The next fall, Andy Griffith entered the University of North Carolina. He was the first in his family to attend college. He planned to enter the ministry.

Andy and his family had been deeply involved in church for years, first with the Baptists and then the Moravians. The Baptist preacher would sometimes point to Andy and tell a church visitor, only partly in jest, "This is our new minister." But according to boyhood friend Garnett Steele, Andy's heart was never really in it; he looked to seminary study partly as a way to evade military service.

"He stood on my front porch," Garnett recalled. "My brother had just come back from Guadalcanal and Espiritu Santo in World War Two, and that was in 1944. And he said, 'Andy, when are you going into the service?'" Andy coolly replied, "I'm not going into the service." He never elaborated. By 1944, the army required all men of eighteen to register for the draft. Many of Andy's friends, including Emmett Forrest and Robert Merritt, eventually served. Ministerial study would provide Andy an exemption.

Andy turned eighteen just before he enrolled in college. He dutifully registered for selective service and underwent the customary medical evaluation. According to Garnett, the tests turned up a herniated disk in Andy's lower back, an undetected injury from age thirteen, when clumsy Andy had fallen from a tire swing in Emmett Forrest's yard.

Suddenly, Andy found himself free from military service—and from the need to become a minister.

Andy's own accounts of the era make no mention of military service or avoidance thereof. He said he switched college majors following a simple change of heart. "My major was sociology, and I hated it," he recalled. "And I was living right by the music department." He said he joined various university bands and glee clubs and choral societies "and everything else I could get in." Finally, he approached the Moravian bishop and asked, "Can I major in music and still be a minister?" The bishop said no. "So I went back and thought about it and prayed about it for two weeks. And then I went back and said, 'I'm going to major in music.'" The bishop replied, "You'll never serve God by singing light opera."

Andy's failure to serve would haunt him for the rest of his days. It was one of those topics that, decades later, Don knew not to raise. Some Mount Airy veterans wouldn't speak to him. "Some people thought he was a draft dodger," Robert Merritt recalled. "It was a righteous, patriotic time."

Andy dove into university life with the same jubilant energy he had brought to the Moravian church. But Andy soon found himself crippled by feelings of inadequacy, a new manifestation of the old fears that had dogged him in grammar school. Back in Mount Airy, Andy had felt second-class. Now, he felt like a fraud.

"I had a wonderful time—and a horrible time—in Chapel Hill," Andy recalled. "I went through every day hoping, just hoping, they wouldn't find out how little I knew, but sometimes they

did. I failed Political Science Forty-One twice. . . .
I guess that was the only record I ever broke at
Chapel Hill."

One night, as he passed Memorial Hall, Andy
glimpsed a poster advertising auditions for a
production of *The Gondoliers*. "I didn't even
know who Gilbert and Sullivan were," Andy
recalled. "Anyway, I decided to go over there, and
I sang a terrible old song, called 'Shepherd, See
Thy Horse's Flowing Mane.' " The next day,
Andy found he had won a part. From then on, he
recalled, "They did a Gilbert and Sullivan almost
every year, and I played the comedy lead in all of
them."

When he was onstage, Andy's fears would
evaporate. He knew he could act. Others knew it,
too. Foster Fitz-Simons, the Carolina dramatist
who directed Andy's university debut, was perhaps the first to recognize the young actor's sway
over an audience. Foster invited his wife, actress
Marion Fitz-Simons, to a rehearsal. As they
watched Andy, Foster told her, "He's got something. I don't know what it is, but he's got
something."

Foster Fitz-Simons led the Carolina Playmakers,
the university's resident repertory company. The
director taught Andy and the other players to "tell
what you know; write what you know." He
encouraged them to craft folk dramas about
"universal truths heard in the kitchen," recalled

William Ivey Long, a Broadway costume designer who grew up as a family friend to the Griffiths. It was in Fitz-Simons's acting classes, William says, that Andy developed a theatrical persona based upon himself, "the ultimate aw-shucks farm boy."

Andy took a job busing tables on campus for "breakfast and eight dollars a week: five dollars for tuition and three dollars to live on, more or less," Andy recalled after his success. "I was a lot thinner in those days than I am now." A voice teacher offered Andy free lessons if he would maintain the sheet music for the glee club. Andy became its president. He appeared in that capacity in a photograph for the university yearbook of 1947, wearing a pompadour and looking a bit like an irritable rockabilly singer.

Andy caught a bigger break when he learned that the old back injury—for which he briefly wore a back brace—qualified him for a program that supported indigent students with disabilities. It paid his tuition. Andy became a dorm manager, a job that covered his rooming costs. He collected laundry for another two dollars a week.

Though Andy's life now centered on Chapel Hill, he returned home on occasion to perform with the Mount Airy Operetta Club, the sort of earnest small-town ensemble Andy would lovingly mock later in *The Andy Griffith Show.* Locals remember the afternoon of November 11, 1946, when the company lulled hundreds of

Mount Airy schoolchildren to sleep with a matinee performance of *The Bartered Bride*. Suddenly, the male lead unleashed a piercing yodel; the vibrations triggered a massive spring-coiled window shade, which flapped up to the ceiling like a startled flock of birds. The children exploded in laughter. Andy, already a shrewd judge of his audience, followed their lead, reviving the moribund performance with slapstick and ad-libbed high jinks. In his final scene, Andy leaped onto the back of another actor and rode him piggyback off the stage. The children laughed and clapped. Andy waved back. It would be his last public appearance in Mount Airy for more than a decade.

In fall 1947, Andy prepared to audition for a production of Haydn's *Seasons* by the Chapel Hill Choral Club. A classmate asked him, "Have you heard Bobby Edwards sing? Now, there's a voice!"

Andy considered, then answered, "I don't know him."

"You *really* don't know Bobby Edwards." Bobby was short for Barbara.

Barbara Bray Edwards came from the Carolina town of Troy. Her father was the superintendent of schools; her mother, Dixie, was a doctor's daughter. "They were a genteel southern-eastern North Carolina family," recalled Robert Edwards King, Barbara's nephew. They were prominent in their town, and Barbara, artistic and pretty, left Troy with abundant promise.

Barbara brought her crystalline soprano to Chapel Hill after completing her degree at Converse College in South Carolina. She wanted to begin graduate work and to explore the fertile arts scene.

"Barbara Edwards was a sweetheart," recalled Carl Perry, a classmate who befriended the young couple and acted with them in a campus production of *The Mikado*. "Her voice was clear as a bell."

One day, a friend pointed Bobby out to Andy. He glimpsed her only from behind: a receding form clad in a matching sweater and skirt, topped with a sweep of rich brown hair tamed into a long bob. A few days later, he saw her almond eyes and her sculpted cheekbones. And he heard her sing.

"They were doing the Haydn *Seasons* and they needed a soprano," Barbara recalled. "So I went in all full of spirit. And Andy was standing behind a baby-grand piano, and I shook hands with Andy, and I don't know, something just happened. So then I sang my little audition. And it just so happened that Andy had waited out in the foyer. I had to say something. So I asked him for a match."

He asked her to coffee. Three days later, he asked her to marry him.

In summer 1946, Andy had considered auditioning for *The Lost Colony*, the long-running outdoor drama that reenacts the founding and mysterious disappearance of the first English settlement in North America. Set on the Carolina shore, the production offered a chance for Andy to continue his dramatic studies through the summer. But he decided against it. "They paid only twenty-five dollars, and I figured I couldn't do that and stay in school," Andy recalled. So, Andy reluctantly returned to Mount Airy and worked in the furniture factory with his father, earning forty dollars a week. This was one of Andy's few encounters with genuine toil, and he hated every minute of it.

The next summer, Andy and Barbara drove to Manteo to join *The Lost Colony*. Andy had never seen the ocean. He was spellbound. In time, Andy would forsake Mount Airy and make Manteo his home.

The actors lived in repurposed naval buildings left over from the war. They rode to the theater on an old school bus. "We had our own swimming hole, our own volleyball, our own eating place, our own beer joint, everything," Andy recalled.

Andy and Barbara were cast into small roles at first. "My dad started out playing a red soldier for the queen," Dixie Griffith recalled. Andy wore tights. When he overheard two women discussing his spindly legs, he took to padding them with newspaper or cotton wadding. By 1949, Andy was playing Sir Walter Raleigh and Barbara was playing Eleanor Dare, mother of the first child born in North America to English parents. Andy and Barbara began to appear together on *Lost Colony* postcards and program covers.

Barbara remained, to this point, the star of the Griffith family. Andy later conceded he wouldn't have won a lead role without his wife, who persuaded *The Lost Colony* director to promote him. But Andy, too, had found his calling. Back on campus, he missed classes and ignored homework whenever he was in a production; in Andy's mind, his career had already begun.

As a theatrical performer, Andy excelled in light opera and outdoor theater. But he sensed his strongest talents lay elsewhere. Most of his fellow thespians made do with established acts. Andy began to create his own, experimenting with song and storytelling, weaving humorous stories among the songs and sometimes even between verses. It was part pop act, part comedy sketch, all suffused with Andy's skill for parodying his own hayseed heritage.

Robert Hurley, a fellow actor and singer at Chapel Hill, hadn't regarded Andy as particularly ambitious until the night Andy appeared at his dorm room to announce he had started "a little nightclub act" in the basement of the student center, where boys brought dates on Saturday nights. Andy was acting as master of ceremonies and looking for talent. He wondered whether Robert and a few others from the glee club might come by and sing. Andy had heard, and occasionally joined, the five friends when their voices rose in tight harmony on the bus to glee club concerts. At the Saturday-night performances, Andy "would play popular songs, and he would tell stories between them," Robert recalled. "I guess that was about his first gig."

After "five years and two summers," as he put it, Andy finally finished college. It was spring of 1949. Andy and Barbara set their wedding for August 22, closing a nearly two-year courtship. It was a Monday, Andy's day off from *The Lost Colony*. The couple traveled to Norfolk and chose a rust silk afternoon frock for Barbara and a navy suit for Andy. The ceremony was held at Fort Raleigh, the national park, in a log-cabin chapel.

"I remember helping pick the flowers and helping decorate the church," said William Ivey Long, whose parents were close to Andy and Barbara. "I remember my father making punch and little sandwiches." There was talk that Barbara's folks were "fancy," William recalled, and "everyone wanted it to look as elegant a wedding as possible."

Andy was Moravian; Barbara was Baptist. They were married by a Methodist minister in a facsimile of an Anglican church. Someone played "Ave Maria" on a vibraharp. No one still living seems to recall how this denominational smorgasbord came about, but it suited eclectic Andy, who started life a Baptist, converted to Moravianism, and would later embrace the Methodist faith.

Andy and Barbara Griffith settled into a rented house outside Chapel Hill. "They lived way out in the country," recalled William Ivey Long. "They didn't have electricity or indoor plumbing. They had a well. Everyone was poor. We shared food."

On Saturday mornings, Barbara would travel to William's house, where she and Mary Long, William's mother, would give each other Toni home-permanent hair treatments. William's father would prepare a vat of vegetable soup and pour it into quart jars to feed both families for the week. William would sometimes deliver the soup to the Griffith mailbox. One time, in what can only be termed an Opie moment, William opened the box to find a bird's nest inside. Andy had put it there to "shake me up," William recalled.

Andy had no permanent job awaiting him as an entertainer, so he took a teacher training course and signed a contract in fall 1949 to teach music at the high school in Goldsboro, in eastern North Carolina. Clifton Britton, stage manager at *The*

Lost Colony, ran the drama department there and was trying to build it into a regional powerhouse against long odds.

"They only had six hundred students," Andy recalled. "He had three hundred of them in his drama department. He won every prize there was. He hired me to come up there as his assistant, teaching drama. The reason I was there was to build up the choral music department so he could put on musical plays. . . . He did every major production that the university would do. He would use students; he would use townspeople."

The job put Andy and Barbara an hour's drive from Raleigh, epicenter of the North Carolina theater scene.

At Goldsboro High, Andy revealed a talent for recruiting students into music study, and soon he had a full roster. But Andy wasn't much of a teacher. "I don't know how to just sit down and talk about one thing," Andy recalled. His cigarette craving would build till the end of class, when Andy would race his students out the door.

In summer, Andy and Barbara returned to Manteo and rejoined the pursuit of their passion. By 1951, they were stars of *The Lost Colony*, the most glamorous couple among its lead actors. Andy and Barbara struck up enduring friendships. "Every night after the show, we'd be partying," recalled George Vassos, a lifelong friend of Andy's. "As soon as it would end, we'd head out for the beer parlor. We'd go out there and drink and dance."

Andy formed a particularly close bond with a *Lost Colony* player named Ainslie Pryor. Ainslie managed the Raleigh Little Theatre, a community playhouse. He was another director, like Foster Fitz-Simons at the university, who thought Andy had something special.

In February 1952, a publicity man heard the Griffiths sing and invited them to audition at the Paper Mill Playhouse, a regional theater in northern New Jersey with an outsize reputation owing to its locale, a short train ride from Broadway. The Griffiths had never been that far north, but they made the trip, feeling very much like country mice.

At the audition, Andy and Barbara lined up with more than two hundred others. Barbara sang "In the Still of the Night," and Andy sang "Dancing in the Dark." They did not get the parts. An auditioner told Andy his voice was "overbrilliant, almost painfully so." Andy could have shrugged off the advice; the auditions were a long shot in the first place. But Andy decided, then and there, to halt his singing career. He would make a living being funny. "Singing had always frightened me, anyway," he recalled.

Ainslie Pryor and his wife came up to meet the Griffiths, offering succor and a gin-soaked tour of New York. On the train ride home, Ainslie told

Andy of a show he was preparing to stage, called *The Drunkard*. It was a melodrama, and Ainslie needed oleo acts, brief skits to distract the audience while the scenery was changed. Andy had some ideas.

Off *The Lost Colony* stage, Andy continued his experiments with skit-based comedy and vaudeville. When *The Lost Colony* curtain fell on Saturday nights, the colonial actors would decamp to the local Shriners club to stage a weekly program of song, dance, and laughs, with Andy as master of ceremonies. The audience was a rowdy mix of *Lost Colony* cast and crew and local townsfolk.

George Vassos would sing the standards "Early Autumn" and "Stormy Weather" with three other men drawn from a local church choir. Barbara would sing folk songs and Andy would accompany her on guitar. Andy would stage his monologues. But the centerpiece of the show was Andy's preacher act. Written with Ainslie, Andy's sometime collaborator, the sketch began with a processional and a string of off-color announcements: "The deacons wish that whoever keeps writing 'Meet me in the basement' on the back of the hymn books would cut it out, because everybody that goes down there tracks mud all over the church." Then, Andy would launch into a backwoods sermon, telling the singsong story of the Preacher and the Bear:

O Lord, didn't you deliver Daniel from the
lion's den
Also deliver Jonah from the belly of the whale
and then
The Hebrew children from the fiery furnace,
the good book do declare
O Lord, if you can't help me, for goodness'
sake don't help that bear!

Gradually, Andy's ambitions for the late-night
vaudeville act would eclipse his interest in *The
Lost Colony*.

It occurred to Andy one night to build a skit
around the most famous lines from *Hamlet*. But he
wasn't sure quite how to do it; "just doing it with
a Southern accent didn't seem funny," he recalled.
Besides, Andy had never read *Hamlet*. He called
Bob Armstrong, his university buddy and *Lost
Colony* costar. Bob came over and walked Andy
through the play. Andy wrote down the names of
the characters and committed the story to memory.
He crafted a monologue, performed it the next
Saturday, and drew huge laughs. "The idea was
that I was selling these books, five great tragedies
by this fella named William Shakespeare who
lived over in the old country," Andy recalled.

Andy didn't write down his skits, but a version
of the *Hamlet* sketch survives on record:

And it's a pretty good show. And the moral
of it is, though, I reckon, if you was to ever kill

a fellah and then marry his wife, I'd be extra careful not to tell my stepson.

Andy had learned to poke fun at his own intellectual limitations, to laugh at his rough edges and his hick heritage—in short, to mock the very qualities that fed his deepest insecurities. He soon learned that those foibles were not his alone. The Shriner audience howled.

"He talked just like we did," recalled Robert Edwards King, nephew of Barbara Griffith. "That's the way we are. We laugh about that stuff."

In spring 1952, Andy gave his notice at Goldsboro High School, over the objections of the principal, who told him, "You're never gonna make any money running around the country." The Griffiths moved back to Chapel Hill, rented a house for eighty-five dollars a month, and began to channel their ambitions into a traveling variety show.

Andy's first impulse was to head straight for Miami and the regional nightclub scene there. Barbara proposed a more practical alternative: They would play the local Rotary Club circuit, driving around the state and performing at any civic function that would have them. If they were good, someone would eventually invite them to New York.

Andy cashed out his $300 in accumulated teacher retirement pay, borrowed $1,000 more, bought a used station wagon, and printed up flyers. He and Barbara lived, for a time, not much better than starving artists. Their parents—Barbara's, in particular—fretted for their future. Andy was giving up a comfortable teaching career. "I really think our families thought we were slightly crazy," Barbara recalled. But Andy was determined, and no one in the family tried to stop him.

"Unique entertainment for your group with Andy and Barbara Griffith," the couple promised in a trifold brochure. "No occasion too small, no job too big. Andy and Barbara Griffith offer one of the most unusual and entertaining programs to be found today. Their act is as versatile as it is warm and appealing to every type of audience."

Andy recalled, "She'd sing. I'd do the comedy. We'd hire a piano player for fifteen dollars. We had our own lighting system. I never used a microphone; never had one."

Andy and Barbara collected listings of every convention or chicken dinner planned in North Carolina for the next six months. "We figured that at least one out of every hundred would have need of entertainment," he recalled. They sent out their brochures. Offers began to trickle in.

Mike King, Barbara's nephew, went with his family to see his aunt and uncle in an early gig, at Fred Koury's Plantation Supper Club in

Greensboro. "They were like a duo," he recalled. "They would play off of each other. One would be the straight guy. . . . They were basically a team, back then."

Around this time, J. B. Childress received a letter from his boyhood friend. Andy had read in the paper that J.B. was the new president of the local Kiwanis Club in Waynesville. "I'm trying to gain some experience in show business," Andy wrote. "I'd like to come to Waynesville and put on a show for you and raise funds." He offered to divide the proceeds evenly with the service club. The Kiwanis board asked J.B. about Andy. J.B. told them, "Well, nobody knows him. He couldn't draw any more people than I could, and I couldn't draw half a dozen." J.B. politely declined.

Andy would not soon forget the slight. A few years later, when Andy was famous, J.B. sent him a letter. J.B. now belonged to the Chamber of Commerce in Charlotte, and the group was looking for a big name to headline a banquet. The organizers wanted Andy. But Andy never replied. A decade after that, Andy invited J.B. and his wife to a performance. That night, J.B. asked Andy, "Why didn't you answer my letter?" Andy smiled and replied, "J.B., why didn't you let me come to Waynesville when I needed some experience?" For the next five decades, Andy would reward loyalty in his friends and hold long and bitter grudges toward those who let him down.

Some months into their new venture, Andy and Barbara found they had a show booked for a group they'd entertained previously. "And I didn't have but one show," Andy recalled. On the way to the gig, Andy assembled a monologue from his memories of playing sousaphone in the marching band at football games in Chapel Hill. "I don't know where it come from, nor why, but that notion came to me in the car on the way to the second job," he recalled. The skit described a "country fella" stumbling upon a game of college football:

"And I looked down thar, and I seen five or six convicts a-runnin' up and down and a-blowin' whistles. . . . And I seen thirty-five or forty men come a-runnin' out one end of a great big outhouse down there. . . . And, friends, I seen that evenin' the awfulest fight that I have ever seen in my life!"

The observer concludes that the point of the game is for the men to run a "pumpkin" from one end of a cow pasture to the other without being knocked down or "steppin' in something." The last bit was a nod to Andy's own scrimmages, long ago, in Mrs. Allred's cow pasture.

Or was it? Barbara once told an interviewer Andy's most famous sketch merely retold a football story Andy had heard from another man, a tale "so blue Andy wouldn't tell it to me." She said Andy simply rewrote it, leaving out the dirty parts.

Andy and Barbara had pledged, early in their marriage, that if either found fame, the other would step back into a supporting role. By spring of 1953, the Griffiths were beginning to draw attention, and most of it was going to Andy.

One May weekend, the Raleigh Little Theatre presented a production of *Ten Nights in a Barroom*. A reviewer in the *Raleigh Times* dismissed it as "two hours of archaic dialogue, missed cues, mysterious hands, dangling sandbags," and such. The writer said the production was salvaged only by Andy Griffith, who came on between acts to perform his new football sketch and another Shakespeare send-up, this one inspired by *Romeo and Juliet*. Andy "could have held the stage all night," the critic wrote, "and no one would have minded."

Andy performed his football sketch that summer at a dinner gathering. A man came running up afterward and introduced himself as Orville Campbell. He told Andy, "We've got to make a record of this!" Andy replied, "Well, Mr. Campbell, if you've got the money, I've got the time."

Orville began to bring a microphone and a tape recorder to Andy's shows. Five times, he tried to record the sketch. Each time, Andy froze because he wasn't accustomed to the microphone. Orville finally captured a good performance that September in Greensboro, at a convention of the Jefferson Standard Life Insurance Company.

Orville released the 45 rpm record on November 14, 1953, on Colonial Records, a tiny Chapel Hill imprint. Side A was the football sketch, which Orville titled "What It Was, Was Football." Side B was the *Romeo and Juliet* sketch. Both were credited to "Deacon Andy Griffith."

They agreed to split the profits. Before long, Orville's record had sold fifty thousand copies, and "Deacon" Andy Griffith was in heavy rotation.

3.

The Bumpkins Take Broadway

Don Knotts lay in bed in the tiny hotel room above Times Square and wondered whether his wife's first night in Manhattan might be her last. *Thump, thump, thump,* went the wall, shuddering from the weight of one body heaving against another in passion, like a sweaty human battering ram. How long could the wall endure this? How long could Kay?

In the service, Don had heard men have sex with each other. But sweet little Kay, the preacher's daughter, seemed so innocent. Now, on this cold January night in 1949, they lay in a fleabag hotel, trying to ignore the horrible noises bleeding across the shabby partition. Don imagined Kay asking herself, "What in God's name have we gotten ourselves into?"

Matters improved the next day. The Knottses rented a room at Ninety-Ninth Street and Broadway. Kay took a secretarial job with Celanese Corporation, a chemical company, for thirty-three dollars a week. Don claimed the twenty-dollar weekly allotment to which he was entitled through the military's 52-20 Club, which guaranteed

84

unemployed servicemen a meager living for up to fifty-two weeks. Don would remain on the dole for only two weeks.

"We would go to a place; the cheapest thing on the menu was spaghetti and meatballs, but it was a white-tablecloth thing," Kay recalled. "And every week we would eat okay until it got to be Thursday, and then it was slim pickings. They had those Automats, where you could eat for forty cents."

Every morning, Don hit the streets to "make the rounds," visiting theatrical agents and trolling for work. After a few weeks, he was clearly getting nowhere. Spent and frustrated, he confessed to Kay, "I don't know how to get into show business." She replied, "Why don't you look up Lanny Ross?"

Lanny had come backstage after one of the *Stars and Gripes* performances overseas and invited Don to look him up in peacetime. Now, in 1949, Lanny was back in New York, hosting a radio show on the powerful Mutual Broadcasting System from station WOR. Taking Lanny up on his offer seemed a long shot to Don, but Kay thought he should at least try. So, Don wrote Lanny a letter. Much to Don's surprise, he received an immediate reply.

Lanny happily adopted Don as a cause. "He introduced me all around, telling all his people how talented he thought I was," Don recalled.

"And he gave me a shot on his radio show." Don couldn't believe his good fortune.

Lanny had plenty of reasons to help Don. One was the powerful bond of fraternity that linked servicemen after the war. Another was Don's prodigious talent, which seemed plain to everyone—save, perhaps, Don himself. A third was Don's manner. Suppliant and self-effacing, Don radiated a complaisant submissiveness when in the company of other men, triggering the same protective impulse as a wagging tail on a stray dog. People wanted to help him.

In his radio debut, Don performed the monologue Lanny had seen him do in the South Pacific, depicting "a sportscaster calling a football game who gets excited and mixes up his words, like, 'They're going back to their puddle. I mean, their huddle,'" Don recalled. Both he and Andy effectively launched their broadcast careers with skits about football.

Lanny sent Don to William Morris, and soon Don was booked on *Arthur Godfrey's Talent Scouts*. Arthur Godfrey was a star-maker, and his *Talent Scouts* was simulcast on radio and television, giving Don, in 1949, his first on-screen appearance.

New York was amid a vaudeville revival, so the William Morris agents dispatched Don to try out his stand-up act in variety shows at theaters in the outer boroughs. When Don arrived at his first engagement, in the Bronx, the booking agent told him to leave his music with the pit band. Don said he had no music.

"No play-on music, no play-off music?" the agent snarled.

"No, sir."

The agent scowled. "Well, give me one of your eight-by-ten pictures to put out front."

"I, uh . . . I don't have any eight-by-ten pictures."

"What?" the agent screamed. "You've got no pictures? Listen, you do ten minutes and get off, you hear me? Not one minute more!"

The booker stormed off. Later, Don heard the man telling someone, "The kid's got no pictures. He's got no music. What kind of an act is that?"

Yet, Don's act drew riotous laughs in the Bronx. Emboldened, Don sought a booking in Manhattan. He got a gig at the Jefferson Theatre on Fourteenth Street in the East Village, where agents went to scout new acts.

"I walked onstage at the Jefferson with all the confidence in the world," Don recalled, "but after about two minutes, I realized I was in Trouble City. . . . These people had seen it all, and I'm sure they knew the punch lines to every one of my jokes. Five minutes went by and I had heard not one laugh. I was beginning to break out in a cold sweat. Finally, one guy in the balcony laughed, and I said, 'Thanks, Dad!' "

That was the end of Don's vaudeville career. He quit William Morris in humiliation and resolved never again to attempt stand-up, convinced it was "not my strong suit." Once again, Don seemed to sell himself short. The agents told Don he simply needed new material; he hadn't written anything of note since his army days. But Don would not be swayed. In the meager weeks that followed, surely the low ebb of his adult artistic career, Don took a job stuffing envelopes. "I'll say this," he recalled decades later. "It beat the hell out of plucking chickens in Raese's grocery."

Don's confidence had abandoned him, but not his ambition. He continued to make the rounds, haunting the agencies and casting offices and popping in to visit Lanny Ross. Don's persistence soon bore fruit. Peter Dixon, Lanny's writer, asked Don one day if he could do "the voice of an old-timer like, say, Gabby Hayes." Gabby was the quintessential geriatric cowboy sidekick, cast alongside Roy Rogers and John Wayne in films such as *Tall in the Saddle* and *Heldorado* to spout authentic frontier gibberish.

Dixon was assembling a revival of the Bobby Benson show, a radio series that had reaped a massive following in the 1930s. It was the stuff of juvenile fantasy: Bobby is an orphan who inherits a Texas cattle ranch and a gang of colorful sidekicks, including foreman Tex Mason, a "red Indian" called Harka, and an Irishman named . . .

Irish. Rounding out the cast is old-timer Windy Wales. Together, they fight off cattle thieves and outwit escaped cons.

Bobby Benson and the B-Bar-B Riders took to the air in 1949 as a summer replacement series on the Mutual Broadcasting System, home to *The Shadow* and Major League Baseball. Radio was still king in those days, two years before the debut of *I Love Lucy*. *Bobby Benson* was slated for 5:00 p.m. on Tuesdays and Thursdays, a thirty-minute segment timed to catch young boys between homework and dinner. Don played Windy Wales.

"That first Tuesday afternoon, I found myself at the microphone with a cast of veteran radio actors," Don recalled. "Let me tell you, I was just about as nervous as a person could be and still function. Pete Dixon [the scriptwriter] was in the control room, and when we went off the air, I sashayed by. He grinned at me. 'Good' was all he said." Don returned home feeling physically ill. "My body ached so much from the entire experience that I thought I was coming down with the flu."

Don's symptoms were anxiety made manifest. Don had performed well in his radio debut. Yet, he fully expected a phone call releasing him from the part. At the very inception of his professional career, Don already suffered from a debilitating pessimism, which combined with his natural fretfulness and budding hypochondria to yield an ensemble of physical ills. At such times, Don lay frozen in bed, sleepless and incapacitated.

The dreaded call never came, and Don returned to the microphone two days later to broadcast the second episode, groggy but relieved.

It was easy work, with no makeup or costumes and no need to memorize the script, which Don held in his hand as he read the part into the microphone. Don would eventually earn nearly $200 a week, which was good pay for the time.

"There was quite a technique to it, knowing how to fade yourself on and off the mike, how to match your voice to the action you were supposed to be engaged in, and keeping your eye on the director as well as your script," Don recalled. "The director directed the entire show from the control room behind the glass, much like an orchestra conductor. Our sound effects man; our organist, who played our musical bridges on the Hammond organ; and in our case, because we were a western, our animal sound man, the man who did all the horse whinnies and dog barks and so on; all had to be woven in with precise cues from the director. The whole thing fascinated me."

In Don's hands, Windy Wales soon emerged as the most colorful character in the *Bobby Benson* cast. A tired, old ranch hand, Windy is faithful and devoted and happily oblivious that his best days are behind him. He spins tales of derring-do, placing himself at the center of fantastic events that, if real, are well past: "Windjammer Wales, they used to call me, back in the days when I hunted whales up near the Arctic!" *Clop-diddy-clop-diddy-clop-diddy-clop.* "Yessiree, fellers, I've killed so many men the cemetery men made me a partner!"

Don's character was derivative, and he knew it. One day, Gabby Hayes himself came storming onto the set. "Goddamn you!" he raged. "You've been doing me on the radio every day and I'm sick of it!" Don stared at him in agony. Then, Gabby's lip trembled and he burst out laughing. Don looked into the control room and saw his producers in hysterics.

The nation's ten-year-old boys laughed with Windy Wales, and they laughed at him. His wheezy tenor was implicitly funny, and his tough-guy bluster made Windy an easy target for mockery from both the narrator and his costars. Windy Wales was the first iteration of Don's comedic caricature of male machismo, his first send-up of all the smirking swagger and action-hero posturing he saw in other men. Windy Wales was Don's absurdist critique of the postwar masculine ideal. The same ironic bravura would come to define Barney Fife a decade later, and Ralph Furley after that.

The revival worked: Bobby Benson again became a household name, at least among prepubescent boys. B-Bar-B riders formed clubs across the nation. Herbert Rice, a British immigrant who owned the show, ordered up a cornucopia of Bobby Benson merchandise and began to arrange publicity tours, dispatching Don and Ivan Cury, the twelve-year-old actor who played Bobby, to rodeos and county fairs up and down the East Coast along with a few hired hands and truckloads of collectibles.

"There were hundreds of things: Bobby Benson bikes, Bobby Benson hats, handkerchiefs, socks, gloves, flashlights, everything," Ivan recalled. "They would get a lot of money. We would get nothing."

In spring 1950, the success of Bobby Benson spawned a local television program, shot at the New Amsterdam Theatre on Forty-Second Street and broadcast live on the brand-new WOR television station. The broadcast prominently featured Windy Wales, signaling the character's rising currency with the Cracker Jack set. At the end of some broadcasts, no doubt to the delight of Manhattan parents, the station gave away a pony.

In one early television episode, Bobby and the gang are trapped in a bunkhouse by the bad guys. As Ivan Cury recalled, the director cut back and forth between live shots of the imperiled friends and a recorded loop of horses galloping through dust, with Tex Mason shouting, "Watch out!" and "Keep your head down!" Bobby and his friends hatch a plan to light a fire and create a smoke screen, providing cover to escape the bad guys. The crew had rounded up some crude smoke bombs; TV was still in its infancy, and visual effects were not yet an exact science.

"They set off a smoke bomb in the studio, and Don was at the door, and there was not much smoke coming in," Ivan recalled. Don began flapping the door open and shut to fan the smoke, which then engulfed the studio. "I couldn't see Don standing next to me," Ivan recalled. "Somebody came in and grabbed me by the arm and took me over to the next set."

The adjoining set was staged for the pony giveaway. The cameras rolled. "And this pony was hysterical, because of all the smoke," Ivan recalled. "Well, this pony couldn't bear it, and so it defecated and urinated at the same time, big, loud, and close to me. Don and the sound guys were hysterical with laughter. The guy on the boom fell off the boom."

By 1951, Ivan Cury's voice was changing and the Mutual radio network began searching for a new Bobby Benson. By the time Clive Rice, Ivan's replacement, joined the cast, *Bobby Benson* was a hit. The producers upgraded from the cheesy Hammond organ to a prerecorded score played by an actual orchestra. The promotional tours continued, with Clive replacing Ivan as the public face of Bobby Benson. Don and Clive traveled in a Boeing Stratocruiser emblazoned with the Bobby Benson logo.

Don and Clive played to huge crowds, but Don loathed the journeys, and he was becoming increasingly paranoid about his health. "He had quite a collection of medications when he was on the road," Clive recalled. "I can remember seeing, for the first time in my life, one of those throat-spray things. He had one of those, and he had this collection of pills he had to take for one reason or another. . . . He was very conscious of anyone who had a cold." Don would fret daily about his health for the next five decades.

Don's *Bobby Benson* duties occupied about four hours of his day, from his arrival at the studio after lunch to the conclusion of the daily broadcast at five thirty. Don was free every morning. He spent those hours making the rounds, visiting casting offices, trolling for parts, and trying to make his mark on television. There was little money to be made, but "everything was up for grabs," and Don sensed opportunity.

He landed a few small parts on television dramas, such as a 1953 spot on *Robert Montgomery Presents*, but he could make no headway in comedies. He telephoned *The Jackie Gleason Show*. "I'd love to do your show," he told the gruff man on the line. "I'm a comedian." After a lengthy silence, the voice shot back, "We got a comedian."

But Don's talent and his winsome personality were about to pay another dividend. Charles Irving, who portrayed ranch foreman Tex Mason on the B-Bar-B, was navigating his own migration to television. In 1953, Irving helped Don land a part on one of the new television soaps, *Search for Tomorrow*. Don later termed it the only serious dramatic role of his television career. He played a neurotic janitor named Wilbur, who spoke to no one but his sister, Rose, portrayed by a young Lee Grant.

"He played a nebbish," Lee recalled. "And he looked like a nebbish. And he was sweet. And he didn't have a chance to be funny, because he was supposed to be dying or something. . . . It was so silly. And we were silly together, because neither of us knew what we were doing."

Daily rehearsals began at 8:00 a.m. The show aired at 12:45 and ended at 1:00, a fifteen-minute broadcast modeled on the format of radio. The schedule left Don time to race over to the Mutual Broadcasting studio for the afternoon broadcast of *Bobby Benson*. One role called for Don to act chiefly with his expressive face, in the manner of a silent film. The other exploited only his emotive voice. Don seemed equally skilled at both.

Wilbur was scripted to appear in only two or three episodes of the soap. But Don played the part so well that Wilbur returned to the program sporadically for two years. Once again, he couldn't believe his good fortune.

"He didn't have to speak," recalled Kay, Don's wife. "And so he didn't have to learn any lines. He loved it."

To this growing repertoire of characters, Don now added a new persona, one that would define his career. The Nervous Man came to Don in a dream; he awoke just as it ended and jotted down some notes. In the dream, a speaker delivers a speech at a civic-club dinner on ladies' night. He feels out of place. He is shaking with fear, and he stammers, stumbles, and apologizes as he speaks. The dream combined two memories.

"Several months earlier, I had attended a luncheon during which one of the speakers was so nervous, his hands were shaking visibly," Don recalled. "He rattled the paper his notes were written on, and when he attempted a drink of water, he proceeded to spill it all over himself. It was a painful thing to watch, but at the same time, amusing."

The second memory concerned Robert Benchley, a comedic actor whose celebrated short film "The Treasurer's Report" had apparently found its way to Morgantown. Benchley's public speaker sits in palpable agony, a dozen pained expressions playing across his face as he strangles his cloth napkin and twiddles his thumbs. Then he speaks: "I am reminded of a story that probably all of you have heard. It seems there were these two Irishmen walking down the street. And they came to a, um, I should have said in the first place that the, uh, store belonging to the Irishman, the first Irishman, the first fellow's store . . ."

Don's sketch combined the fluster and unease of Benchley with the palpable terror of the fretful luncheon speaker. Don's character coughs and sputters and clears his throat. His speech, when it comes, veers from one faux pas to the next: "[Y]ou ladies would probably complain less if we stopped kidding you so much, calling you nicknames. For instance, Tom there, our president —hi, Tom—is always calling his wife, Claudia— hi, Claude—is always calling her the Old Woman. I happen to know that Claude is only forty-two. Well, that is, what I meant is, she's not nearly as old as she looks. . . ."

The darting saucer eyes, the pursed lips, the shuddering hands, the knotted brow, the quaking, overcaffeinated voice: Don's comedic persona took wing in that scribbled sketch.

Don was ecstatic. To that point in his career, he felt that his every performance had been derivative. Here, finally, was a character pulled from Don's own mind.

Don set up an audition at the Blue Angel, a nightclub on East Fifty-Fifth Street with quilted walls. The owner watched the routine in silence, sitting alone in the middle of the long, narrow room. When it was over, Don recalled, the owner pronounced it "the most boring thing he'd ever seen." Don went home, crestfallen, and tucked the routine back into his subconscious, presumably for good.

Between *Bobby Benson* and *Search for Tomorrow*, Don's schedule was growing increasingly hectic. His soap-opera talents kept Wilbur alive far longer than Don had expected. (Lee Grant was not so lucky: Sponsors fired her over alleged communist sympathies. Two other actresses stepped in to play Wilbur's sister.) Meanwhile, Don's radio voicings on *Bobby Benson* proved so popular that the producers created a spin-off program called *Songs of the B-Bar-B*, which eventually expanded from five minutes to a full half hour. By 1955, the spin-off had moved to television, and Don found himself in a scramble.

"My day went something like this," Don recalled. "I would arrive at the studio for *Search for Tomorrow* at eight a.m., off the air at one, then lunch, then off to rehearse for *Bobby Benson*. Then grab a cab to the television station, where Jim McMenemy"—*Songs of the B-Bar-B*'s writer-director—"would read me the tall tale I was to tell while I was changing into my cowboy costume. I would more or less memorize it as he told it. Off the air at eight p.m., then dinner, then take the subway home to learn the lines for the next day's *Search for Tomorrow*."

Don and Kay's first child, Karen, had arrived in April 1954. In 1955, to lighten his load, Don quit the television version of *Bobby Benson*, leaving him the radio show and the soap opera. Not long after, *Bobby Benson and the B-Bar-B Riders* was canceled, a casualty of the waning radio era. Around the same time, Wilbur was eased out of *Search for Tomorrow*. And, just like that, Don was unemployed.

Joblessness bred desperation. "The nest egg was dwindling rapidly," Don recalled, "and there wasn't a job in sight. My spirits were sagging, and with the responsibility of a family now, I was, for the first time, beginning to feel I would have to throw in the towel."

Between visits to casting agencies, Don would rest his feet at Cromwell's Drugstore, nestled inside the RCA Building at Rockefeller Center, a notorious actor hangout. Don's stoolmates included Tony Randall, later of television's *Odd Couple*, and Jonathan Winters, then a young, wild warm-up comic. Another of Don's cronies was Frank Behrens, a struggling television actor. One day, Don was pondering his fate over coffee at Cromwell's when Frank happened by and asked, "Have you looked into that *No Time for Sergeants* thing?"

Don replied, "What the hell's a *No Time for Sergeants* thing?"

"You haven't read about it? It's a new play.

Maurice Evans is going to produce it on Broadway. They're looking for Southern types. It ought to be right down your alley. Here." Frank pointed to an article about the new production in a trade paper. "I think this is the last day they're seeing people."

Don scanned the article. "You're right!" he cried. "They stop seeing people at five p.m. today, and Maurice Evan's office is clear down in Greenwich Village."

Don looked at his watch. It was four thirty. He leaped from his chair, dashed out of the restaurant, and ducked into a subway station.

Don arrived at the office of Maurice Evans at five o'clock. His production was adapting a best-selling book by Mac Hyman, a Georgian who had crafted a novel from his experiences as a Southerner in the military. Evans was not a Southerner but a British-born thespian who had brought the first full-length *Hamlet* to the modern American stage—although contemporary readers will more likely remember him as Dr. Zaius in the postapocalyptic film *Planet of the Apes*.

Don ran to the desk. "I'm sorry," said the man behind it, "but I'm afraid you're a little too late. Mr. Rogers isn't seeing any more people." Emmett Rogers was Maurice Evans's companion and the play's associate producer.

"Please?" Don begged.

The man rose and entered the casting room.

He returned with a forlorn look. "I'm sorry."

Don was near tears, his face a mask of raw sorrow. He turned and slumped toward the stairs.

He was about to take his first step down when the receptionist called him back. "You looked so sad, I went back and pleaded."

Once again, Don's puppy-dog charm had elicited an outpouring of human compassion, this time from a total stranger.

Don was ushered into the casting room. Emmett Rogers "greeted me abruptly," Don recalled, "and I had the feeling he was going to give me the bum's rush, so I started spitting out my credits as fast as I could, being careful to drawl as much as possible."

It worked. "All right," Rogers said finally, "we're reading people Monday morning at the Alvin Theatre."

Don read *No Time for Sergeants* over the weekend. The narrator was one Will Stockdale, a backwoods Georgian, whose isolated family and country values represent a sort of last stand for rural America against assimilation into the wartime machinery of a mechanized society. The book plants this simple, guileless individual within the jaded bureaucracy of the military. The military tries to break him; instead, he breaks it. Don took particular interest in the part of Ben Whitledge, a smaller, smarter sidekick to Will. It seemed a natural fit.

At 10:00 a.m. on Monday, Don arrived at the Alvin Theatre at Fifty-Second and Broadway. "I could hear my heart pounding in my ears," he recalled. "I was determined and yet, at the same time, frightened beyond description." Finally, Don was called to the stage and asked to read Ben Whitledge, the very part he had prepared. When he had finished, Emmett Rogers came running down the aisle. "He seemed all excited," Don recalled. "I could tell he loved my reading." His excitement ebbed, though, when Maurice Evans joined Rogers in the footlights.

"That was veddy good, Mr. Knotts," Evans said, "but I'm afraid you might be just a little too tall. Ben Whitledge should be quite short."

Awaiting a second reading, Don fretted about the "too tall" remark. He was only five eight and a half. How could he make himself shorter? In desperation, he tore the heels from his one good pair of shoes, shortening himself by an inch. Don returned to the theater and struggled to stand upright on the crippled shoes. The effort was wasted: Maurice Evans still thought Don was too tall. The producers told him he'd hear from them in a week or so.

That week seemed the longest in Don's life. "I was learning that a big part of an actor's life is waiting for the phone to ring," he recalled. Finally, the producers called. Don had two small roles in the play. The work paid union scale, eighty-five dollars a week. Still, it was a Broadway show, and Don sensed it might be a turning point.

Maurice Evans had awarded the sidekick part of Ben Whitledge to Roddy McDowall, his fellow countryman and, a decade later, fellow ape. Roddy was actually a hair taller than Don; but, unlike Don, Roddy had made a movie with Elizabeth Taylor.

One chilly September morning, Don returned to the stage of the Alvin Theatre to read through *No Time for Sergeants*, still bitter.

"My name is Maurice Evans," the producer said. "You may call me Mr. E. I will work you very hard and pay you very little." He paused for polite laughter. "Let me introduce our star, Mr. Andy Griffith."

In the final days of 1953, Andy and Barbara Griffith left North Carolina and took a suite at the Park Sheraton Hotel in Manhattan. Just a few months earlier, Andy wouldn't have dreamed of moving to New York. All that changed when he met Dick Linke.

Richard O. Linke was born in Summit, New Jersey, a leafy New York suburb, the son of German immigrants. He studied journalism at Ohio University and went to work for the Associated Press at Rockefeller Center. Then he left to join a PR firm run by a former newsman, where he did press for Perry Como on *The*

Chesterfield Supper Club radio show. He eventually moved into record promotion, working for the Capitol and Columbia labels and briefly running his own firm, where he handled Doris Day. In 1953, Dick was head of promotion at Capitol.

One day that fall, Dick was sitting in his New York apartment, eating breakfast at noon; it had been a late night. The radio DJ was showcasing other stations around the country. That day, the signal was coming from North Carolina, and the recording caught Dick's ear:

". . . It was that both bunches full of them men wanted this funny-lookin' little punkin to play with. . . ."

Orville Campbell had pressed an initial five hundred copies of "What It Was, Was Football" and dispatched them to radio stations around the state. The record became a regional hit. It caught the attention of Capitol's man in North Carolina. He alerted Hal Cook, national sales manager at Capitol.

Hal was Dick's boss. Now, in different ways, each man had heard of Andy Griffith. In December, Dick and Hal flew down to Chapel Hill to meet with Andy and Orville Campbell, carrying a Capitol Records contract. When Dick walked into the meeting, Andy whispered to Orville, "His teeth are too close together." To Andy, the slick New Yorker might as well have been Jimmy Cagney.

"And we went over every word of the contract," Dick recalled. "They were always worried about Northerners: Were we going to take them?"

By the meeting's end, Dick had purchased "What It Was, Was Football" for $10,000, splitting the sum between Andy and Orville. Andy was now a Capitol recording artist at $300 a week. Dick also signed on as Andy's manager, though he remained a Capitol Records employee for the time. Dick and Hal felt they could trust no one else to manage Andy, the guileless country boy. During the meeting, Hal telephoned his superiors at the home office and boasted, "I have found a real Li'l Abner." Andy swallowed his bile.

Andy and Barbara used the $5,000 advance to repay their debts. They took an apartment in Kew Gardens, Queens. Dick and Andy started work together on January 4. As they crisscrossed Manhattan, Dick noticed Andy had a charming Southern habit of saying "I 'preciate it" at every chance. After he'd heard it twenty times or so, he told Andy, "Hey, do me a favor. Say that all the time. When you autograph pictures, write, 'I 'preciate it.' And someday, that'll be a household word."

Dick smothered Andy with attention. "Dick told me where to live, where to buy food," Andy recalled later. "He didn't suggest; he *told* me. He led me to agents; he personally took me to auditions." For most of a decade, Andy had depended on Barbara for counsel. Now, Dick delivered an ultimatum: "Either I'm going to have to make the decisions, or Barbara is." Andy considered and made his choice, telling his wife, "Well, Barbara, I won't be asking you any more what you think." Barbara graciously yielded to Dick, and the Griffiths and Linkes became dear friends. Yet, the power shift marked a turning point in both relationships.

Dick got Andy a meeting with Abe Lastfogel, head of the William Morris Agency. Lastfogel was one of the most powerful men in show business. But when Andy walked into the office, he recognized neither the name nor the smallish man who owned it. Lastfogel was there with his wife, Frances, and Danny Kaye, whose presence gave Andy a hint of the man's gravitas. "They put on my record," Andy recalled, "and I don't remember anybody laughing at all. But when it was over, Frances leaned over to Abe and said, 'Sign him.' "

The agency booked Andy onto Ed Sullivan's *Toast of the Town*. The Capitol Records reissue of the football sketch was on its way to selling a million copies, making it one of the bestselling comedy records in history. Ed Sullivan was so taken with Andy that he wanted to book him for eighteen appearances. But Andy was untested on the national stage, and Abe Lastfogel would give Sullivan only four nights. Abe's instinct would prove prescient.

"Deacon" Andy Griffith debuted on *Toast of the Town* on January 10, along with singer Dolores Gray, the Copacabana Dancers, and an act called Joyce's Camels. Andy followed the camels. He performed the skits on both sides of the "Football" single. And he bombed, as anyone in the viewing audience could tell.

Andy could not recall his performance afterward, except that no one had laughed. To add insult to injury, Ed Sullivan scolded the comic after the broadcast for the adult theme of the "Romeo and Juliet" sketch, telling him, "Andy, don't ever work blue." Andy's *Toast of the Town* run would end after a single night.

Nonetheless, the spot earned Andy his first national press, short items in the January 18 issues of *Time* and *Newsweek*. The latter publication pronounced him on "the verge of a big-time career."

Undeterred, the William Morris agents booked Andy at the Blue Angel, the same Fifty-Fifth Street club where Don would audition his Nervous Man routine. On the first night, the agency packed the room with celebrities and friends, including Henry Fonda and James Garner. Andy drew big laughs. But after the show, Abe Lastfogel came up and told him, "Now, I want you to go anywhere you can and learn how to entertain." Andy was mystified—until the next night. "And the next night," Andy recalled, "I was by myself, and I died."

Andy did two shows a night for nearly a month, and he never recovered his mojo. After the club had emptied, Andy would walk the streets of New York, trying to figure out how his act could have gone so quickly south after the trip north. Like Don before him, Andy was learning that success back home in no way guaranteed success in New York. Both men had come to the city and bombed: their hayseed humor died in Manhattan clubs.

"He needed a lot of work," Dick Linke recalled. "With Andy's kind of comedy, you couldn't put him in New York, you couldn't put him in big cities. A Jewish comic, you put him in the Catskills, but with Andy, we had to talk about putting him down around the South and Southwest."

Andy spent the next fifteen months on the road, in his car, working the Southern nightclub circuit. He would polish his delivery and timing with a growing repertoire of monologues that played off Northern stereotypes of Southern rubes.

He went to Miami and did a stint as resident comic for Eddy Arnold, the country singer, at the Olympia Theater. "And I scored, and I got my security back," Andy recalled. "I got my self-confidence back. Same material. Same stuff."

Andy went on to a two-week stand at a hotel in Atlanta, and he scored again. He worked as far west as Denver, and he ranged north from Florida to the Carolinas, earning as much as $1,500 a week. In September 1954, he returned to the University of North Carolina to perform his football sketch at halftime in an actual college football game.

Lawrence Laurent, entertainment writer for *The Washington Post*, later recounted seeing Andy at one of those early shows. Andy was playing the Mosque, a cavernous auditorium in Richmond, Virginia, on a bill of "hillbilly" performers that included country singer Jimmy Dean. "Deacon Andy" took the stage and performed the vaudeville tune "A Good Man Is Hard to Find" with his fervent, Southern-revivalist delivery. "The effect on the audience was electric, more compelling than anything I had ever seen," Laurent wrote. "The crowd shouted with Griffith, responded to his every gesture and lapsed into a strange, almost reverent silence" when he was finished.

Andy began to upstage more famous acts. One night, after Andy opened for Mae West, Mae's manager approached him and told him to do a different act in the second show. Andy dug out an old folk song called "In the Pines" and revived his preacher character, sermonizing and stomping his foot. It was, if anything, funnier than what Andy had done in the first show. Mae loved it. Andy was promptly fired.

During the long, lonely hours on the road, Andy sometimes tuned in to the Mutual radio network to catch an afternoon broadcast of *Bobby Benson and the B-Bar-B Riders.* His favorite character was "an old man who told tall tales, named Windy Wales."

Several months into Andy's nightclub tour, an old friend from the North Carolina theater sent him a copy of the bestseller *No Time for Sergeants*. On an airplane to Denver, Andy found time to read it. The book began, "The thing was, we had gone fishing that day and Pa had wore himself out with it the way he usually did when he went fishing. I mean he went at it pretty hard and called the fish all sorts of names. . . ."

Andy was intrigued. Will Stockdale's satirical observations of military rigmarole reminded Andy of his own monologues. When he returned to New York, Andy went straight to Abe Lastfogel's office at William Morris. He told him, "If there's ever anything that I can play, this is it." Andy sent a copy of the book to Dick and conveyed the same message.

No Time for Sergeants was a hot property, and the rights had already been sold. But Andy would not give up. This was the role he'd been born to play.

Andy telephoned the author, Mac Hyman. Mac coughed up the name of his literary agent. Andy found the agent and stormed into his office. The agent tried to let Andy down easy: "Andy, you have to know that this is a number one bestseller and it's been on the bestseller list ten, fifteen weeks. It's gonna be a play and a movie and a television show."

The meeting gave Andy the edge he needed. No one in New York seemed to know about the television production, which was being staged by the storied Theatre Guild for broadcast March 15, 1955, on *The United States Steel Hour*. There was still time for Andy to read for Will Stockdale. Andy was the first actor to arrive at the audition.

Alas, Andy had spent the previous year honing his stand-up comedy skills, to the detriment of his acting. His audition fell flat. "I didn't read well because I didn't know how to read," he recalled. Andy pleaded with the producers: "I'm a talker, not a reader." They were unmoved. Andy retreated to the waiting room, his mind racing: How could he salvage the role of his life?

For want of another plan, Andy struck up a conversation with a random woman in the waiting room, hoping to draw attention to himself. She took the bait, asking Andy, "What do you do?"

"I work nightclubs."

"You sing?"

"No, I talk."

"What do you talk about?"

"Oh, Shakespeare, *Hamlet*, *Romeo and Juliet*, opera, ballet."

"*Hamlet*? Do you read it?"

"No, I tell it."

"Well, how does it start?"

Andy took the cue: "It's called *Hamlet*. And it was named after this young boy Hamlet that appeared in the play, and it was pretty good, except they don't speak as good English as we do. . . ."

One by one, actors, executives, and secretaries filed into the room to hear Andy's monologue. "It sounds like a bad B movie, but it happened," Andy recalled. "As I went along, each of them would go out and get somebody else."

The random woman was Armina Marshall, a director of both the Theatre Guild and the *Steel Hour*. When Andy had finished, she took him by the hand and led him to Alex Segal, the director. She told him, "I have Will Stockdale."

The United States Steel Hour broadcast was nothing more than a televised play, filmed on a stage with theatrical sets before a live audience. When it commenced, Andy was terrified, just like on Ed Sullivan's stage and at the Blue Angel. But when Andy began to speak, the audience responded, first with smiles, then with chuckles, then with laughter. Andy fed on the reaction. His terror fell away and his frozen body thawed.

The teleplay opens with Andy seated alone on a chair. "Howdy, I'm Will Stockdale," he says, his intense gaze and broad smile warming the camera. "I'm fixin' to tell you some of the things that happened to me in the draft." He produces a

Jew's harp and commences to play, then to sing: "Whoa, mule, you kicking mule / Whoa, mule, I say / Well, I ain't got time to kiss you now / My mule's run away. . . ."

The viewing audience that night included Maurice Evans, who was to direct the play on Broadway. Maurice had found his Will Stockdale.

That September, inside the Alvin Theatre, Andy and Don sat down at a table together for the first time for the inaugural script read-through. They had yet to meet. Don was "as nervous as a cat," he recalled, "but I couldn't get over how good Andy Griffith was. . . . When we finished, I was certain of two things: this play was going to be a hit, and a lot of people were going to know who Andy Griffith was."

On the first day of rehearsals, Andy stood in the wings and watched as "this thin little man came out." It was Don. "He was a young fella then, but he put on an old voice and introduced Will Stockdale." Andy couldn't place the man, but he recognized the voice.

On the second day of rehearsals, Don wandered out the stage door and found Andy sitting on a fire hydrant. Andy was whittling. Don didn't think he had ever seen an actor whittle.

"Excuse me," Andy said. "Are you Windy Wales?"

4.

Nervous Men

It was a miracle Andy and Don met at all.

Both men had wound up among the rejects in the waiting rooms of their respective *No Time for Sergeants* auditions. And at the decisive moment, each had refused to concede defeat. Their improbable comebacks were a testament to their ambitions.

Yes, Don confessed, he was Windy Wales. He was frankly stunned that Andy—or anyone else past adolescence—had even heard of Windy Wales.

"Sheee-it, yes!" Andy cried, breaking into a broad grin. "I knew I recognized that voice!"

They talked for a few minutes. Andy explained that he had listened to *Bobby Benson* on the radio to pass the long hours on the road between shows. Each man was surprised to learn the other actually hailed from the South. Though *Sergeants* was a quintessentially Southern production, most of the cast and crew seemed to come either from New York or Great Britain. There weren't many Southerners on Broadway. Finding a kindred spirit gave each man a measure of comfort.

"Both of us were inherently shy people, but now

the ice was broken," Don recalled. ". . . Our friendship had begun."

Backstage, Andy and Don spent their spare moments playing mumblety-peg, a school-yard game from the Mark Twain era that involves throwing a pocketknife at one's foot. This shared heritage bolstered their friendship immeasurably.

The producers could cut anyone from the *No Time* cast at will during the first week. Naturally, Don worried himself sick, contracting one of the worst colds of his life. When the week was over, Don shifted his angst to the director. He expected to learn a lot from the great Morton DaCosta, who would go on to direct *Auntie Mame* and *The Music Man*. But DaCosta rarely spoke aloud. After two weeks, he had not said a single word to Don.

Finally, Don approached him. "Mr. DaCosta?"

The director "whirled around and looked at me as if he had never seen me before in his life," Don recalled.

"Yes," Morton croaked.

"Well, I . . . er . . . uh . . . er . . . Am I doing it all right?"

"Yes."

It was the only conversation they ever had.

The schedule for *Sergeants* called for three weeks of rehearsals and three weeks of out-of-town "tryouts" in New Haven and Boston. In addition to a preacher role, Don was cast as a corporal who tests Will's manual dexterity with a steel-ring puzzle. This would prove a far more consequential casting.

Ira Levin's script calls for an "officious little Corporal." Don played the part with palpable tension, rapping his fingers on his arm as Private Stockdale walks in.

The corporal silently motions Will to sit. "What we do here, Private, is to evaluate your manual dexterity on a time scale in relation to digital-visual coordination," the corporal announces, sounding like a highly caffeinated carnival barker. He holds up the steel rings. "Two irregular steel links, which can be interconnected . . . thusly." He smoothly joins them. "I separate them . . . I join them." He sets a stopwatch as the sergeant cautions Will, "Whatever you do, don't get nervous."

As the corporal and sergeant converse behind him, Will wrenches open one link with inhuman strength, threads it through the other, and then twists it into a knot. "I'm done," he announces.

"Done?!" the corporal cries. "In fourteen seconds? He . . . look what he . . . look!" the corporal says, gazing at the twisted steel.

"He put them together, didn't he?" the sergeant barks.

The corporal is defeated and deflated. He seems ready to cry.

The skit was short, but Andy and Don played so well off each other that their little scene seemed to burn a bit brighter than the rest of the production. "It's there or it's not there," Andy would remark decades later. "And it was there with us."

Don quickly learned that Andy's perfectionist zeal matched his own. The New Haven audience was laughing nonstop that first week, but one night, the show didn't play so well. Don ran into Andy after the curtain fell. Andy began to pick apart the performance. Don surely felt the same impulse, but he tried to soothe his new friend with false levity, telling Andy, "You can't win 'em all."

Andy, ferocity flaring in his eyes, spat back, "You can damn well try!"

October 20, 1955, was opening night at the Alvin Theatre in New York. It fell to Don to walk onstage and introduce Andy. As Don stood in the wings, he feared he might faint and felt certain he could not move. He finally summoned the strength to stagger out and deliver his lines, although he could not recall having done so when the performance was over. Then Don retreated offstage and glimpsed Andy, who was hobbling forward in a state that made Don look positively relaxed. "I've never seen a man so frightened," recalled Roddy McDowall, Andy's costar.

Then, Andy began to speak. "And a couple of people giggled," McDowall recalled, "and then they began to applaud. Watching from the wings, you could see old Andy's confidence coming back."

McDowall had heard about Andy's magic. That night, he saw it: Andy could perform a powerful scene with another character and then turn around, break the fourth wall, and engage with the audience in the seats. "He played Stockdale— right to the people," McDowall recalled. "And they loved it. He'd spot a lady in the second row all doubled up with laughter, and he'd laugh right with her."

At intermission, Andy's manager, Dick Linke, raced out into the lobby to gauge the reaction of the newspapermen. "Everyone was there," he recalled. "Ed Sullivan, Earl Wilson. And they said, 'Dick, you've got a star on your hands.'" When Andy had taken his last curtain call, the cast repaired to Sardi's, the Forty-Fourth Street restaurant where actors gathered to await the reviews. Andy knew nothing of this tradition and had made other plans, but he was easily persuaded to come along. He walked in to a standing ovation.

The critics were pleased. "A thespian nobody stepped into full stardom," *Newsweek* pronounced. *The New York Times* noted Andy's potent chemistry: "All he has to do is walk on the stage and look the audience straight in the face. If the armed forces cannot cope with Will Stockdale, neither can the audience resist Andy Griffith." *No Time for Sergeants* would play for 796 performances.

Andy and Don quickly grew close. Don admired

Andy's abundant talent, and Andy came to adore Don's sweet vulnerability. Both men were bumpkins who had come to New York and had found ways to sell their Southernness to a national audience.

"We had similar backgrounds," Don recalled. "When we talked about our relatives, they all seemed to be the same. Our sense of humor clicked."

Andy and Barbara would drive out to visit Don and Kay at their home in suburban Dumont, New Jersey, or Don and Kay would drive in and pick up the Griffiths at their apartment in Queens. It was the martini era, and the two young couples made the rounds of giddy Manhattan cocktail parties. At one such gathering, the host served potent drinks. Diminutive Kay soon found herself lying woozy on a couch. She looked over to another couch, and there lay big Andy, just as sick as she.

When they were together, Andy and Don would sit and talk for hours, dishing dirt on their costars and their fellow Broadway travelers.

"They talked about everybody they knew," Kay Knotts recalled. "They just loved to talk about people. I always thought, women get accused of being gossips, but no one could beat these two. . . . Men very rarely are as intimate as they were together."

Andy and Don traded stories of the Old South,

of dusty towns filled with old men whittling outside country stores, of lonely widows pickling cucumbers for the state fair, of lazy evenings spent strumming guitars and singing hymns on the front porch. Andy told Don of the bourgeois scorn that had shaped his childhood. Don told Andy of the household demons that had shaped his.

"One thing we've talked about a lot is the way a comedian is born," Andy recalled. "Don says a comedian is born out of either unhappiness or embarrassment, and at some time in life, perhaps when you're about three or five years old, you start to learn to protect yourself. When you're laughed at, you turn it to your advantage."

Andy and Don came to trust each other for counsel, perhaps even above their wives, and certainly above their managers. Those men were Northerners. Andy and Don would consult each other before making big decisions.

Alas, the spouses didn't hit it off quite so well. Kay Knotts was a minister's daughter, raised with enough domestic savvy to be a good wife and mother. Barbara Griffith was the daughter of a schools superintendent, reared around hired help, a Southern aristocrat who thought dirty dishes and discarded socks were carried off by elves. Whereas Kay was first and foremost Don's wife, Barbara saw herself as a fellow entertainer; on the North Carolina stage where she and Andy had met, Barbara was the star. Don's success put food on Kay's table. Andy's success drove a wedge between him and Barbara, who watched her own career drift away. The final straw came when a television producer approached Barbara and offered her a bit part on a show if she would persuade her husband to take the lead. That day, she vowed to leave show business.

Back in college, "she was the big girl on campus, and he was just a hayseed," Kay Knotts recalled. "When he became famous and was picked up on Broadway, I think she felt left out, and that bothered her a lot. And she had problems with domestic things. . . . She would never drive on the freeway. Margaret Linke"— Dick's wife—"had to take her around and about. I had her fill in for a bridge game I had once, and she was very uncomfortable there."

Once, at a dinner party, Don and Kay watched in horror as Barbara lurched up from her seat, dead drunk, and launched into a seductive dance, a bit like Brigitte Bardot in the film *And God Created Woman*. "It was very embarrassing," Kay recalled. "Barbara, she had problems, lots of problems. She drank too much. It was another codependency relationship, I think. I think Andy was very consistent, but Barbara wasn't."

No Time for Sergeants made Andy a celebrity. A group from Mount Airy traveled to New York for the premiere. They were Andy's old classmates, kids "from prominent families" who "thought they were a bit better than he" and had ignored Andy until he made it big, a former classmate recalled. Now, they asked to go backstage for autographs. Andy turned them away. This wasn't Andy being a prima donna: it was a grudge, one that would endure for five more decades.

No crowds gathered for Don Knotts. He remained, for the time, a talented bit player.

"I had finally gotten my salary up to one hundred and ten dollars a week," Don recalled, "but that still wouldn't quite pay the bills, so I had to hustle for TV work on the side." It wasn't just about money: Don wanted to stay active in television because the TV medium was growing and *Sergeants* would not last forever. "I was on the backstage pay phone quite a lot," Don recalled. "Some of the actors would tease me. 'Hey, why the hustle?' they would say. 'Relax. You're in a hit.' But looking ahead had already become my modus operandi. It's the only way to survive in show business."

Don's performance did not go entirely unnoticed. Other *No Time* actors immediately noted the electricity he stirred onstage, both alone and with Andy. "I didn't feel he was a small part at all," recalled Earle Hyman, perhaps the only original *Sergeants* cast member still living. "He would pop his eyes, as we say down home, and the audience would just holler. They loved him."

As the play concluded its first season, Andy got word that he was being considered for the lead role in the next picture from Elia Kazan, one of the hottest directors in Hollywood. Kazan had made *On the Waterfront* with Marlon Brando. Now, he and his collaborator, writer Budd Schulberg, wanted to take on the rising power of television. Schulberg's script for *A Face in the Crowd* chronicles the rise and fall of a hillbilly singer who transforms into a powerful television personality under the sway of a young female producer, a Sarah Lawrence intellectual who becomes smitten with his brutish charm and plucks him from obscurity. She creates a monster, and "Lonesome" Rhodes rampages through the second half of the picture like Godzilla through Tokyo. Lonesome Rhodes was a composite of several men who had wielded outsize influence on popular culture in Andy's lifetime: Will Rogers, the cowboy philosopher who shaped national politics in the 1920s and 1930s; Arthur Godfrey, the folksy but mercurial variety-show host; and Elvis Presley, the Mississippi crooner who unleashed sexual frenzy in teenaged girls.

R. G. Armstrong, Andy Griffith's friend and fellow North Carolina thespian, recommended Andy to Kazan. The director went to three showings of *No Time for Sergeants*, liked what he saw, and short-listed Andy for the part. But a series of meetings left Budd Schulberg unconvinced. "Griffith could give us the hillbilly stuff all right," Schulberg recalled, "but what about the power madness that dominates the whole second half of the picture?"

Andy scarcely needed the work. He was gainfully employed on Broadway. But he thirsted to play Lonesome Rhodes. He persuaded Kazan to hold one last meeting at Gallaghers Steakhouse on West Fifty-Second Street. Andy had gone to the earlier meetings as Will Stockdale. He arrived at this one as Lonesome Rhodes. "I knew I had to do something outrageous or I wouldn't get the part," Andy recalled, "because everybody in town was out for it."

Kazan and Schulberg wanted Andy to prove he could play a monster. Andy thought he could. He asked Kazan, "Have you ever heard of Oral Roberts?" Andy told Kazan of the Oklahoma faith healer—how Roberts would line up the faithful at a table, seize their heads in his hands, and say, *"Heal."* Then Andy grabbed Kazan by the ears, squeezing the head of the great director between his palms. Fever washed over Andy's face as he gazed in Kazan's eyes and cried, *"Heal!"**

Kazan was rattled, but convinced. Andy had the part. Kazan loved Andy's intense natural charm and hoped to exploit it by building Lonesome

---

*While Andy recounted making this pitch to Kazan, manager Dick Linke said the last-ditch appeal was in fact directed at Schulberg.

Rhodes into a poignant, disarming brand of villain.

In August 1956, Andy left the cast of *Sergeants* to begin filming *A Face in the Crowd* in Piggott, Arkansas, a dusty town in cotton country. Kazan drafted its entire population into service as extras.

Andy had never acted on the big screen. As Kazan readied the first shot that required real acting from his star, he pulled Andy aside and told him, "The camera is an amazing piece of equipment. It sees everything. All you have to do as an actor is find what the character's feeling and what he's thinking, and if you feel it and think it hard enough, it will come out in your eyes and you won't have to show the camera anything."

The first shot called for Patricia Neal's character, Marcia Jeffries, to encounter Lonesome Rhodes on a dirt road and lure him back to her uncle's radio station. Kazan coached Andy: "Now, Patricia Neal there wants you to go to work at that radio station. You don't want to go work at the radio station. But look at Patsy Neal. Can't you think of something you'd like to do with her?" They got the shot in a single take.

"And then he and I started a connection," Andy recalled. "Every morning he'd call me into his office and tell me everything he expected to see that day in terms of color, moods, mood swings. . . . Then he'd say, 'Go figure out how to do that.' He is a great teacher, but he preferred to let you figure it out. And I did. It was hard, hard work. It took three months to shoot it, two months to get over it."

The production returned to New York in late August and set up at a studio in the Bronx. Kazan wanted to unleash in Andy all the anger, self-pity, and violence Kazan envisioned in Lonesome Rhodes. The director began asking Andy about his childhood, prodding for gaps in his emotional armor: "Remember all those people who said you'd never do anything but teach?"

"That doesn't bother me," Andy replied. "I'll tell you some things that do."

Andy told Kazan of the time in fourth grade when he was chasing a girl who wanted to be left alone. Finally, she dispatched him with the command "Get away from me, white trash." That term, Andy explained, "means rejection to me." Thereafter, when Kazan wanted to summon his actor's wrath, he would walk up and whisper, "White trash," in his ear.

On many days, Andy took Lonesome Rhodes home with him. "He became the part," Patricia Neal recalled. "He wanted to be that character, and it began to be him." Andy unleashed many torments on Barbara in the big, empty East Side apartment they had rented since that spring with his *Sergeants* earnings. In one outburst, he splintered three doors. "I did a lot of things to Barbara," he recalled. "The thing was, I actually felt the power of Lonesome Rhodes. I'll tell you the truth. You play an egomaniac and paranoid all day and it's hard to turn it off by bedtime."

A Face in the Crowd was Andy's greatest single performance. Yet, much as he wished to, Andy would never again work with Kazan.

Toward the end of 1956, Don made a fateful decision. He exhumed the old Nervous Man character from two years earlier and tried it out on the cast of *No Time for Sergeants*. He still hoped the Nervous Man might be his master-piece—a parody of the Eisenhower-era masculine ideal, and a perfect match to his delicate, vulnerable frame. The Nervous Man wore his emotions on his sleeve, just as Don did.

The Blue Angel manager had hated Don's sketch. The *Sergeants* cast loved it. "This was more like it!" Don recalled.

There is another version of the story. Andy claimed it was he, not his *Sergeants* cast mates, who rekindled Don's passion for the Nervous Man sketch. He said Don performed the skit for him several months earlier, while Andy was still in the Broadway cast.

"He came up to my dressing room one night and did a bit for me," Andy recalled. "It was a man who had never made a speech before. . . . And he took this little piece of paper and it was shaking like that." Andy demonstrated with a violent tremor.

"Is it funny?" Don asked when he was done.

"Lord, Don, that's brilliant." Once Andy had stopped laughing, he begged his friend to take the sketch to *Tonight*.

Tonight was NBC's edgy and audacious foray into late-night television. Host Steve Allen had essentially invented the genre, introducing such conventions as the opening monologue, the celebrity interview, and the house band. Allen could be irreverent, even mischievous, much like the early David Letterman, who channeled Allen's spirit three decades later.

Andy Griffith had a warm regard for Steve Allen. After the Ed Sullivan debacle, Allen had almost single-handedly restored Andy's confidence in appearing on live television. Allen thought Andy had died on *Toast of the Town* because the studio design had put Andy a good twenty feet from the front row, too far away for him to work his magic with the audience. For Andy's first appearance with Allen, "they brought out two stools," Andy recalled, "where Steve and I would sit. I would do these monologues to Steve, and Steve would get tickled and laugh out loud. The more he'd laugh, the more the audience would laugh."

For Don's own *Tonight* debut, on November 8, 1956, he penned a sketch that presented his

Nervous Man character as a last-minute replacement for a television weatherman. For his second outing, Don became a Nervous Conventioneer.

Allen was hooked. These were "monologues of [Don's] own creation," he recalled, "that I at once recognized as classics in the Benchley tradition," which indeed they were. After Don's third appearance, Don was told he'd be written into Allen's other television vehicle, a Sunday-night variety show that pitted the rising host against Ed Sullivan. In 1957, the network would pull Allen from *Tonight* to focus his full energy on the contest with Sullivan.

In January 1957, Andy flew to Hollywood to film the screen version of *No Time for Sergeants*. He brought Don west to spend a week with him and Barbara in their rented LA home and reprise Don's Broadway role. Don was one of a few from the play invited to join the film, at Andy's request. Don left for California three days after the birth of his second child, Tom. Don loved his family, but work came first. Kay understood.

One night that week in the temporary Griffith residence, Don awoke in the guest room to what sounded like a tinny recording of Andy and Barbara in bed. Don soon divined that someone had left the house intercom system on. All night, he heard Andy and Barbara tumble from one extreme of passion to another: fighting, screaming, crying, then falling into bed and making love—then fighting, screaming, and crying again.

That winter, Don began work on *The Steve Allen Show* as a fill-in for Tom Poston, a young comic who played a befuddled goof in a regular skit called "Man on the Street," probably the best-remembered sketch from the Steve Allen era by dint of sheer repetition. Allen would walk up to Tom Poston and ask, "And what is your name, sir?" Tom would roll his eyes in cranial agony until Allen finally gave up. Then he would move on to Louis Nye, who played a *Mad Men*–style sophisticate. He launched a sort of catchphrase with the salutation "Hi-ho, Steverino!"

Don's Nervous Man completed the comedic triangle. For Don's first appearance on *The Steve Allen Show*, the writers inserted him into that week's "Man on the Street," quaking with fear. When Allen asked, "Are you nervous?" Don replied, "Noop!" His bug-eyed exclamation brought down the house. It was, Don recalled, "the biggest laugh I'd heard in my life."

They asked Don back week after week to perform new "Man on the Street" material. Don wrote some of it himself.

"My name is K. B. Morrison, and I used to work in a munitions factory."
"What does the *K.B.* stand for?"
" 'Kaboom!' "

"You say you *used* to work in a munitions factory. You don't work there anymore?"

"It isn't there anymore!"

Poston, Knotts, and Nye were becoming an item. *The New York Times* celebrated the trio in a fall 1957 article: "Their tomfoolery on the Sunday evening program has been drawing an impressive amount of mail from appreciative viewers. Much of it comes from college students." Their edgy skits were attracting the same demographic that would flock to David Letterman in the 1980s and Jon Stewart in the 2000s.

In mid-1957, Steve Allen's producers persuaded Don to give up his small part in *No Time for Sergeants*; with eight shows a week, the theater work conflicted with Don's rehearsal schedule for *Steve Allen*. Don was characteristically reluctant to relinquish a paying gig.

As his star ascended, Don's aversion to live television escalated from discomfort to terror. His Broadway run was over, and the hour-long Sunday *Steve Allen* broadcast was very nearly Don's only concern. His life grew comparatively idle, and his neuroses expanded to fill every free moment. He couldn't sleep at night for fear he would bomb the next day.

Kay, his long-suffering wife, could only roll her eyes. "His habit would be to take to his bed for about three days if he had a show coming up,"

Kay recalled. "If he had a show on Sunday, he would go to bed on Friday and stay there, resting up. And that would just drive me up the wall."

Back in childhood, when Kay's family returned home from church, her minister father would grill her on the success or failure of that day's sermon. Now, Don was doing the same thing. "I had to make sure all of the people were out of my home by the time Don came home," she recalled, "because I had to tell him how great he was, and everything had to be positive. And maybe a couple days later we could really discuss it."

Steve Allen preferred to operate on the edge of chaos. He favored minimal rehearsal. No one was allowed to utter any joke's punch line until airtime. Don didn't like that. He became afflicted with stage fright so severe that he would go lie down somewhere before an impending performance, sometimes warning Allen that he might not return. But he always did.

Louis Nye and Tom Poston liked to improvise. "Not Don," writer Herb Sargent recalled. "He would take old routines that he had perfected and build them into our show, polishing them, adapting them. He left nothing to chance."

The most terrifying moment in Don's television career came on *Steve Allen*. One Sunday, Don had prepared a monologue on a political candidate speaking to his staffers. When the floor manager offered to put it on the teleprompter, Don declined. But in the middle of the monologue, Don froze. "My mind went totally blank," he recalled. "I had no idea what my next line was. I looked around helplessly. The teleprompters were dark and still. I was all alone out there and there was no help to be gotten from anything or anyone." Don began to frantically ad-lib, sputtering nonsense. That was precisely what the audience expected from *Steve Allen*, so no one batted an eye. Don finally remembered his lines, finished the speech, staggered offstage, and collapsed.

Though it was fretful work, television fame had its perks, and Don soon began to partake. One Sunday, for Don's birthday, Tom and Louis planted a prostitute in Don's dressing room during the live broadcast. When the three returned to the room after a sketch, they pushed Don inside and locked the door. Other cast and crew had gathered outside to watch the fireworks. Through the door, they began to hear Don's howls of protest: "Don't do that. I have to change. I'm on next. You're not helping."

Don might have welcomed the visitor at another time. Just now, though, he had to perform, and Don approached such appointments with religious zeal. When Tom and Louis finally opened the door, Don emerged, red-faced, to a round of "Happy Birthday." He was furious. He couldn't believe his friends would spring a prank at such a time. He cursed them. Then he rushed to the stage and did his sketch. It went well, and everyone shook hands afterward. Don turned to leave.

"Where are you going?" Tom asked.

"I'm going upstairs and finish," Don replied.

"Don, I'm so sorry. We sent the girl home."

"That's all right. I'm going upstairs and finish anyway."

Backstage at *Steve Allen*, Don struck up a friendship with a theatrical manager named Sherwin Bash. Though still in his twenties, Sherwin had connections: he was the son-in-law of Ray Bloch, musical director for both Jackie Gleason and Ed Sullivan. But Sherwin's success rested on more than that: he was one of the first managers to pounce on the rising stars of television.

"Most of the people I considered important in the entertainment business, they didn't like television," Sherwin recalled. "In television, you worked twice as much and you got paid half as much." Radio was easy: no makeup, no wardrobe, no lines to learn. Radio attracted stand-up comics. Sherwin gravitated toward comedic actors—men, such as Tom Poston, Louis Nye, and Don Knotts, who could play parts on television. Sherwin envisioned a career for Don in television and film, "and not one that would burn out."

Sherwin visited Don and Kay one night at their home. "I remember him telling Don how much money he was going to make and how famous he was going to be," Kay recalled. She didn't buy it, but Don signed up. It would be a five-decade relationship.

Sherwin already viewed Don as the shadow leader of Allen's trio of "bananas." "Even though Don was supposed to be this introverted, quiet character, I realized that he was sort of the strength of the three of them," Sherwin recalled. "Don had this remarkable ability. He could not only remember his own lines, he could remember Tom Poston's lines and Louis Nye's lines. He was like a pillar to them."

In summer 1959, *The Steve Allen Show* migrated to Hollywood and took up residence at NBC Color City, a Burbank studio built for television, a step up from the repurposed radio studios in New York. For the 1959–60 season, the program was renamed *The Steve Allen Plymouth Show* and moved from Sunday to Monday. The show also went from live broadcast to tape and was sweetened with a laugh track, a spool of pre-recorded laughter added at moments when the producers wanted the viewing audience to know something funny was happening.

The Knotts family moved west that June. They purchased a two-story Spanish colonial in Glendale, a sleepy bedroom community not commonly associated with Hollywood glitterati. Glendale was, in fact, a magnet for John Birch conservatives, and Kay didn't like the place. Don attempted to mollify her by building a pool in the backyard.

Most of the *Steve Allen* gang lived west of Hollywood. Don lived east. He set himself apart from the others, just as he had done in New York. "I would see Kay at the studio," Sherwin Bash recalled, "but they were so far away that we never really socialized. If you planned to go to dinner with Don and Kay, you had to leave the day before."

Don quickly warmed to the California ethos. The ceaseless sunshine and the towering palms seemed worlds removed from hardscrabble Morgantown. Don looked forward to a comparatively serene existence on the retooled *Steve Allen* show. For nearly the first time in his career, he would not be performing live. If he forgot his lines on a taped broadcast, they could simply rewind the tape. Now, it seemed, Don could finally get some rest.

But his mind wouldn't settle for long. Soon, Don began to worry that the coming changes would sap the program's rhythm and energy. He felt sure the laugh track made the *Steve Allen* team less funny. "When I questioned whether or not a certain joke would work, the answer was often 'Don't worry about it. The laugh track will love it,' " he recalled. Don loved the relaxed atmosphere of a taped show, but he feared the magic was gone.

The new show was much like Don's new Glendale home: relaxed, comfortable . . . and bland. At the end of the season, *The Steve Allen Plymouth Show* would be canceled.

In May 1957, Andy traveled to North Carolina for a publicity tour to mark the release of *A Face in the Crowd*. He spoke to state legislators in Raleigh, closing with the enigmatic words, "I'd like to wish you all the common sense in the world." The next day was Saturday, June 1, Andy's birthday. To mark the occasion, Andy returned—finally—to Mount Airy, where town leaders declared it Andy Griffith Day. A motorcade steered up US 52 into town. Then, Andy paraded down Main Street, flanked by marching bands and political glad-handers as he waved from the back of a convertible. Town leaders presented Andy a ceremonial key to the city.

The only thing missing, one attendee recalled, was spectators. The event had been poorly advertised. "There were a few people on the sidewalk, but nothing like anybody expected," recalled Robert Merritt, the president of Andy's high school class. "So here you had this celebrity, a ticker-tape parade, and no ticker tape, and no people."

Andy Griffith Day concluded with a showing of *A Face in the Crowd* at the Earle Theatre. As patrons filed in, Andy stole upstairs to the balcony. Mike, his fourteen-year-old nephew, followed at a polite distance. Andy sat down, alone, and watched his old friends and class-mates settle into seats for the film. He watched, rapt, as the lights dimmed, the crowd fell silent, and the film crackled to life on the screen. "He was just taking it all in," Mike recalled. Finally, Andy saw his name appear across the giant screen. As it faded, and the picture began, Andy rose to leave.

Andy would not again appear publicly in Mount Airy for forty-five years.*

On June 14, a camera crew filed into the Griffiths' Sutton Place apartment on Manhattan's East Side to film *Person to Person*, a live celebrity interview program hosted by Edward R. Murrow. *Person to Person* was tailored to bring viewers inside a celebrity's home and, to some extent, inside their lives. Murrow probed a bit deeper than Andy might have liked.

"Barbara," Murrow asked, turning to Mrs. Griffith, "I know you used to sing and dance and act. You doing anything of that sort now?"

Something flared in Barbara's eyes. She replied through clenched teeth, "Not right now, Ed. I guess one career in the family is enough." She let the words hang in the air. "However, I would like to—"

---

*Not, at least, as a guest of the city. Andy did return to town more than once to speak at graduations and other semipublic events.

Andy broke in. "I hope . . . Barbara is a good actress and singer—"

"Thank you," Barbara said, with more than a trace of sarcasm.

"—and one of these times, I want us to do a movie or a play together."

Murrow had stumbled upon the central tension in their relationship. He pressed on, inviting Andy to play a song for him, and for Barbara to sing it. Andy picked up a guitar, the one Lonesome Rhodes had played in the movie, and began to strum. Barbara's melancholy soprano rose in song:

I gave my love a cherry without a stone
I gave my love a chicken without a bone
I told my love a story without an end
I gave my love a baby with no cryin' . . .

Something in Barbara's voice rendered this lovely moment unspeakably sad. Andy and his interviewer were struck dumb. Then, Andy found his voice and drawled, "And you could just go on and on." And the moment was gone.

That fall, Dick Linke quit his job in the record industry to manage Andy full-time. His friends were incredulous. A music publisher cornered him on a train and asked, "Dick, you have a good job at Capitol Records. Why would you leave that for a hillbilly?" Dick replied, "Lemme tell you something. He's not a hillbilly. He's a mountain-billy from North Carolina. And I have an intuition for talent. And this guy's gonna be a big star, believe me."

Now that Andy had fame, he was ready to build a family. The Griffiths purchased fifty-three acres of forest and sand on the Carolina coast, a waterfront estate just up the road from *The Lost Colony* stage where Andy and Barbara had spent summers together. The land and nine-room house had cost them $30,000. Among the denizens of tiny Manteo, the Griffiths would be royalty.

"Now, no matter what happens, we know that's home, the place we can really be free," Andy told an interviewer. "We can fly to Hollywood or New York or wherever else I got to be, but Manteo, that's home."

Both Andy and Don saw themselves as loners. With his move to Glendale, Don had planted his family a few suburbs away from friends and associates. Now, Andy would spend his summers at a distance of 2,750 miles.

In fall 1958, the Griffiths adopted a son, unable to conceive their own. Andrew Samuel Griffith Jr. had been born the previous December. The following year, Andy and Barbara would adopt a daughter, Dixie, to complete the family.

The year also saw the release of the film version of *No Time for Sergeants*; it earned both critical acclaim and a cool $9 million, ultimately ranking as the fourth-highest-grossing film of 1958. *The New York Times* called it a "minor classic," and critic Bosley Crowther predicted Andy "will have a hard time shedding himself of the aura" of Will Stockdale. They were prophetic words.

Andy wasn't the only one finding fame. Back in Mount Airy, proud Geneva Griffith held court at the Snappy Lunch, the diner Andy had frequented in high school. She would stand by the window with a Coke, waiting for the matinee showing of *Sergeants* to let out. "She'd just stand there," recalled Charles Dowell, the diner's owner. "Then, she'd walk over to the lobby and sign autographs."

Warner Bros. looked to *No Time for Sergeants* as a template for Andy's next role. The result was another military comedy, *Onionhead*, rushed out five months later as a blatant cash-in. Posters announced, "That wonderful 'No Time for Sergeants' meathead ANDY GRIFFITH is back as Onionhead."

In fact, *Onionhead* was not another madcap farce but a comedy-drama about a lovelorn cook on a Coast Guard ship. It was a serviceable film, but few filmgoers saw it, and fewer knew what to make of it. Andy, typically, was his own worst critic, calling the film "terrible bad."

A few months earlier, in March, Andy had starred in a woeful television production of *The Male Animal*, an adaptation of a Broadway play.

"Strictly a turkey," the *Los Angeles Times* reviewer opined, "and I'm afraid most of the fault lies in Andy's performance."

In just a few years, Andy had gone from unknown to Broadway star to box-office king—to has-been. Suddenly, his phone wasn't ringing, and panic was setting in.

"Well, we was sittin' around with the William Morris fellows," Andy recalled, "and I hadn't done a thing in that year. Not a blessed thing. And I asked 'em if there was any pictures comin' up that I might do, and they hawed about it a bit and said, well, no, there wasn't. So I right out asked one of 'em, 'Has anybody asked for me?' And I guess this sort of caught him off guard because he said, quicker'n he'd meant to, 'No.' "

Andy asked Dick Linke if he should begin to phase out his hillbilly accent. "Sure," Dick deadpanned, "that's fine, if you want to get out of show business."

On April 23, 1959, Andy returned to Broadway as the lead in a musical adaptation of *Destry Rides Again*. The name was apt: *Destry* had already cantered through a novel and three films, the lead character interpreted by Tom Mix, James Stewart, and Audie Murphy. Now *Destry* was retooled as a vehicle for Andy's comeback, an odd turn of events for an actor whose Broadway debut was only four years past.

Destry was "half a hit," Griffith recalled. "What

I mean by half a hit is, we stayed open—just barely. Monday through Thursday we were on twofers—two tickets for the price of one—and on holidays—Thanksgiving, Christmas, and the like—there was a sign out front that said, 'Matinee Today.' " The songs "were mundane at most," Andy recalled. "The dancing was what kept that show open."

Don went to see *Destry* before his family left for Hollywood. After the show, Don met his friend backstage and told him, "Ange, it's fun the way you danced there." But Don could tell Andy wasn't emotionally invested in the work and knew the performance was nowhere near what Andy could be. It was time for his friend to try something else.

5.

Andy Takes a Deputy

Inside the Last Chance Saloon, on the set of *Destry Rides Again*, Andy Griffith mulled his future. At thirty-three, Andy sensed he was on a downward trajectory. In the New York and Hollywood of the 1950s, one flop could sink a promising career. Andy wasn't likely to get another crack at a leading film role after *Onionhead*, and now his Broadway currency was in decline.

Andy had yet one more card to play: television. Though well entrenched by 1959, television was nonetheless viewed as the least desirable option for a performer—an actor's Last Chance Saloon. "I'd always been afraid of it," Andy recalled, "because I figured if you strike out there, that's it."

Andy and his manager, Dick Linke, set up a meeting with Abe Lastfogel at William Morris. Andy told him, "Mr. Lastfogel, I've struck out in movies and now on Broadway, and I don't want to go back to nightclubs, so maybe I'd better try television." Lastfogel went to see Sheldon Leonard, the powerful producer of television's *Danny Thomas Show*. He asked if Sheldon knew of Andy. Sheldon replied, "Yeah, he did a record, a funny record." Lastfogel said, "He'd like to do television. Can you think of something for him?"

It didn't take Sheldon Leonard long to respond. "Thinking of something for a personality is the easiest part," he recalled. "Andy Griffith, country boy. What's the show going to be? He's going to be a country boy."

One winter night in 1959, Sheldon traveled to New York, where Andy was in a 472-show run of *Destry*, to see him backstage.

"I was told that a man named Sheldon Leonard would come to see me one night," Andy recalled. "A little time went by and I didn't think much more about it. And one night, after the show and curtain calls—which didn't take very long—I passed the stage door on my way to my dressing room. There was a man standing there smiling. I kind of smiled back and went on. I thought I had seen him before—maybe playing heavies in movies."

Born in 1907, Sheldon Leonard Bershad attended Syracuse on scholarship and attained a modest fame playing bad guys in a string of films, characters with such names as Pretty Willie, Lippy Harris, and Jumbo Schneider. Most infamously, Sheldon played Nick, the hard-hearted barkeep in *It's a Wonderful Life* who hurls Jimmy Stewart into the snow. By the late 1950s, Sheldon had tired of acting and ascended into management, serving as both producer and director of the Danny Thomas vehicle *Make*

Room for Daddy. The program would remain on the air for eleven years, one of television's longest-running sitcoms. Tall, dark, and handsome, Sheldon demonstrated a brilliant mastery of the television medium and an uncanny ability to match personalities to shows.

Sheldon escorted Andy out to Forty-Fifth Street. "We went to his favorite bar on Eighth Avenue and sat and had a beer and a sandwich, and I told him the idea we had, which was to make him sheriff of a small town," Sheldon recalled.

The conversation spawned a series of meetings between the two men and Dick Linke at the elegant Hotel St. Moritz. At the first meeting, Andy listened intently, said little, and left uncommitted. Sheldon was impressed: most actors would jump at the chance to star in their own show. At the second meeting, Andy sat and nodded politely. But then he broke his silence, raised his voice in an exaggerated Carolina drawl, and set about probing the producer on everything from the program's financing to its artistic direction. Sheldon was stunned; Dick Linke just smiled.

At the third meeting, Sheldon and Andy shook hands on *The Andy Griffith Show*. When the contracts were signed, Sheldon asked Andy, "Why all this advance rigmarole?" Andy replied, "Jest wanted to know who I wuz dealing with."

To Sheldon, the entire challenge of television lay in finding a personality to build a show around; once he found his personality, the show would write itself. And Sheldon knew he could write a show for Andy. He plotted to insert Andy into a small town and surround him with characters to whom he could react; Sheldon felt that Andy's gift lay in the unsung art of reactive comedy. He envisioned Andy as a broadly comedic bumpkin, not unlike Andy's Will Stockdale character in *No Time for Sergeants*.

To Andy, it sounded like a mishmash of tired Southern clichés and unflattering stereotypes. He particularly disliked Sheldon's notion of casting Andy in multiple roles, playing not just the sheriff but also the town's newspaper editor and justice of the peace, all for madcap effect. Andy thought to himself, "This will last maybe two weeks."

Yet, Andy agreed to everything Sheldon Leonard proposed. He wasn't investing in the show so much as the man who had proposed it.

Sheldon wanted to present the new character as a guest star in an episode of *Danny Thomas*. It was a consummate Hollywood deal: To film a pilot for *The Andy Griffith Show*, as was the custom, would have cost $50,000. Presenting it instead as an episode of *Danny Thomas* allowed Sheldon to sell the new show while also delivering a *Danny Thomas* episode at no extra cost to the sponsor, General Foods. Sheldon and Danny Thomas would own shares of the resulting *Griffith Show*, if one materialized, making them business partners with Andy and his manager and lining everyone's pockets. "I didn't realize it," Sheldon recalled, "but I was inventing what is now called the spin-off."*

Sheldon put *Danny Thomas* writer Artie Stander to work on a pilot. Andy got a week off from *Destry* and flew to Hollywood in January 1960 to film it. He arrived on a set buzzing about this larger-than-life actor, Kazan's wild man, and the magical chemistry he could brew with a live audience. But when rehearsals started, it seemed that Andy had left his mojo in New York. He was as flat as stale pop. The cast and crew whispered behind his back, "What is this magic they're talking about?" But as rehearsals progressed, Andy recalled, "I got looser and looser. And when they brought the audience in, I was on top of it, and whatever I bring happened."

A week on the set of *Danny Thomas* gave Andy an eyeful of the nascent television industry, and he didn't like what he saw. "The first day, Artie Stander, Danny Thomas, and Sheldon Leonard yelled at each other all day," Andy recalled. Andy pulled Sheldon aside and told him, "If this is

---

*Griffith was not, in fact, television's first spin-off. *The Honeymooners* began as a recurring sketch on the *Cavalcade of Stars*, which Jackie Gleason hosted, making it a sort of spin-off. And the CBS sitcom *December Bride* spawned the offspring *Pete and Gladys*, which debuted in September 1960, one month before *Griffith*.

what television is, I don't think I can handle it." Sheldon replied, "Andy, the star dictates what the attitude will be on the set. Danny likes to yell, so we all yell. If you don't want to yell, nobody will yell."

The pilot, broadcast on February 15, 1960, opens with a hand-drawn sketch of Andy's face, looking a bit like a sinister ventriloquist dummy, and a voice-over announcing, "Tonight's special guest: Andy Griffith." Then, the camera reveals a first glimpse of Mayberry, a modest set constructed on the *Danny Thomas* soundstage. The lens descends to a street, where Andy sits in his Ford Galaxie 500 squad car, escorting Danny and his family back into town. Danny has been caught running a stop sign. The story, titled "Danny Meets Andy Griffith," invokes a 1950s New Yorker's nightmare of driving through the rural South.

"You picked on the wrong guy this time, Clem," Danny warns.

"Name ain't Clem," Andy replies, with a wide smile. "It's Andy. Andy Taylor." On that cue, the audience breaks into polite applause.

Bits and pieces of *The Andy Griffith Show* are already there, but some are in the wrong places. The town drunk shambles onto the set, announces, "I'm under arrest!," and locks himself in his cell. But he is not Otis, and he is not played by Hal Smith. Frances Bavier comes to see Andy, but she is not Aunt Bee; she is Henrietta Perkins, a widow who is behind on her taxes. Little Ronny Howard is there; but Don Knotts is not. Sheriff Taylor has no deputy.

Don and Kay spent that evening playing bridge at the home of Pat Harrington, Don's friend and costar on *The Steve Allen Show*. Pat, awaiting a guest role on *Danny Thomas*, halted the proceedings at nine o'clock to watch that night's episode. He switched on the set, and Don glimpsed the face of a friend.

Andy and Don had lost touch since their time together in the cast of *No Time for Sergeants*, half a decade earlier. Now they were three thousand miles apart—Don in Hollywood, Andy in New York—and their correspondence had fallen off. Andy was unaware *Steve Allen* had been canceled. Don had no inkling Andy was working on a television show.

Now, as Don beheld Andy on Pat Harrington's television set, it struck him that there might be a place for him in Mayberry. A part on Andy's new show might just rekindle Don's career—and their friendship.

The next day, Don telephoned Andy in New York. "Listen," he said, "don't you think Sheriff Andy Taylor ought to have a deputy?"

A long pause followed.

In that silence, Andy must have weighed the pros and cons of adding his friend to the *Griffith* production. Don's comic talent would unquestionably elevate the show. The two men had already proved how well they could play off each other. Besides, Andy loved having Don around. If there was a downside, perhaps it was the danger that Don's comic star might one day outshine Andy's own. Dean Martin had watched this happen with Jerry Lewis, all the critics ignoring the straight man and lavishing praise on his funnier partner. Yet, Andy loathed the hayseed part that had been assigned him in Sheldon Leonard's pilot. He cringed at the thought of portraying another simpering Southern stereotype, trolling for yucks with a gap-toothed grin and scenery-shredding pratfalls. With a deputy, especially a wide-eyed, manic comedic dervish such as Don—why, maybe then Andy could reshape Sheriff Andy Taylor into something palatable, something enduring.

Andy's voice crackled back onto the line: "That's a hell of an idea! I didn't know you were out of a job."

"Yes, Steve was canceled."

"Lord! Call Sheldon Leonard."

The friends eventually decided that Don would approach Dick Linke, and that Andy's manager would convey Don's pitch to Sheldon. Andy telephoned Sheldon, too, and told him he wanted Don. Thus, barely a week after the pilot aired, Don found himself walking into Sheldon's office on the Desilu lot. Don had a sheaf of old scripts tucked under his arm, a ruse to create the impression he was brimming with offers rather than conspicuously unemployed.

Sheldon was savvy. He played it cool, acting as if Don had to convince him a deputy in Mayberry was a good idea. In an hour-long meeting, Don recalled, Sheldon "prodded me with questions about what I thought this deputy character should be like." Don had "no preconceived ideas," but he knew he didn't want another reincarnation of his Nervous Man, any more than Andy wanted to ape Will Stockdale. The character of Barney Fife took his surname from Fife Street, back in Morgantown. Don envisioned playing him as a grown man with the mentality of a nine-year-old boy, given to flights of Tom Sawyer fancy and prone to wear his emotions plainly on his face.

There was no formal audition. Sheldon dismissed Don coolly, telling the fretful actor that his idea "would be taken under advisement." Decades later, Sheldon recalled that his original thought was to hire Don for a single episode.

He kept Don waiting for three agonizing weeks. Don filmed his final *Steve Allen Show* in the interim. He was now officially out of work. He sat by the phone. Finally, Sherwin Bash, Don's manager, called to relay the offer: the part was his. Don nearly fainted with delight. "I had a good feeling about this," he recalled. "I had a real good feeling, even before it started."

However fateful the casting, Don Knotts wasn't the first or even the second actor hired to populate Mayberry.

Sheldon Leonard's first impulse was to give Andy a son. Ronny Howard was the progeny of Rance and Jean Howard, New York actors who had met in college. Ronny was born while Rance served in the air force, touring the country and entertaining the troops. "Backstage, Jean would have Ron in a bassinet or in her arms," Rance recalled. By age two, Ronny was attending his parents' rehearsals and performances. One day, Rance discovered Ronny had an uncanny talent to learn lines, apparently by osmosis, as the boy could neither read nor write. Father and son began to entertain friends by reciting scenes from the play *Mister Roberts* from memory.

In fall 1959, five-year-old Ronny was cast in a television pilot called "Mr. O'Malley." Hosted by Ronald Reagan as part of the series *General Electric Theater*, "Mr. O'Malley" was based on the intellectual comic strip *Barnaby* and meant to launch a comedy-fantasy series about five-year-old Barnaby (Ronny) and his fairy godfather.

Sheldon saw the pilot, and he liked Ronny. He met with Rance and told him he wanted Ronny to play Andy Griffith's son on his new show. The boy would be named Opie, after the Southern bandleader Opie Cates, a favorite of Andy's. Ronny was bound to the *Mr. O'Malley* show by

CBS. That didn't seem to bother Sheldon. He told Rance, "The show will not sell." Rance asked why. "Because the show is fantasy," Sheldon said, "and fantasy is not selling on TV now." The two men agreed to a contingency plan: If *Mr. O'Malley* sold, Ronny was free to do it. If it didn't, he would do the *Griffith Show*. "And of course, Sheldon was right," Rance recalled. *Mr. O'Malley* didn't sell.

The second permanent addition to Mayberry, Frances Bavier, was a product of Columbia University and a veteran of stage and screen, endowed with a dignified air and a transatlantic finishing-school accent. Her manner was haughty and patrician from the day she walked into the Forty-Eighth Street Theatre in New York, fresh out of acting school in 1925, and announced to director Howard Lindsay, "I'm a graduate of the American Academy of Dramatic Arts."

"Get her a chair!" the director cried, feigning awe. "We'll write a special part for her!" Oddly enough, they did. Frances made her Broadway debut in the farce *The Poor Nut*. Better parts followed. Then she was cast as a grandmother in the Broadway hit *On Borrowed Time* while still in her thirties, and her career trajectory changed. Frances evolved from ingenue to matron and amassed many screen and television credits.

On-screen, Andy, Opie, and the future Aunt Bee melted hearts. General Foods, sponsor of

Danny Thomas, purchased the series before the pilot had even aired. They loved it for its Americana appeal, for Andy's warm smile, and for the budding magic of Mayberry.

Griffith was budgeted for thirty-two episodes at $58,000 apiece, or about $1.8 million for its first full season. Dick Linke knew that he and his client weren't big names in Hollywood; all of Dick's career, and most of Andy's, had played out in New York. For either man to wield real clout on the *Griffith Show*, both would need to ante up. Dick approached Bank of America and borrowed several hundred thousand dollars, enough to make Andy half owner of the show and to give them, together, a majority stake. The remaining shares would go to Sheldon Leonard and Danny Thomas. Griffith's ownership interest would give him a measure of artistic control. In time, the arrangement would also make Andy and Dick wealthy men.

Don Knotts had no ownership stake in the *Griffith Show*. Instead, the producers signed him to a single season, and then to a five-year contract, at a starting salary of $1,250 an episode, or about $35,000 a year. "I worked out this terrible deal for him, where he ended up making no money in five years," lamented Sherwin Bash, Don's manager. The producers lowballed Don, playing on his insecurity and concealing their eagerness to sign him. Still, it was good money for a tele-

155

vision actor in 1960, and Don bore none of the risk that Andy assumed by investing in the series.

Andy took ten days off the *Destry* production, claiming a back injury. Sheldon Leonard descended on Andy's home in Westchester County with two writers in tow. Together, they developed a half dozen story lines that would become the first episodes of the *Griffith Show*. The plots betrayed the group's artistic and commercial ambitions.

One story, "The New Housekeeper," felt like a retooled pilot, with Andy coaxing a reluctant Opie to accept Aunt Bee as a matronly surrogate for his dead mother. Another, "The Guitar Player," set the stage for much singing and dancing to come. But the most fateful of these half-baked ideas was "The Manhunt," the first teleplay written to spotlight Deputy Barney Fife.

Everyone attending the meeting at the Griffith home that day sensed what they might have in Don, a man who could set off paroxysms of laughter before he even opened his mouth. His piercing, saucer eyes evoked the mute expressiveness of the great silent-film stars. His gangly frame, wiry but fragile, diminutive and stooped, seemed somehow trapped between adolescence and old age. His face was a canvas of raw emotion, so expressive it was almost painful to look upon. But no one at the meeting yet knew what Don would do with the part he had created for himself.

One more key role was yet to be cast. As executive producer, Sheldon Leonard would oversee the entire project, but not the day-to-day management of actors, locations, and scripts. For that, he needed a line producer. He approached Aaron Ruben.

Born to Polish Jews in Chicago, Aaron Ruben emerged as a gifted comedy writer, and he wrote for the best, first on radio with Burns and Allen and Milton Berle, then on television with Phil Silvers and Sid Caesar. Sheldon hired Aaron at the urging of Andy and Dick Linke, who appreciated both Aaron's talent and his Zen-like calm. Over time, Aaron would contribute more than any other single person, save perhaps Andy and Don, to the words and images that elevated the *Griffith Show* above the run-of-the-mill television program in the first half of the 1960s.

Aaron met with Sheldon Leonard, who told him, "Television isn't a director's medium, television is a producer's medium." The most important ingredient is the script, Sheldon said, and you need someone in charge of that script. Aaron was hooked.

Aaron Ruben went to meet Andy Griffith at his home in Rye, New York, and was surprised when Andy did not invite him inside. They settled onto the steps of Andy's back porch. Andy asked, "Ya hunt much?" Aaron replied, "Hunt?! I've never hunted in my life." But then talk turned to Andy's show, and they found common ground. Andy and Aaron (and, later, Don) would be friends for life.

After the turbulent week in Hollywood filming his pilot, Andy knew a few things he would do differently on *The Andy Griffith Show*. Andy wanted his own soundstage to be productive but relaxed. He envisioned cast and crew functioning like an extended family: exchanging gifts at Christmas, eating lunch together at the commissary, playing music in the dressing rooms, even staging the occasional practical joke. And he couldn't wait to share those moments with Don.

The Andy Griffith Show would be shot with a single camera, like a movie, the scenes filmed out of sequence and without an audience. The format guaranteed the production would focus on character, story, and human interaction. That was how Andy wanted it. Most situation comedies of the day, including *Danny Thomas*, were filmed with three cameras before a live studio audience. That format generated a natural laugh track and a wonderful chemistry between audience and performers, who fed on the energy in the room. But the actors played for laughs, an impulse that could distract actors and writers from building character and plot. "I hate those three-camera shows," Andy once said. "You can work on values all week, and the minute you bring two hundred people in, all your values go out the window."

Filming a one-camera comedy in 1960 meant sweetening it with a laugh track. Andy was uneasy with the laugh track. His concern may have come from Don, who believed the laugh track had killed *The Steve Allen Show*. Andy persuaded the *Griffith* producers to try an experiment: screen a filmed episode before a live audience, record the laughter, and add it to the tape before broadcast. A few early *Griffith* episodes were broadcast with "live" laugh tracks before the network pulled the plug on Andy's costly experiment. He and the producers reached a sort of compromise: *Griffith* would use a laugh track, but sparingly.

The *Griffith Show* would be shot at Desilu Studios, the production company founded by Lucille Ball and Desi Arnaz and responsible for many of the best television programs of the 1950s and 1960s, including *I Love Lucy*, but also *Star Trek*, *The Dick Van Dyke Show*, and *My Three Sons*. The lot was called the Motion Picture Center and sat on Cahuenga Boulevard near Melrose, a white art deco compound with an arch of overlapping concrete rectangles stretching above the main driveway. Its soundstages were notoriously leaky; "Don and I used to do scenes when it rained, and it would often rain in between us," Andy recalled.

The sets for the first *Griffith* episodes were "few and simple," *Griffith* scholar Richard Kelly writes: the courthouse, where most interior shots were filmed; the living room, kitchen, and porch of the Taylor home; the barbershop; the mayor's office; and the inside of the filling station. Exteriors were mostly shot on a back lot half an hour away in Culver City named Forty Acres. It had first been used by Cecil DeMille on his silent films of the 1920s and had provided the backdrop for the classics *King Kong* and *Gone with the Wind.*

The minimalist musical theme came from Hollywood composer Earle Hagen. He and the producers had been "beating our brains out for a couple of months" for an appropriate theme when Earle awoke one day "and thought, that thing ought to be simple enough to whistle. And it took me about ten minutes to write it," he recalled. He recorded a simple, whistled demo, backed with a string bass and drums, and took it to Sheldon Leonard. Sheldon loved it. "I tell you what," Sheldon said. "I'll shoot Andy and Ronny walking along the lake with a couple of fishing poles over their shoulder." Earle's demo became the final theme. "I never whistled before in my life," Earle recalled, "and never since."

On the first day of production, in summer 1960, the core cast and crew of the *Griffith Show* drove up to the back entrance of the Desilu lot, parked along Willoughby Avenue, crossed the street to the gate, and walked past Tiny, the guard, into the concrete compound. The group gathered in a conference room to read the script for the first episode, "The New Housekeeper." Sheldon Leonard would direct, one of only two times he oversaw a *Griffith* episode personally.

Don arrived looking "a little nervous," Rance Howard recalled, possessed by the same paralytic first-day angst that had vexed him in most of his previous jobs. He was buoyed, though, to know that he would be working on a calm one-camera production, not a torturous live shoot. And he sensed great talent gathered around him. Andy asserted himself immediately as the group's benevolent leader. Don recalled it later as "one of the most delightful days of my life."

The next Monday, the crew drove up into Franklin Canyon, above Beverly Hills, to a bucolic spot with a reservoir that supplied water to the city, populated with the sort of indeterminate flora that could just as easily be North Carolina as California. Assistant director Bruce Bilson shouted, *"Roll it!"* The crew filmed the scene Sheldon Leonard had ordered up to accompany Earle Hagen's theme music. The twenty-second sequence called for Andy and Opie to amble along a dirt road, and for Opie to lob a rock into the water.

"They came walking down the road," Bruce Bilson recalled, "and the kid threw a rock in the lake, and it didn't get in the lake. So we did another take, and the kid threw the rock, and it didn't go in the lake. And so I said, 'Okay, propman, get behind that bush down there, and when I say, "Throw it," throw it.' " Bilson shot the scene a third time. Opie underthrew again, but this time, the propman lobbed a stone into the

161

reservoir. In the resulting shot, careful viewers will note a slight, gravity-defying lag between Opie's throw and the consequent splash.

The canyon would serve as the backdrop for many subsequent picnics and manhunts. Andy and Barney would occasionally launch a leaky rowboat into the reservoir and fish—a delicate undertaking, given that they were rowing in the city's drinking water.

Andy, Don, and the rest of the cast settled into something approaching the nine-to-five schedule that would typify the *Griffith Show* for the next eight years. The core players would gather at nine o'clock on Thursday mornings to "read down" the script for the next week's show, as the script supervisor kept time with her stopwatch. Then, they would read the script for the following week, to give the ensemble an early feel for whether that script worked and, if it didn't, what changes might be in order. Then, most of the cast would be dismissed. Aaron Ruben would stay behind with Andy, Don, and the directors to work on rewrites. Friday morning, new scripts would be handed out, and the cast would begin rehearsals on the soundstage. Shooting would commence at eight o'clock Monday morning and would continue through Wednesday.

The first episode filmed, "The New House-keeper," seems to have been written largely as a concession to the network and the sponsor,

General Foods, whose representatives were eager to reaffirm the heartwarming backstory set up in the pilot. The episode established Andy as a winsome widower, introduced Aunt Bee as his matronly housekeeper, and posited a tender relationship between Andy and Opie. "The New Housekeeper" also illustrated what the program might have become without Don. Andy dominates, reprising the exaggerated drawl of his *Hamlet* days and generally playing the buffoon.

Ron Howard later recounted his first impression of Barney Fife: "Andy and this man were talking very quietly. Andy was a lot bigger than that fellow. And they were talking, and I couldn't really hear much, but I started watching. All of a sudden, this very quiet man, Don Knotts, became a complete bundle of nerves. Cameras were rolling. I think he was tapping his pocket and saluting and knocking his hat off. . . . I remember turning to my dad and saying something like 'Is that man crazy?' And he said, 'No, no, no. He's a very funny actor.'"

Don made the most of his first real scene, a ninety-second exchange in the sheriff's driveway, saying with a stiff salute, "Deputy Barney Fife reporting, sir, with an important message."

"Barney, I've told you, you don't have to do that." Andy smiles. "This ain't the army. You see, it's just me and you."

"Well, shucks, Andy. I want to do good on this

job. Even if it's just deliverin' messages, I want to do it right."

"Well, I know you do, and I admire your attitude."

"You see, Andy, I want the folks in this town to realize that you picked me to be your deputy because . . . Well, you looked over all the candidates for the job and you judged their qualifications and their character and their ability, and you come to the fair, the just, and the honest conclusion that I was the best suited for the job. And I want to thank you, Cousin Andy."

The exchange gave the *Griffith* producers a glimpse of the magic that could unfold when Andy and Don shared a scene: Barney's almost unbearably taut delivery, the twinkle of love in Andy's eyes, and the impeccable timing that linked the two actors. Sheldon Leonard recalled, "There was such an electricity, there was such chemistry apparent on the screen when we saw it in the dailies in the next day after we shot it, that we all looked at one another and we said, 'Well, that's it. Let's get [Don] tied up, let's make sure he's a part of the show.' "

Sheldon approached Don and offered him a contract.* Don's pay would top out at $3,500 an episode, or about $100,000 a year, in season five.

---

*In a 2005 interview with Bill Dana, Don said Sheldon first offered a one-year contract, but extended it to five years "after I had been on the show about a month or so."

He was guaranteed an appearance in ten of every thirteen episodes; soon enough, though, Don would be begging to get even a single week off.

Andy and Don thought they had a hit. But most television shows fail, and no one would know *Griffith*'s fate until the first episode aired that fall. By that time, at least ten episodes had been filmed. "We liked it. It was fun. It was funny. Everybody was good," recalled Bruce Bilson, the assistant director. "But we were working in a vacuum, on two big soundstages on Cahuenga Boulevard."

One day about six weeks into production, Andy found himself in the men's room, standing next to a studio electrician named Frank. He hadn't spoken to Andy once in those six weeks. Now, he turned to Andy and said, "You'll be in the top ten in six months."

As the premiere neared, the *Griffith* producers began to mull which of the filmed episodes should be first to air. The network brass chose "The New Housekeeper." Andy and much of the creative staff preferred "The Manhunt," the second script filmed. The reason was Barney Fife.

"The Manhunt" opens with Andy and Opie fishing in the reservoir. As they pull their rowboat to shore, Barney tears down the dirt road in his Galaxie 500 squad car.

"Sheriff. Sheriff!" Barney bellows, leaping

from his patrol car. "Sheriff, you'll never guess what's happened! Somethin' big!"

Andy calmly asks, "Well, what is it?"

Barney's eyes bug out. "Biggest thing ever happened in Mayberry. Real big. Big! Big big!"

The story would win the 1962 Writers Guild Award for best comedy writing in a television series. With this episode, the first to feature Don, the cast and crew began to sense that something special was playing out in front of the *Griffith* camera. Whenever Andy and Don would take the stage, Don's eyes would widen and his body would tense as he transformed into Barney, and Andy's eyes would warm with adoration, and some primal comedic force would be unleashed. "The Manhunt" recast the Mayberry universe. It was still Andy's show; but for the next five years, most of the laughs would go to Barney.

"By that episode," Andy recalled later, "I knew that Don should be the comic and I should play straight for him, and that made all the difference. All the difference . . . The event of Don on this show changed the whole groundwork of it. Because every comic character that came on, we added them as fast as we could find them, and I played straight to all of them."

By stepping back, dialing down his Will Stockdale shtick and retreating into the role of straight man, Andy Griffith brought balance to Mayberry and immortality to his program. As the production evolved and the cast grew, Andy Griffith would emerge as one of the hardest-working straight men on television, his timing and gravitas elevating the artistry not just of Don but, later, of such comedic talents as Howard "Floyd" McNear and Jim "Gomer" Nabors.

"To be a straight man is a wonderful position," Andy recalled later. "You are privileged more than anyone else—to be in the scene and to watch it, too. I could watch Don Knotts and Frances and the rest with a thousand times more delight than anybody in the audience ever could, because I'm between the camera and you on most shots and I'm closer to Don's eyes than you can ever be. There's no more joy than that, I can tell you right now."

Andy was always walking around the set chuckling and shaking his head over something Don had said. Don, for his part, had never worked with a better partner.

"Our timing was alike," Don recalled. "I could almost tell when Andy was going to come in, and he said he could do the same with me. And Andy found Barney funny. I think that helped, too. I could see sometimes in Andy's eyes that he was trying to keep from laughing, which would help me try to be even funnier. And Andy was like the ultimate straight man. He was the best you could imagine."

Neither Andy nor Don received a writing credit on the *Griffith Show*. But both men made enormous contributions to the Southern-flavored scripts almost from the start. Andy insisted that Don get a seat at the table when the *Griffith* elite gathered to fine-tune a coming episode. When a script had holes to be plugged, Andy would turn to Don and say, "Why don't you see if you can write up a funny little thing to put in there."

The collaboration would yield Andy and Barney's first classic routine. The team was polishing the script for "Ellie Comes to Town," which would be the fourth episode to air. As the *Griffith* producers reviewed the pages, Don sat in his chair and scribbled on a sheet of paper. Then he turned to Andy and said, "Hey, Andy, I just memorized the lawman's code. Try me out." Andy turned to Don with palpable delight and said, "Okay, Don, go ahead." Don handed Andy the sheet of scribble, slipped into character, and asked the sheriff to test his recall of what he'd written. Aaron Ruben and the others sat mesmerized as Don led Andy through the routine, in which Barney boasts of his memory skills and then proves unable to recall a single word.

"Wanna just check me on it? I know the whole thing," Barney tells his sheriff in the finished episode. He hands Andy the text.

" 'Rule number one,' " Andy recites. "All right. Go ahead."

Barney sits, concentrates, knits his brows, clears his throat. A grave expression crosses his face as he looks up at Andy: "You wanna just give me the first word?"

"Okay: 'An.' "

" 'An,' " Barney repeats. " 'An.' 'An'?" He looks at Andy quizzically.

"Yeah. 'An.' "

"You sure?"

"I'm lookin' right at it."

" 'An.' 'An' . . ." Barney sighs. "Uh, you wanna just give me the second word?"

" 'An officer.' "

"Oh, yeah. 'An officer' . . . 'An officer' . . . 'An officer' . . . 'An officer' . . . 'An officer' . . ." Barney sinks his head in his hands, twirls in his chair, and thuds his forehead against a coat tree.

The exchange goes on for more than two minutes, with Barney twisting his face and disheveling his hair in agony. It reaches a comic crescendo as Barney barks back the final words of the code, moments after they leave Andy's mouth.

Most of the scene was shot with Andy and Barney reading their lines in separate takes, so Andy wouldn't lose his composure on camera. The final seconds were shot in a single take, Andy struggling mightily to spit out his words without exploding in laughter. The camera quickly cut away to a shot of a sober Andy.

"You wanna go over it again, or you think ya got it?"

"I got it," Barney replies.

An adolescent Don Knotts poses with Danny the dummy. Inspired by Edgar Bergen, Don sent away for a mail-order "Ventrilo" in junior high school and learned to throw his voice. Danny would earn Don his first pay as a performer.

The seventh-grade class at Rockford Street Grammar School in Mount Airy, North Carolina. Andy stands at the top right. Childhood friend Emmett Forrest is in the front row, wearing a tie. The tall girl to Emmett's far left is Angie Marshall, who would be Andy's first love.

Andy poses for a high school–era portrait, already sporting an unruly mop and a Lincolnesque brow. He was a bit too clean-scrubbed to fit in among the other working-class boys in Mount Airy.

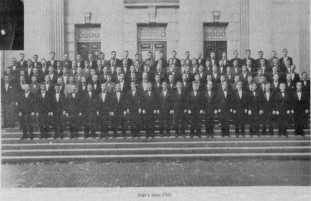

Men's Glee Club

Under the direction of Paul Young the Men's Glee Club has completed another successful season. Greatly reinforced by the influx of veterans, the club had a full schedule opening with the University Day program in October. A highlight of the year was the Christmas Concert in December, a combined program with the Women's Glee Club. A tour of several cities of the state was another main event, a trip in April to women's colleges in Virginia, and the Spring concert on campus.

OFFICERS

Andrew Griffith...............................President
William Smith...............................Vice-President
Charles Stanford...............................Secretary
Richard Cox...............................Business Manager
Don McFarland...............................Advertising Manager

ANDREW GRIFFITH
President

216

A page from the 1947 *Yackety Yack* yearbook, presenting "Andrew Griffith" as president of the men's glee club at the University of North Carolina. By this time, Andy's hair was tamed into a lopsided pompadour, his face trimmed to a hungry scowl.

171

Don (*center*) entertains the troops with the *Stars and Gripes* revue, his ticket out of the trenches in the Pacific theater. Note the conspicuous absence of Danny: legend has it Don threw the dummy overboard so he could ditch ventriloquism for skit comedy.

Don performs with child actor Clive Rice in *Bobby Benson and the B-Bar-B Riders*, a radio Western on the powerful Mutual Broadcasting System. Though not yet thirty, Don was cast as Windy Wales, a Gabby Hayes–style old-timer who spouted authentic frontier gibberish.

Andy and Don perform the manual dexterity skit in
No Time for Sergeants during its celebrated Broadway
run, joined by costar Myron McCormick. Andy and
Don met during rehearsals for *Sergeants*. It was
Andy's first star turn. Don had only a small part,
but their chemistry was immediate.

Andy romances Patricia Neal in *A Face in the Crowd*.
Andy delivered his strongest single performance in the
Elia Kazan masterpiece as Lonesome Rhodes, a simple
country boy transformed by mass media into a
power-mad monster.

Andy with Barbara Edwards, the elegant Chapel Hill diva who became his first wife. This picture was shot on a trip back home after Andy's first blush of fame up north.

Don as the Nervous Man on *The Steve Allen Show*. Don's breakout character came to him in a dream; Andy persuaded him to put it on television. To this day, fans of a certain vintage remember Don most fondly for his *Steve Allen* work.

Andy with his wife and parents on the Griffiths'
fifty-three-acre spread on the Carolina coast, bought
with Andy's *No Time for Sergeants* riches. Carl
Griffith's knee-slapping humor inspired his son.

Andy and Barney
shoot their first
scene on *The Andy
Griffith Show*. The
production was
supposed to
revolve around
Andy, but once
producers saw the
magic between
Andy and Don,
they set about
reordering the
show around their
relationship.

Andy and Don with executive producer Sheldon Leonard (*at right*) and producer Aaron Ruben (*facing camera*) in the writing room. A humble supporting actor wasn't normally permitted to join the producers in tweaking scripts, but Andy insisted Don get a seat at the table. Within weeks of the *Griffith* debut, Andy and Don were writing entire skits for their characters.

Don with Kay, his college sweetheart and first wife. Unlike Barbara Griffith, Kay had no theatrical ambitions. Nonetheless, some observers mistook her for a young Debbie Reynolds.

Andy and Barbara with their adopted children, Dixie and Sam. Andy labored to give his children a normal life, but Sam would descend into alcoholism. He died at age thirty-seven.

Don poses outside his home with Kay and their children, Karen and Tom. Most of the *Griffith* cast lived in the fashionable communities west of Hollywood, but Don lived east, in the sleepy bedroom community of Glendale.

A publicity still featuring Don with Andy and his television son, Ronny Howard. In fathering Opie, Andy drew inspiration from the powerful father–son bond between Ronny and father Rance Howard, a mainstay on the *Griffith* set. With Barney around, it sometimes seemed Sheriff Taylor had two sons.

6.

A Hollywood Friendship

One chilly morning in winter 1960, Sherwin Bash drove out to Forty Acres, the Desilu back lot in Culver City, to visit Don, his ascendant client. He found him huddled beneath a blanket, warming his hands at a flaming garbage can beside Andy; they looked to Sherwin like a pair of hoboes. Andy emerged from beneath his own blanket, strode over to Sherwin with a broad smile, and said, "Ah want you to meet two big stars in showbiz!"

Andy and Don had been in showbiz long enough to know a hit when they saw one. By that winter, it was clear their show was both better crafted and more plainly likable than most anything else on television that year. The first batch of teleplays by Jack Elinson and Charles Stewart explored the childlike frailty in the characters who surrounded Sheriff Andy Taylor and introduced some of the peccadilloes that would immortalize the show. Here was Otis, a lovable drunk who let himself in and out of the jail cell; Barney, a deputy of such juvenile dimensions that the sheriff entrusted him with only a single bullet; and Aunt Bee, a woman of such myopic hospitality that she insists on delivering lunch to Andy and Barney at the jailhouse. The procession of drunks, vagabonds, farmers, doting aunts, and sundry eccentrics must have reminded Don of the West Virginia boarding-house where he was raised.

But the critics were not convinced. "The New Housekeeper," the syrupy story chosen to launch the series on October 3, drew middling reviews. *Variety* found the episode "more sentiment than comedy" and, at moments, "dangerously close to the maudlin." A squib in *Time* magazine offered both praise and condescension, declaring Griffith and his show "good for laughs, all of them canned." This would be a recurring theme in press coverage to come.

The morning after *Griffith*'s television debut, assistant director Bruce Bilson raced into the makeup room to find Andy and Don already comparing notes with their new director, Bob Sweeney, and makeup man Lee Greenway. "I said, 'Boy, everybody I spoke to just loved the show,' " Bruce recalled. "And the makeup man said, 'Yeah. Me, too. Everybody loved it.' And Andy said, 'Everybody I spoke to loved it, too.' And Sween said, 'Everybody I spoke to just said, "What a wonderful show." ' And Andy said, 'Yeah, when I came in this morning, Tiny at the gate said, "Great show last night." ' "

"And Sween said, 'That's where I heard it,' "
Bruce recalled. "And Don said, 'That's where I
heard it.' And that was the great moment when
we thought everybody loved us, because of Tiny
at the gate."

Bob Sweeney—"Sween"—joined the *Griffith*
ensemble just as it went on the air. The new
director was forty-one and had risen to fame with
a San Francisco radio show called *Sweeney and
March*, as part of a comedy duo. Bob had done
some television acting, and he knew Sheldon
Leonard, who hired him on a hunch.

"He had never directed before," recalled
Bridget Sweeney, Bob's daughter. "He read
every book he could get on the subject."

Bob replaced Don Weis, a capable hand who
had directed nine of the first ten episodes. The
producers "were feeling around for chemistry, for
somebody who Don and Andy responded to,"
Bruce Bilson recalled. "And Sween turned out to
be that guy." He marched onto the soundstage one
morning and announced, "Sweeney's the name,
comedy's the game." Then he assembled the cast
and crew for the first shot of that week's episode,
"The Christmas Story." He was so flustered that,
instead of "Action," he yelled, "Cut!"

Sween would direct the next eighty *Griffith*
episodes.

The October 1 *TV Guide* introduced *The Andy
Griffith Show* to its 20 million subscribers in a

story titled "Doin' What Comes Natural" and featuring a photograph of Opie perched on Andy's shoulders. It described Andy "bursting into show business like an undammed waterfall." Don drew only a passing mention.

The next week brought the "Manhunt" episode to air and introduced the first addition to this ensemble of lovable kooks, Hal Smith. Born forty-four years earlier at the northern tip of Michigan, Hal came to Hollywood and eventually landed a utility role on *The Adventures of Ozzie and Harriet.* He was invited to the Desilu lot to read for the role of Otis the inebriate, one of a few parts from the pilot that Sheldon Leonard planned to carry forward to the series. Like many Mayberry roles, this one might have run its course as a single appearance. But Hal fit it so snugly that Aaron Ruben took him aside after the episode wrapped and told him, "Hal, this might develop into quite a part for you."

The fourth episode, "Ellie Comes to Town," would roll out twenty-three-year-old Elinor Donahue, a fresh face in Mayberry and potential love interest for Andy. A former child actress from Tacoma, Washington, Elinor had spent the previous six years as the eldest daughter on the landmark series *Father Knows Best.* She was as well-known in Hollywood as either Andy or Don, and she arrived to the show as its presumptive leading lady, her name announced ahead of

Don's in the credits. She would last just one season.

Elinor was cast on *Griffith* as a lady druggist who arrives from up north to replace her retiring uncle at the Mayberry pharmacy. "It was sort of a loose premise to get a female in town of Andy's age," Elinor recalled. But Andy was eleven years older than Ellie, who, months earlier, had been playing someone's college-age daughter. The pairing must have left viewers a tad uncomfortable.

The producers wanted a courtship in season one and a wedding in season two. Elinor was radiant on-screen—perhaps a bit too radiant, a debutante among gap-toothed farmers. But it became immediately apparent that no sparks would fly. When Andy wooed Ellie, the overall impression was of a benevolent uncle reluctantly courting his prim niece. Behind the scenes, Andy quietly called off the wedding.

"There's things ah can do, and things ah cain't," Andy told an interviewer. "Love scenes are one ah surely cain't."

There would be no wedding for Ellie, nor for lovely Joanna Moore, fiery Aneta Corsaut, or any of the other women paraded through Mayberry as romantic interests for Andy, through the entire eight-year run of *The Andy Griffith Show*. The real "marriage" in Mayberry was between Andy and Barney.

That winter, in a *Los Angeles Times* interview,

Elinor hinted at simmering tensions on the set, at Andy's dissatisfaction with his leading lady and refusal to marry her on-screen. "And I'm inclined to agree with him," she said. "The show would then become something like a *Sheriff Knows Best.*"

Elinor soon found herself with a lot of free time on the Mayberry set. As the season lengthened, she was written into fewer episodes and given fewer lines.

"Andy would say, 'You know, why don't we give Ellie's line to Don and have Don say that,' " she recalled. "And so my lines got taken away. But they worked when Don said them. They were funny when Don said them. They weren't funny when I said them."

Andy and Don enjoyed nothing on the Desilu set so much as performing together. When they worked one-on-one, Don would sometimes torture Andy by pursing his lips in a certain way, or cocking his head, or flexing his eyebrows— there were so many ways he could break Andy up. He would do it again and again, until Andy would finally clutch his sides and say, "Stop it, you son of a bitch."

In his own gentle way, Don was every bit as much the perfectionist as Andy. On those rare occasions when he felt Andy hadn't set him up just right, Don would lean in and quietly ask, "You wanna come in a little earlier there, Ange?"

Sometimes, as the two stood waiting for the

crew to calibrate the stage lights, they would sing church hymns, with Don on the high harmony. Before long, Andy and Barney were harmonizing on camera, as well.

Off camera, they worked up little off-color skits to amuse the crew. In one, Andy stood straight-faced while Don narrated a mock advertisement: "I thought I was impotent. I tried everything. I went to doctors. I went to psychiatrists. I went to chiropractors. I took shots. And then I met her, and . . . [bursting into song, with Andy in harmony] 'Love lifted me . . .' "

"We spent every day together," Andy recalled. "We'd sit side by side, talk or not talk. Every day. And one day he admitted that his full name was Jesse Donald Knotts. And he hated his first name. Well, I've always had a mean streak, and I started calling him Jess."

Don already called Andy "Ange," the nickname from his Carolina childhood. In time, those were the only names either man used for the other. These were honorifics, a treasured inside joke. They stuck till the day Don died.

Episode 7, "Andy the Matchmaker," revealed an emerging theme in the *Griffith* scripts. In Mayberry people would go to any length to shield each other from hurt. Barney storms into the sheriff's office and threatens to resign over a whimsical poem someone has written at his expense on the wall of the bank, alleging the deputy is incapable of catching a crook. Andy plots to revive his deputy's confidence by manufacturing a crime for him to solve; Barney has never actually collared a criminal, crime being so scarce in Mayberry. Andy summons Barney to the drugstore, where Ellie, the druggist, claims someone has made off with twenty-four dollars. Barney tries to console Ellie but can scarcely contain his glee at her misfortune. He produces a canister of fingerprint powder and promptly spills it, setting off a fit of sneezing. Don's performance is magnificently manic, and the camera cleverly cuts away from Andy and Ellie when they can no longer keep from laughing.

Andy wasn't yet entirely comfortable with his own character. Story conferences were leaving him less and less to do. It became increasingly clear that Andy's role was to solve problems, not to create them. His character was coming to resemble a benevolent parent in a room full of riotous children. The best jokes were going to Barney. At home, watching the dailies one evening, Barbara turned to Andy and said, "Honey, you're too samey."

At the script table, surrounded by the regular Mayberry cast, Andy aired his misgivings. His bosses were horrified. Aaron Ruben took Andy aside and told him, "You know, you're the star of the show, and they look to you, and if you're going to express misgivings about where we're going, how do you expect Don, or Frances, or the kid, or the kid's father, to get up that energy and that morale that we need?"

It wouldn't happen again.

The January 2, 1961, broadcast of Episode 13, "Mayberry Goes Hollywood," introduced another new face to Mayberry: Howard McNear as Floyd the barber. Howard had gotten his start at the Savoy Theatre in San Diego in the 1920s. He had worked hundreds of roles in radio, television, and cinema, most notably as grumpy Doc Adams on the radio series *Gunsmoke*. His delivery was quirky and unpredictable: Howard would mumble and stammer and mutter before fixing his eyes on a costar and uttering some comedic chestnut. "You never knew which look or gesture or reading you were going to get from Howard, and he usually caught you completely off guard," Don recalled. "I cannot tell you how many takes I ruined, breaking up at Howard."

The October 26 issue of *Variety* put *Griffith* at No. 8 in the Nielsen ratings, just ahead of *Candid Camera*. Not yet a month old, *Griffith* had cracked the top ten, where it would remain for the rest of its eight-year run. "One of the most remarkable, and unexpected, successes of this television season has been the popularity of *The Andy Griffith Show*," wrote Lawrence Laurent, television critic for *The Washington Post*. "This is an unpretentious comedy, and it was not expected to do much opposite the ABC-TV powerhouse, *Adventures in Paradise*."

"Unpretentious" was code for "rural," "hick," or worse. But the show was an undeniable hit. *Adventures in Paradise* vanished from the airwaves two years later.

Andy's success aroused envy in his peers. One day, Andy and Don were eating lunch in the Desilu commissary along with directors Bruce Bilson and Bob Sweeney. Up walked Danny Thomas, the star of *The Danny Thomas Show* and part owner of Andy's new show. Danny patted Andy on the back and said, in his most patronizing voice, "There's my little moneymaker."

Another grudge was sown; Andy would neither forgive nor forget the remark. "We never ate in the commissary again," Bruce recalled.

By 1961, Andy was his own little moneymaker. He owned a Carolina waterfront estate, half of the *Griffith Show*, and parts of a shopping center, a record store, and two music companies; and his résumé included a hit record, a smash play, a blockbuster movie, and now a top-rated television show.

In January, *The Andy Griffith Show* made the cover of *TV Guide* for the first of eight times. A two-part story portrayed the enigmatic Andy as "a hard worker and a hard worrier," vexed by self-doubt: "He begins his day of worries at 5:30 a.m. when he props a script against the toaster at home and reads intensely while he has his cereal and coffee. He is often on the Desilu lot half an hour earlier than anyone else and seems surprised to find nobody around at 7:30 a.m."

The article depicted the working Andy as an ensemble of tics and quirks, ritually tweaking his ear or rubbing his nose as he guzzled coffee and pawed through *Griffith Show* scripts. "If he is frustrated or angry, he prowls the set, rampaging in all directions and mussing his curly hair until it looks as though he had spent the night in a hayloft. He writes appointments on slips of paper and then loses them, a habit he's had all his life." Once, while greeting visitors to the set, absent-minded Andy found himself fervently shaking hands with Barbara, his wife.

The piece made Andy sound like a disheveled madman. Andy's costar assured the reading public that he was not. "Some comedians are tight inside," Don Knotts told the interviewer, "but Andy is warm. You can get close to him."

When the camera wasn't rolling, Andy seemed intent on running his show like a big ole family picnic, with song and dance, food and drink, and much general merriment. Lee Greenway, the makeup man, kept a five-string banjo on hand. After lunch, Andy would grab his guitar and the two men would begin to play and sing. Don would join them sometimes, adding a warbly counter-tenor and occasionally breaking into a soft-shoe dance.

Lee was a man of the world and a champion skeet-shooter; he would become one of Andy's closest friends. He played a great straight man to Andy and Don backstage, "kind of like Ed McMahon," Ron Howard recalled. "They'd start singing these hymns or these country tunes. And he'd get Andy singing, and doing these kooky harmonies, and he'd be laughing his head off."

Apart from Andy, members of the cast and crew barely noticed Don when the cameras were off. He would retreat to a corner and sit with a polite smile, all but invisible—until Andy appeared and awakened his muse. "Don could make Andy laugh until he was crying," Ron recalled. "He would do bits. He would do comedic sermons. He would tell stories about going to church when he was a kid. This kind of stuff would absolutely melt Andy. It would just slay him."

Don was naturally shy. And he was frequently tired; he would exhaust himself with a high-energy performance at the start of the day, and toward the end of a ten- or twelve-hour shoot, he would begin to drag. "Barney ran around the whole day, talking his head off," Don quipped later, "and Andy just sat there and grinned."

Andy loved to horse around with Don, taking particular delight in any opportunity to shatter his aura of quiet repose. (Don was quite the antithesis of Barney in this regard when he was not on camera.) Once, while Don was napping on a cot between scenes, Andy picked up a film canister and dropped it on the floor, awakening Don with a bug-eyed start that would have surely drawn a laugh on-screen. Don would get Andy back by making lewd gestures during his close-ups. Few others on the set dared play practical jokes on Andy.

Andy began to spend ever-longer days at the Desilu lot. Always a smoker, Andy now put away four packs a day, along with the endless cups of coffee that he and Don would sip to stay sharp.

"I remember my dad coming home. Often he still had makeup on," recalled Dixie Griffith, Andy's daughter. "My brother and I, we would eat dinner first, in the kitchen. And he and my mother would eat later in the dining room. He tended to go to bed pretty early. He was exhausted." Dixie would see more of her father on weekends: "He would often be in the pool. We had this great lounge chair that floated, and it had these Styrofoam arms, and I remember him reading his scripts in the pool, and I'd be splashing around."

Andy was a workaholic, and he loved being on his set, enjoying the daily celebration of jubilant creativity he had assembled around him. "All these characters were friends of mine, both on the screen and off the screen," he recalled. "Everything was so grand." At work, anyway. Andy admitted later that his marriage to Barbara was "going sour" by the time the *Griffith* project was under way.

In fourteen years with Andy, Barbara had watched her artistic currency steadily decline, from university diva to Manhattan socialite to bored Hollywood housewife. "Barbara's life changed from New York to LA," recalled Robert Edwards King, her nephew. "New York was a very vibrant thespian community. When she got out to California and lived in the suburbs, that was a sedate lifestyle, and she wasn't very much involved. She probably did become less happy at that point."

Andy and Barbara still knew how to go out and have fun. They spent many evenings with Don and Kay, sometimes as guests at the home of Pat and Marjorie Harrington. Everyone loved how Andy's radiant warmth drew forth flashes of droll wit from the normally reticent Don. Barbara, tall and stately, would charm the group with stories of her own. She confided one night that Sam, their son, had stumbled into the master bedroom while she and Andy were making love, drawn by his mother's moans and convinced his father was hurting his mother. She told the story not with shame but with pride, born of a happy love life.

Don, too, arrived home late many evenings. "He worked very long hours. Sometimes twelve hours," recalled Karen Knotts, his daughter. "If he'd missed dinner, he would always come up to our room and say good-night to us." One night, she said, "I just couldn't go to sleep, and he bought me a little radio, and I left it on all night, and it cured me of my sleeplessness."

On weekends, Don would disappear into the bedroom with his script. "He would take each line and break it down maybe thirty ways," recalled Karen, who would sit and listen outside the door as her father searched for just the right inflection. When he was satisfied with his delivery, he would repeat the line still more times, until he felt he was locked in. Then, he would put the line together with the others. "It was like a concert pianist learning a new piece," Karen recalled. Only then would Don emerge from the bedroom, hand the script to Kay, and ask her to rehearse it with him.

Kay, unlike Barbara, was reasonably content in the role of Hollywood housewife. But Don's marriage, like Andy's, had become strained.

Don had entered therapy toward the end of the 1950s, shortly before the move to California, to deal with his insomnia, his phantom illnesses, and the crippling anxiety that would put him in bed for days before a performance. The therapists had dispensed pills, and by 1960, Don was hopelessly addicted. Ensconced in California, Don sought out Dick Renneker, a prominent Hollywood psychiatrist. Dick began seeing Don and quickly surmised what lay at the root of his maladies. Even as he entered middle age, Don was still haunted by the old childhood fears that he was going to hell—because he had never been possessed by the holy spirit, had never writhed on the revival-tent floor, had never spoken in ancient tongues. Dick asked Don, "Well, do you believe in God or not?"

Don replied, "No, I don't."

"Well, then, say, 'F— you, God.' " Raising his voice, Dick pointed toward the ceiling. "Look up there and say, 'F— you, God.' "

Don raised his eyes skyward and vented three decades of fear.

Dick persuaded Don to go off sleeping pills, cold turkey. For four consecutive nights, Don found no sleep. On the fifth night, he went outside and took a long swim in the backyard pool. Then he came back inside, crashed into bed, and slept. The addiction was broken.

Without Dick's help, "I'm convinced my dad wouldn't have made it," Tom Knotts said. "He would've committed suicide or something, he was so screwed up."

Dick helped Don pull his life together. So did Andy, whose friendship and constant companionship in those *Griffith* years lifted both men's spirits.

Kay started her own sessions with Dick Renneker. While both partners made swift progress, the therapy seemed to push them in different spiritual directions. After more than a decade of marriage, Don and Kay were growing apart. "We had a very, very close relationship," Kay recalled. "And then it was just changing."

Andy and Don sometimes squired Betty Lynn, Barney's girlfriend on the *Griffith Show*, to lunch at a hamburger shop across from the studio. One day, on the way back, Betty turned serious. "Listen to me," she told them. "You're married to your first wives, who have probably gone through a lot with the two of you. Now that you've gotten to be big stars, you're going to have women all over you. But you'd better watch out. Those women who have stood by you, you should value that. You'd better watch your step." The men laughed at her. "They thought I was so funny," she recalled. "I was being sincere."

On this topic, Betty had expertise born of Hollywood experience. A native of Kansas City, Missouri, Betty worked her way from radio to Broadway to a contract at Twentieth Century–Fox, where she compiled a lengthy film résumé along with various television guest spots. One day in 1960, she got a phone call from the *Griffith Show*. "I had seen the show only twice, but I laughed so hard," Betty recalled. She went to the Desilu studio and read for producer Aaron Ruben and director Bob Sweeney. Though Betty never signed a contract, she would appear in twenty-six *Griffith* episodes.

When Betty worked, Andy and Don "would kind of incorporate me into their lives for that day," she recalled. It didn't hurt that Betty, a natural, freckle-faced redhead, was the only available young woman among the regular cast outside of Elinor Donahue, and Ellie didn't fraternize much with Andy or Don.

Betty debuted in "Cyrano Andy," the twenty-second episode and the first of many to put Andy and Barney on a double date. The story opens with Andy and Barney sitting on adjoining couches. Andy is paired with poor Ellie, still gamely playing out the sad charade of on-screen romance; when Andy reaches over for Ellie's hand, she leaps like a frightened cat. Ironically, the script calls for precisely this sort of tension between the other couple in the room, fretful Barney and his new girlfriend. As Barney drops Thelma Lou at her door, she pauses for a good-night kiss. Instead, Barney blurts out, "Next time I'll tell you all about the assembly and the oiling of a .38 caliber revolver," before scurrying off.

The episode ends with one of the funnier sequences of the first season. Barney and Thelma Lou are seated on the couch, finally about to close in for their kiss, when Andy bursts in, asking, "Hey, Barney, ya want some pie?" "Pie's fine," Barney says, dismissing Andy. Barney leans in for his kiss, and again Andy appears at the curtain, asking, "Ya want some cheese on your pie?"

"Cheese is fine," Barney barks. Andy leaves. Barney and Thelma Lou close in to kiss—and Andy bursts in again: "Ya want cream and sugar in your coffee?"

"Yeah! Yeah!" Barney explodes. "Cream an' sugar an' pie an' cheese an' I'll get it myself!" As he storms off the set, Andy and Betty are fit to burst from suppressed laughter.

"Barney was such a sweet but pitiful little character, in a way," Betty recalled. "I can still see him suddenly turn and look at me with those big blue eyes. I don't know how I kept a straight face. But I did. I had to."

In time, Betty would find she had real-life feelings—not for Barney, but for his television boss. "I had a crush on him," she recalled. "But he was married, and [Barbara] was a lovely lady." Betty once told Andy, "I wish you were twins, because that way there would be one for Barbara, and one for me." Andy, for his part, liked to flirt with his single costar. "After Elinor left and he had no other girl to relate to, he'd sit and visit with me sometimes, hold my hand," Betty recalled. "He was a tease. Sometimes it would make me a little angry. Other times it wouldn't." In one well-traveled publicity shot, Betty sits with Andy, smoking a cigarette, her hand resting on his knee. Publicists airbrushed out the cigarette, but not the hand.

Years later, Betty presented Andy a portrait of

himself and asked him to sign it. He returned it with the inscription "You were Don's girl, but you should've been mine." Betty never displayed the photo, she said, "because I didn't want to hurt anyone's feelings."

Don, too, seemed to have a soft spot for Betty: "He had poetry he'd written that he would read to me," she recalled. But neither relationship passed beyond friendship. Betty would remain friends with Andy and Don till the end.

Andy's on-screen romance with Ellie the druggist would prove less enduring. At the end of the first season, Elinor Donahue left Mayberry. She asked out of her three-year *Griffith* contract, acting before the producers could fire her. No one fought to keep her, and that hurt.

Whatever Ellie's faults, the *Griffith* producers had not expected to lose her. Plans were already afoot to release a record of Earle Hagen's music from the show for the second season. One track was titled "Ellie's Theme." Earle sent the recording to Ellie. "I got tears in my eyes when I heard it," she recalled.

A few years later, Elinor spotted Andy at a Christmas party. They hadn't spoken since her departure. "He must hate me," Elinor said to Dick Linke, Andy's manager, who was standing nearby. "Don't be silly," Dick said. But Andy had indeed taken Ellie's departure personally.

"I walked up to [Andy] and I tapped him lightly

on the arm, and I didn't know what to expect," Elinor recalled. "I said, 'Mr. Griffith? I want to tell you how sorry I am if I upset you for having left the show.' He said, 'No, no, don't give it another thought. We didn't know how to write for you. That's all it was.' And he gave me a look that told me I was dismissed."

On May 16, 1961, six days before the final broadcast of the season, *The Andy Griffith Show* won its first Emmy. The award went to Don, for best performance in a supporting role. The show itself was nominated in the comedy category, but lost to *The Jack Benny Show*. It was hard for either Andy or Don to argue with that; Jack was their idol. In his acceptance speech, Don memorably told the crowd, "I don't know what to say. I've always been a prepared loser."

It occurred to Don, then, that after years of inhabiting docile, submissive characters on stage and screen, he had come to regard himself as a loser. He had projected that image so well that the public had embraced him as a loser. And now that success had made him a winner. Don treated himself to a celebratory round of golf.

The friendship between Andy and Barney was now the central dynamic on this quintessentially male program. The relationship trumped every other, including even the tender father-son bond between Andy and Opie. By the end of the first season, Ronny Howard had effectively lost his second billing on the *Griffith Show*, and that suited him just fine: a seven-year-old boy didn't need that kind of pressure.

Many *Griffith* scripts played like instructional films on parenting. For a model, Andy and his writers looked no further than the real-life relationship between Ronny and his father, Rance, that rare Hollywood parent who seemed to manage both his own affairs and his child's with dignity and sense.

Early in the first season, Rance recalled, "a script came in where Opie had all these smart-alecky lines, kind of flip and kind of sassing his dad." That was the relationship between Danny Thomas and child actor Rusty Hamer on *The Danny Thomas Show*. "And so the writers were just transferring what they did with Rusty to Ron and Opie." At a script meeting, Rance piped up, "You know, these lines, the direction you're going with Ronny's dialogue, it'll get you laughs right now, but it will seem like he's a smart-ass kid, and you'll want to slap him down. And in a year or two, when he gets a little older, it's not going to be funny."

After the meeting, Andy came up to Rance. "You know what, Rance? You're right about that, between Andy and Opie. We're gonna change it. We're gonna try to develop a relationship between Opie and Andy the same as your relationship with Ronny."

Everyone on the *Griffith* set witnessed the dynamic between Rance and Ronny in its full complexity. One day, Rance surprised everyone on the set by bending the child star over his knee and administering a spanking. It happened only once. Ronny doesn't recall the pretext, except that he "was probably acting up" and not concentrating on his work. The whole set grew quiet, and Rance made a little speech worthy of a *Griffith* script: "Anywhere you are—I don't care who's watching, I don't care what's going on. I have only one job, and that's to be your father, and that's to teach you right from wrong. And nothing about that job embarrasses me."

The Howards rented a bungalow on Cahuenga Boulevard near the Desilu lot so Ronny could go home for lunch. On days when Ronny had baseball games, the entire *Griffith* production shuffled its schedule to shoot Opie's scenes first. The family kept home movies of Ronny frolicking on the back lot, his personal playground, where he would take out mitts and play catch with Don between shots. (Andy looked the better athlete but threw "like a girl," Don confided to a friend, years later. *"Don't ever tell him I said that."*)

On the set, "they took one of the dressing rooms and made it into a little schoolhouse," Rance recalled. When the time came for little Ronny to do a scene, assistant director Bruce Bilson would summon him from his schoolroom with a cry of

"Ronny, *hyeeeaaa*," and Ronny would come running. He preferred work to school.

Though Andy turned to Rance many times for counsel on his relationship with his fictional Mayberry child, the two never spoke of Andy's own children, Sam and Dixie. Rance doesn't recall seeing either child on the Desilu set.* Andy kept his home life at home.

Karen and Tom Knotts did make the occasional appearance at their father's workplace. "I was visiting my dad on the set once," Karen recalled. "And I was extremely slow, everything I did, because I was always daydreaming. And I was in the lavatory, just daydreaming, and my dad and Andy were outside the door talking. And all of a sudden Andy said, 'Don, I love Karen, but she is so . . . darn . . . slow!' " Don sheepishly called into the restroom, "Are you done?" And on the other side of the door, Karen heard Andy deadpan, "You're one tough dad."

With "Bringing Up Opie," on May 22, 1961, the first season was over and the *Griffith* ensemble had completed thirty-two episodes. For the second season, they would produce thirty-one more. That schedule put enormous pressure on Sheldon Leonard, Aaron Ruben, and the *Griffith* writers to

---

*Dixie Griffith herself didn't recall ever visiting the *Griffith* set. But press clippings suggest Sam did appear at Desilu a few times, toward the end of the program's run.

produce material during the summer hiatus. The next seven years would see many recycled stories and reheated jokes. "The never-ending maw of the camera heartlessly devoured a script every week," recalled writer Harvey Bullock.

At season's end, Sheldon summoned several writing teams to his office for a three-day "seminar." His aim was to get a head start on the next season by brainstorming and stockpiling ideas. The ritual was unusual in the television industry—and with good reason: union rules forbade such meetings because they amounted to unpaid work.

"We'd sit around and just bounce ideas off each other," recalled Aaron, the producer and lead writer. " 'How about one where Aunt Bee enters homemade pickles in the county fair?' 'How about one where Opie meets a hobo who has a great influence on him?' 'How about one where Don gives somebody a ticket for something ridiculous, a ticket for jaywalking?' I was the one sitting there with the yellow legal tablet, writing as fast as I could."

When the seminar was over, Aaron would take his family to Europe for a month of well-earned vacation. He would return to find a stack of scripts on his desk. Such little feats of planning probably helped elevate the *Griffith Show* above the standard run of television sitcoms in the 1960s.

The *Griffith* camp would approach the second

season with some distinct advantages. They now had a solid cast of regulars with established personalities and predictable quirks. By season two, the writers knew exactly how Barney would overreact to an escaped con, and what Andy might do to rein his deputy in.

They also had a stronger sense of place. It's hard to fathom now, but Mayberry began its life as an anonymous Southern town, rendered without reference to any real city or state. The origin of the name is debated. Decades later, Andy told Larry King it had been coined by Artie Stander, the writer who penned the pilot for *The Danny Thomas Show*. But the name might also have come from Andy's own memory. Mayberry was the name of a community in Patrick County, Virginia, the birthplace of Geneva Griffith, Andy's mother.

For half a century, Andy would deny Mount Airy and its denizens the credit they obviously deserved for inspiring and populating Mayberry. He claimed Mayberry took shape around the script table, "from the imaginations of Don Knotts, me, Aaron Ruben, Sheldon Leonard, and whoever was writing or directing."

But over time, the correspondence between Mayberry and the North Carolina of Andy's childhood became obvious. Winston-Salem, the nearest large city to Andy's home town, is introduced in Episode 3. Episode 17 alludes to

Fancy Gap, a Virginia town just across the state line. In Episode 23, Aunt Bee has a sick relative in Mount Pilot, a play on Pilot Mountain, a local landmark. Subsequent scripts have Andy and Barney journey to the mighty metropolis of Raleigh. This was Southern realism, and Southern sitcom viewers hadn't seen anything quite like it.

One *Griffith* hand who wanted to know more about Andy Griffith's North Carolina was its director, Bob Sweeney. Between seasons, he and Andy traveled there for a two-week visit. They crisscrossed the state, and Bob watched Andy interact with dozens of Carolinians, the better to see Mayberry through Andy's eyes.

"Andy took him to this old lady's house in the country, up in the mountains," said Bridget Sweeney, Bob's daughter. "They had to trot through this field to get to this little shack she lived in. She made them tea and gave them a little bourbon and talked to them for a couple of hours. He had the best time with her and watched Andy interact with her and watched Andy interact with everybody, which made him understand them better. But when they were leaving, she said, 'Now, you be careful of that field, it's full of copperheads.' And they ran through that field like their feet were on fire."

Andy and Barbara Griffith had been living with their children and maid in a $650-a-month Spanish-revival rental home in Pacific Palisades, a secluded enclave north of Santa Monica along the Pacific Coast Highway. In summer 1961, they purchased a spacious eight-room house at Toluca Lake, a town in the eastern San Fernando Valley framed by television and movie studios. They bought it from Gordon MacRae, star of the films *Oklahoma!* and *Carousel.* The house sat on a single-acre lot, large by Hollywood standards but a mere postage stamp by comparison to Andy's Manteo spread.

Don's Emmy win ended any debate over who was Andy's second banana in Mayberry. Their friendship became the theme of the season to come.

With characteristic humility, Andy told the press his partnership with Don was nearly the only reason he turned on his television Monday nights. He told the *Chicago Tribune*, "I hate to see myself on the screen. Except when I'm doing something with Don. We can almost feel one another breathe —that man is so good you just can't believe it. He is so intense, he looks at me so deeply, he's trying so hard that half the time I just bust up right there on the set and we have to start all over."

By this time, Andy had retreated so far from the center of the Mayberry stage that, at times, it seemed as if he were sitting in the audience. Andy's character gave viewers someone with whom they could identify, a soothing presence amid all the comedic high jinks. Without Andy, *Griffith* risked alienating at least half the nation —those who were neither rural nor Southern. Andy served as their surrogate. His knowing grin and gentle quips reminded the urban sophisticates that his show was satire. His arched eyebrows and half smiles told viewers that he knew how ridiculous his friends looked, and he loved them anyway, and so should they.

Everyone knew Andy worked best as Mayberry's straight man. Yet, accepting that role put Andy's artistic sensibilities in conflict with his competitive spirit. On the Desilu lot, Andy would sometimes scan his script, frown, and ask, "When do I get some of the jokes?"

7.

A Slight Thread of Insanity

Season two of *The Andy Griffith Show* revisited scenes from two Southern Gothic childhoods, Andy's in Mount Airy, Don's in Morgantown, sweetening them with happy Mayberry endings.

The scripts came from several pens but seemed to draw from a single source: Andy's and Don's painful journeys through youth. Many of their memories were too dark for a television comedy. The *Griffith Show* allowed them to recast the stories as tender Mayberry parables. Perhaps this was a way for the two men to exorcise some childhood demons.

The season-two opener, "Opie and the Bully," finds Opie surrendering a nickel to a neighborhood urchin every morning on his way to school. Barney vows to investigate and stalks the boy around Mayberry, peering through a round hole cut from a newspaper. When he sees Opie hand over a nickel, his lips purse in fury. Barney tells Andy, who persuades Opie to make a stand. "It's fine and dandy to give away somethin' because you want to," Andy tells his son, "but not because you're scared the other fella's gonna give you a punch in the nose if you don't." He tells Opie that he himself stood up to a bully when he was a child, and that when the rogue punched him in the nose, "I didn't even feel it."

Opie finally summons the courage to face the bully. As he sets out for the confrontation, he turns once more to Andy and asks, "You sure you didn't even feel it?" Wordlessly, Andy lifts Opie into his arms and hugs him.

It seems as if, in that moment, the last trace of Will Stockdale drains from the face of Andy Griffith. In episodes to come, Andy would still pivot between a deep upland twang and the gentler Chapel Hill lilt, between the broadly grinning bumpkin of *No Time for Sergeants* and the sage, Lincolnesque patriarch of *Griffith*. But as the months and years passed, the ear-to-ear grins would be fewer, giving way to more furrowed brows and warm, fatherly eyes.

The episode "Opie's Hobo Friend" offered another nuanced lesson on civics and parenting. The script leaned heavily on guest star Buddy Ebsen, a colorful character actor who would resurface the next year at the helm of another "rural" sitcom, *The Beverly Hillbillies*, perhaps the most successful of many *Griffith* imitators. In this story, Ebsen plays David Browne, a rail-yard vagabond not unlike the nomads who wandered in and out of the Morgantown boardinghouse run by Elsie Knotts. Buddy's hobo flouts the rules. He swipes sandwiches from Andy's patrol car, liberates gumballs from the corner machine, and feeds Opie roast chicken purloined from someone's farm. Opie is entranced—until the hobo finally exhausts Andy's goodwill. The hobo brags, "I live the kind of life that other people would just love to live, if they only had the courage." Andy responds with a brief, brilliant summation of the essence of parenting: "You can't let a youngin decide for himself. He'll grab at the first flashy thing with shiny ribbons on it. Then when he finds out there's a hook in it, it's too late."

All through the first season, Andy and Don had labored in story conferences to leaven the *Griffith* dialogue with words and phrases that sounded properly Southern. By season two, the writers—virtually all of them Northern—were finding that language themselves. "Somewhere in the genes, some other force was tapping the typewriter keys," recalled writer Harvey Bullock. "I found myself having Andy *carry* Helen to the dance; fat folks became *heavyset;* the gas station became the *fillin'* station; ladies didn't perspire, they *felt the heat;* people had *half a mind* to do things or were *just fixing to.*"

The writers soaked up Mayberry vernacular from previous scripts and listened to Andy and Don spin tales on the set. And they reached back into their own childhoods, in small Midwestern towns and large East Coast cities, to reclaim sweet memories. These rhetorical artifacts weren't particularly Southern or Northern, urban or rural: they were universal. The earnest realism of the *Griffith Show* was becoming a collaborative effort.

Once, early in the second season, director Bob Sweeney cued little Ronny at the doorway to the sheriff's office, and the child actor balked.

"What is it?" Bob asked.

"Well, I'm not sure a kid would say it that way."

"Well, how would he say it?"

Ronny said the line the way he thought a kid would say it. (Decades later, he remembers the scene but not the exact words.)

"Well, say it that way," Bob told the boy. Then he said, "Action!"

Ronny stood grinning.

Andy looked over. "What's the matter, youngin?"

Ronny said, "That's the first suggestion of mine that you've taken."

And Andy said, "That's the first one that was any damn good. Now, let's go rehearse the scene."

For Ronny's eighth birthday, the *Griffith* cast and crew chipped in to buy him an eight-millimeter movie camera. Ronny set about making a home movie, which he titled *The Chase*. It starred his father, Rance, as a hobo who steals a pie, a plot not unlike that of "Opie's Hobo Friend."

Ronny took careful note of Andy's skills as

211

benevolent boss of the Mayberry set and keeper of the *Griffith* flame. Ron remembers sitting through a Thursday script-reading: "It was pretty funny, and it was pretty outrageous. It had Andy and Barney being pretty goofy. And when it was over, people were smiling, and they were happy, and then Andy said, 'I think we're gonna have to rewrite this script.' And there was kind of a silence because everyone had thought it was a pretty funny script, and one of the producers said so. But Andy said, 'Yeah, I think it's funny, too.' He said, 'We're not *The Beverly Hillbillies.*' "

The producers now routinely approached Andy and Don when the show ran a minute or two short. The pair would retreat to a corner of the script room to write. It was filler, yes—some of the most inventive filler ever glimpsed on television. Their meandering dialogues were becoming a trademark of the *Griffith Show*. "You wouldn't know where it was coming from," Ron Howard recalled, "but all of a sudden it would be one of the greatest scenes the show ever offered."

The absurd little skits brought something unique and timeless to the screen. Hedda Hopper, the Hollywood gossip columnist, called it "a slight thread of insanity": that twinkle in Andy's eye, and that tremor in Barney's frame, betrayed just a hint of Carrollian madness in sunny Mayberry.

One of those sessions probably yielded the opening scene between Andy and Barney in "The

Pickle Story," perhaps the most beloved *Griffith* episode. The camera finds the pair in the sheriff's office, alternately humming and singing the hymn "Tell Mother I'll Be There" as they shuffle papers, a tender moment of shared reverie.

"The Pickle Story" celebrates the simple virtue of empathy: recognizing the feelings of another and, in the case of utopian Mayberry, going to comic lengths to protect them. Writer Harvey Bullock later recalled that the story had emerged at one of Sheldon Leonard's brainstorming conferences. Others say the inspiration came from Don's bitter hatred for cucumbers, acquired while eating them in prodigious quantity during the war.

Aunt Bee walks into the sheriff's office and announces that she has brewed a batch of pickles. For Andy and Barney, this is dire news: Aunt Bee's pickles are inedible. They watch a fly land on one and die. Yet, they cannot bear the thought of hurting Bee's feelings. "I don't know how I can face the future," Barney moans, "when there's eight quarts of pickles in it."

Andy and Barney empty Aunt Bee's jars and replace her toxic pickles with surrogates bought from a store. The ploy backfires when Aunt Bee enters her pickles in a contest at the fair. Now, Andy and Barney must choose between hurting Aunt Bee's pride and perpetrating a fraud. They decide the only solution is to eat all the pickles themselves.

The story further defines Andy as Mayberry's archetypal father. He labors to protect not just Aunt Bee's feelings but also those of her arch-rival, Clara, whose pickles eventually win the contest. Andy realizes the pickle contest is all Clara has. She tells the sheriff, "It's a great comfort to know there's something I can do." Like so many in Mayberry, Clara has no family but the town itself.

In fact, there was a distinct dearth of traditional families in this quintessential family show. Andy was a widower, Barney a bachelor, Aunt Bee a spinster. Floyd the barber and Otis the drunk both purportedly had spouses, but they were rarely seen. The lesson of Mayberry, Ron Howard later asserted, was that "a community can be a family. The town of Mayberry is one big family."

Part of the program's unique appeal was its pleasing invocation of simple virtues in a turbulent time. *The Andy Griffith Show* was anachronistic. The denizens of Mayberry wore clothing of uncertain vintage and hair of indeterminate style and drove cars of unspecified age. Scant mention was made of current affairs or changing times. Telephone calls were placed through a human operator, and no one seemed to own a television set.

"Andy used to say that 'even though we're making this show in the sixties, Mayberry is really the town I grew up in, in the forties,' " Ron

Howard recalled. Andy encouraged cast and crew to discard their contemporary affectations and treat the production as a journey through the past. That spirit would infuse every episode of the *Griffith Show*, inspiring viewers to reach back to their own tender memories of smaller towns in simpler times.

When current events did creep into Mayberry conversation, they were invoked in defense of the good old days, or in a sort of mocking defiance of the change simmering all around.

"People are in too much of a hurry nowadays," a barbershop customer intones at the start of Episode 48, "The Manicurist," broadcast in January 1962. "What happened to the fine art of settin', just settin' and starin'?"

"Ohhh, that's the finest thing in the world," Andy chimes in, "settin' on the porch on a moonlit night, starin' up at the sky. That's what probably folks will do when they get to the moon: They'll set on the porch up there and stare down here."

Andy was remarkably adept at shielding his production from the turmoil outside; on the streets of Mayberry, it seemed as if the sixties had never happened. He was somewhat less successful in shutting out the tumult in his own home. One morning, Andy arrived on the set with his right hand in a cast. The official line was that he had injured it while building a toy garage for his son, Sam, according to Griffith biographer Terry

Collins. In fact, Andy had put the hand through a door—or a wall; accounts vary—during a particularly explosive argument with Barbara.

On-screen, yet another story was told: Sheriff Andy had broken his hand while apprehending some crooks. In the opening shot of the March 1962 episode "Aunt Bee, the Warden," Andy emerges from the squad car looking as if he has been worked over, with a bruised face, disheveled hair, puffy eyes, and a torn uniform, an odd sight in tidy Mayberry. It was hard to tell which of the injuries were real.

Andy had spoken openly and honestly about the darker angels of his nature—his bitter grudges, his explosions of temper, his attraction to drink—since his *Face in the Crowd* days. Even now, immersed in the bucolic Mayberry universe he had created, Andy could not entirely purge Lonesome Rhodes from his soul. Friends winced at the thought of spending an evening in the Griffith home. By the 1960s, Andy and Barbara were feuding openly, and drunkenly.

"His and Barbara's relationship was insane," recalled Bridget Sweeney, who spent many childhood evenings as their guest. "They used to bust up furniture and break windows and break walls. . . . They were like the battling Griffiths. The way they talked to each other was awful, and the guests would be so uncomfortable."

As the *Griffith Show* rolled on, the contrast

between Andy Griffith's fictional world and the real one would grow yet starker.

Anyone who had missed the first sixty episodes of the *Griffith Show* could watch the episode "Andy on Trial" that April and come away understanding why this docile comedy connected so powerfully with viewers, and why the program's central character looked so pleased every time his spindly deputy walked on-screen.

"Andy on Trial" revisits themes first aired in the Danny Thomas pilot. Andy arrives at the office of a big-city sophisticate and attempts to arrest him for a neglected speeding ticket back in Mayberry. Andy insists the executive return to town and pay the fine as a matter of simple propriety.

The vengeful executive owns a newspaper. He dispatches a glamorous Rosalind Russell type to gather dirt on the seemingly unimpeachable sheriff, and the reporter quickly pegs Barney as an easy mark. Over milk shakes, she tricks the deputy into a prideful soliloquy of self-aggrandizement at the expense of his boss. "The kid is a little lax," Barney blusters, appraising the sheriff.

The executive publishes a hit piece on Andy, airing vague allegations of corruption and negligence. An overeager state prosecutor orders a hearing to weigh Andy's fitness for office. He calls Barney to the stand and confronts him with his own statements against his employer: Isn't it true that Sheriff Taylor allows prisoners to let themselves in and out of their cells? That he takes the patrol car out on personal errands?

Horrified at the effect of his own braggadocio, Barney is seized with a rare moment of self-awareness: "The truth is, sometimes I get carried away with myself. When I was talking with the young lady there, I—well, I got to braggin' a little bit. I guess that's one of my faults. . . . Why, Andy's the best friend I got in the whole world. And as far as I'm concerned, he's the best sheriff, too."

Andy, Barney explains, "is more than just a sheriff. He's a friend. And the people in this town, they ain't got a better friend than Andy Taylor. . . . The only ruckus you'd ever have in Mayberry is if you tried to remove him from office. Then you'd have a riot."

Andy sits, impassive, through the speech, which Barney delivers with surprising pathos—driven, no doubt, by their powerful real-life friendship.

In May 1962, a week after the end of season two of the *Griffith Show*, Don appeared—alone, this time—on the cover of *TV Guide*.

"As the undersized, undergutted Deputy Barney Fife on *The Griffith Show*, Knotts more often than not snatches scenes right out from under the star's nose," Richard Gehman wrote. "With a word, usually blurted in a panicky way, or a gesture, usually awkward, he quietly pulls the audience's attention to himself."

Curiously, the star of *The Andy Griffith Show*

didn't seem to mind. "Ah've never been a straight man before in mah life, but Ah'm glad to be one with him," Andy told the writer. "Man, he's so good."

The writer likened Andy and Don to Damon and Pythias, the characters from Greek legend who symbolize loyalty and trust in friendship. When Pythias is sentenced to death, Damon offers himself as collateral while Pythias returns home to say farewell to his family. It wasn't a bad analogy: Andy had sacrificed himself, in a way, so that Don could thrive at the center of the *Griffith Show.*

"Playing a scene, even one consisting largely of pantomime, they suddenly will stop, exchange meaningful glances, look at the director, Bob Sweeney, and shake their heads," Gehman wrote. " 'We goofed,' they say. Then they go at it again until it *feels* right."

Andy and Don didn't like to watch unedited footage of their work, Gehman explained. Instead, they would wait until the finished episode aired and watch it together. When that wasn't possible, they would dissect the episode by telephone just after the broadcast had ended.

Neither Don nor Andy expected star treatment. Neither man had his own chair on the *Griffith Show* set. Late one afternoon, Don, exhausted, plopped down in a canvas chair that belonged to the cameraman. A mortified crewman shooed him out of it. Something inside Don snapped. "Hey, Reggie," Don cried to the prop master. "Come here! I want a chair with my name on it."

"We don't do that in this company," the prop master replied.

"We're going to do it now," Don seethed.

"You're serious, aren't you?"

"Yeah. I am deadly serious. I'd like to have a chair by tomorrow, with my name on it."

Unbeknownst to Don, Andy was standing right behind him, grinning broadly.

"Reg," Andy said finally, "I want one, too."

When Andy and Don walked onto the set the next day, two brand-new canvas chairs sat in dramatic repose, beneath spotlights, with SHERIFF and DEPUTY SHERIFF stenciled on the backs.

On May 22, Don accepted his second Emmy Award at the Sheraton-Park Hotel in LA, with typical levity. "You know," he told the crowd, "for the first time in my life I'm really shaking?"

The *Griffith Show* itself earned a nomination in the category of outstanding humor program, but lost to *The Bob Newhart Show.* Apart from Don, the *Griffith Show* would get no love from the Academy of Television Arts & Sciences for five more years. It was a remarkable drought: *The Dick Van Dyke Show,* by contrast, earned twenty-five nominations and fifteen Emmy Awards between 1962 and 1966.

In an interview that spring, Don hinted at

ambitions beyond the *Griffith Show*: "I frankly prefer feature movies. If I had my choice, that's what I would do the rest of my life."

On an airplane ride from New York to Los Angeles, Don found himself seated next to Hedda Hopper, grande dame of Hollywood gossips. They chatted; Hedda asked lots of questions. Not till later did Don realize he was being interviewed. "Don Knotts to Star in Cinema Fantasy," the *Los Angeles Times* headline announced on May 9.

For all his television success, Don yearned for a film career. That spring, he was offered his first starring role. In this military comedy, adapted from the Theodore Pratt novel *Mr. Limpet,* a nebbish from Brooklyn wants to fight the Nazis but is rejected by the navy due to his poor eyesight. Fate and animation intervene: Henry Limpet falls into the ocean and transforms into a fish, who learns to guide American destroyers to German submarines.

The Incredible Mr. Limpet was one of the first feature films to intersperse live action and animation over much of its running time. Animators created a fishy caricature of Don. To visually link the characters, the filmmakers fitted Don with a pince-nez; animators drew matching spectacles on the fish.

Andy visited the set, where he and Don entertained the cast and crew of *Limpet* with improvisational skits, sometimes as a pair of

World War II veterans, sometimes as zookeepers.

In another routine, Andy "played like he was in some big convention hall, and it was a convention of sex therapists," recalled Carole Cook, the Lucille Ball protégé who costarred in *Limpet*. This was a bit Andy and Don had polished at cocktail parties. Andy would introduce Don: "We've got a wonderful speaker today. Some of the language will be very technical and clinical, because we're talking about sexual things." Then Don would stand, take a deep breath, summon his most earnest voice, and announce, "Now, I like a gal with a red bush, and I'll tell you why. . . ." And that was the skit. Those words, from that mouth, were enough to bring the house down.

While it may be Don's best-known film today, *Limpet* confounded the heads of the Warner Bros. studio in 1962. Don's character was meant to be "quiet and amusing" rather than riotously funny, Don recalled, and the movie's charms were subtle. One day, Jack Warner sent a memo to director Arthur Lubin that read, "You've got a funny actor down there. Why don't you give him something funny to do?"

Don wasn't the only one with plans beyond *Griffith*. Assistant director Bruce Bilson left the production in summer 1962 to join *Route 66*, an ambitious drama filmed on locations across the nation. "I never worked with Andy again," Bruce recalled in a recent interview. "And I tried, and I asked an agent, and I never figured out until three months ago why I never worked for him again. And it was because I left the show and I didn't come back, and I never explained why."

Bruce learned the same lesson Elinor Donahue had learned five decades earlier, and others before her: Andy Griffith expected loyalty. When he didn't get it, he neither forgave nor forgot.

The Griffiths retreated to their Manteo compound for the summer hiatus, as was now their habit. Barbara's sister Mary arranged for her son Mike to spend a month with his wealthy aunt and uncle on the Carolina coast. Mike King was eighteen and had just finished his first year at the university in Chapel Hill.

"It was way off the beaten path. But it was this gorgeous little island. It had all these little hideaways that were completely private," Mike recalled. "The population was like a small fishing village. It was a great place to hide, and party. There's nothing there. You could do little things like get in a little boat and row over to a little island and do whatever you wanted to do."

Andy and Barbara had fallen in with a clique of freewheeling couples around their age, and Mike recalled that they partied harder than him. Once, Andy came home with stitches in his face. He explained to Mike that he had fallen and cracked his head in his boat after a bout of drinking.

"They were going to the 'camp,'" Mike

recalled, "which I found out later meant the island where they partied. This would be an all-day event. They would go early afternoon and fire up the grill and start the drinks going, and it went on into the night. And there was a lot of, how do you say, *sex* going on, I realized later, or I realized some then, among the various people involved in these parties, and some of the people were married. It was a pretty wild bunch."

Andy loaned Mike his beloved '55 Ford station wagon and put him up in the servants' quarters off the kitchen of the Griffith home. Mike mostly kept to himself; but the walls were thin. "I heard them come in one night," Mike recalled. "And they got in a fight, the raised voices. I think he was accusing her of flirting. And then I hear this *pow,* and this slap, and then I hear sobbing.

"So then they came in the next day for lunch, and Barbara was outside at a cabana, a table with an umbrella, having lunch, with sunglasses on, and Andy was waiting on her, serving her. She took her glasses off and had a black eye."

For all he saw and heard that summer, Mike left Manteo still revering his uncle Andy. Andy was famous, but he was also a decent fellow, the sort who would hand you a twenty-dollar bill and the car keys on a Friday night.

Whatever drama might be playing out at home, Andy remained an impeccable professional on the set. On the break between seasons two and three of *The Andy Griffith Show*, producers Sheldon Leonard and Aaron Ruben gathered the writers for another marathon writing seminar, a chance to sketch out script ideas and hand them out among the teams. All went well until Andy Griffith walked in, and the air was sucked from the room. "For writers to listen to other writers is a near miracle," writer Harvey Bullock explained. "For them to listen to an actor is totally beyond belief." But Andy knew his audience, and he handled them masterfully.

"When the story meeting began, Andy did something wonderful—nothing," Harvey recalled. "Not a word the first morning, just some nodding and laughing, 'enjoying hisself.' He surpassed himself that afternoon. He referred to some of the past shows written by those in the room as 'real outstanding.' . . . We were ready to bronze him." By the end, the writers were actively encouraging Andy to speak. He began to offer down-home Southern anecdotes. He told them of a newspaper story he'd read about a thief in Raleigh who stole some cows by putting horseshoes on their feet. A few months later, Andy's memories would become a *Griffith* episode titled "The Cow Thief."

Sheldon Leonard and Aaron Ruben did their best to parcel out scripts such that each of the regular characters was featured in turn, like a pitching rotation—Barney one week, Opie the next, Aunt Bee or Floyd the week after that. Writers loved to build stories around Barney. If they had a least favorite subject, it was probably Andy himself. "He was a tough guy to write for, because he was perfect," Harvey Bullock recalled. "No foibles at all. We really had to labor on his scripts."

By season three of *The Andy Griffith Show*, character actor Howard McNear had emerged as perhaps the funniest of the comedians working alongside Andy and Don. The writers featured Howard in Episode 74, "Convicts at Large." On a fishing trip, Barney and Floyd stumble across three burly women who have escaped from the local prison and commandeered a cabin in the woods. The women easily overpower the two milquetoasts, setting off a ludicrous hostage situation. Barney and Floyd are utterly dominated by "Big" Maude Tyler, a broad-shouldered, lantern-jawed, thoroughly mannish con, played by veteran character actress Reta Shaw. *Griffith* never got weirder.

Shortly after filming completed, Howard suffered a massive stroke. As 1963 dawned, the captains of Mayberry found themselves sorely in need of another actor with his gifts.

They would find him singing opera at a club in Santa Monica.

8.

Men in a Hurry

The Horn was an artifact of authentic Hollywood: a Santa Monica cabaret owned by Rick Ricardi, the vocal coach from Twentieth Century–Fox; the sort of place, Andy recalled, where you could "order a cup of coffee and stay from nine till two and never see the same act twice." The room knew no musical boundaries and drew a motley mix of big stars, studio insiders, and brash newcomers like James Thurston Nabors.

Born on June 12, 1930, in Sylacauga, Alabama, Jim Nabors grew up singing in the glee club and church choir. His father was a cop. His mother worked at a truck stop. She also played the piano by ear, a talent she bequeathed to Jim.

Jim joined the Delta Tau Delta fraternity at the University of Alabama and began writing skits to perform at frat parties, mostly song parodies, not unlike the act Andy Griffith had assembled at the University of North Carolina a few years earlier. Jim graduated and moved to Los Angeles in hope that the dry weather might ease his asthma. He got a job at NBC, stacking film in the warehouse and making deliveries, before being promoted to film cutter.

In time, Jim retooled his fraternity act and took it to the Horn. He would talk in an exaggerated Alabama drawl, then rear back and unleash an aria from *Pagliacci* in a shimmering tenor. Then he would stop, mid-aria, and revert to his molasses drawl: "Waal, you see, there was this clown fella, and everyone thawt he was a real happy fella with that painted smile and awl, but he warn't happy a bit, cause . . ."

Jim was caricaturing his own provincial heritage, invoking an ensemble of unflattering stereotypes drawn up by Northerners and urbanites. He was doing with *Pagliacci* what Andy Griffith had done with *Hamlet*.

One Sunday in fall 1962, a mutual friend brought "this strange-looking man" to Andy Griffith's Toluca Lake home and dropped him off, intent that the two should meet. "I gave him a bathing suit and let him get in the pool, and I took him for a drive in the car," Andy recalled. Two weeks later, the friend escorted Andy to the Horn to see Jim perform. "I didn't want to go," Andy recalled. "But the man got up and was electrifying." Afterward, Andy caught up with Jim on the sidewalk outside. "I don't know what you do," Andy told him, "but it's magic, whatever it is." Andy pledged, "If a part ever comes up on our show, I'll give you a call."

Jim thought to himself, "Sure." Two weeks later, the telephone rang.

The *Griffith* producers wanted to expand the regular cast to include another comic, someone who could play a dim-witted gas-station attendant named Gomer Pyle. Producer Aaron Ruben thought he had already found his man: George Lindsey, a former college football quarterback and Broadway actor who had migrated to Hollywood and landed several bit parts on television. "He read for me and he sounded very good, a real pro, and I was about to hire him," Aaron recalled. "And Andy came in after rehearsal one day and said, 'Have you already hired the guy to play the filling-station attendant?' And I said, 'I'm about to.' And he said, 'Before you do, would you meet somebody?'

"So in comes Jim Nabors. He has a script, he reads, and what he lacked in professionalism and experience he made up for with a certain naive charm that he had. And I said, 'Andy, let's try him. He sounds good.'"

Jim couldn't believe the part was his. He told the *Griffith* producers, "Guys, I gotta level with you, I never acted."

Andy drawled, "Ain't nothin' to it."

Andy ushered Jim onto the set. He assembled the cast and said, "This week, our guest star is Jim Nabors. Everybody be real nice to him and go real easy on him, because he's never done this before."

Jim joined the *Griffith* ensemble for "Man in a

Hurry," broadcast on January 14. When shooting commenced, Frances Bavier walked up to Jim and asked, "Is this really your first time?" He nodded. Frances retreated behind the camera to watch. Jim read his part as if he were standing onstage at the Horn, giving a performance too broad for television. Between takes, Frances called Jim over. She told him, "Darling, the camera never misses anything. It never misses a wink or a blink or a smile. I know you're from nightclubs. You don't have to do any of that expository, expressive acting. Just settle down and be yourself."

The *Griffith* producers thought Gomer's Alabama drawl was a bit much. Andy reassured them, "Heck, a lot of the boys back home talk like that." Don looked out for Jim in the weeks to come, pulling him aside in his quiet way and whispering instructions into his ear so that Jim wouldn't unwittingly step in front of his costar on the next take.

Andy and Don were stunned, first at Jim's talent and then at his swift rise. Each of them had spent long years honing his craft, while Jim had arrived at the *Griffith Show* seemingly fresh off the bus from Alabama. Yet, the chemistry among the three transplanted Southerners was immediate. And the best was yet to come.

Mayberry was forever at odds with the world beyond its borders. Some outsiders came to town and stirred up trouble, such as the irreverent Buddy Ebsen in "Opie's Hobo Friend." Others arrived to stir up trouble only to find themselves pacified— even transformed—by Mayberry's charms, such as Danny Thomas in the original *Griffith* pilot. Mayberry was more than a town: it was a philosophy to be propagated, a gospel to be spread.

This was never more evident than in "Man in a Hurry," the *Griffith Show*'s finest episode. The story began as a variation on the stuck-in-Mayberry theme first explored in the pilot. Malcolm Tucker, a businessman bound for Charlotte, trudges into town on a Sunday morning, looking for a mechanic. Played by Robert Emhardt, a veteran character actor, Tucker represents "the typical well-fed, no-nonsense, impatient, successful businessman," Aaron Ruben recalled. In other words, he is a stand-in for every harried woman and man in our nervous world.

Malcolm Tucker is not a bad man, just a busy one. He arrives in town expecting folks to hop to, unaware that Mayberry on Sunday is closed for business. "I've got to get that car fixed now, today, this minute," Tucker cries. "I've got to be in Charlotte. Can't you understand that?"

Andy and his friends cannot. Nothing in their lives is so urgent that it can't wait till tomorrow. Tucker journeys to Wally's filling station and finds Gomer, the simpleton. He appeals to Gomer for help. Gomer treats Tucker to a soliloquy on what a fine job the absent Wally would do, were he only there to fix the man's car.

Overcome by desperation, Tucker leaps into Gomer's battered pickup and drives off. Andy runs him down; but instead of arresting him, the sheriff invites Tucker into his home. Tucker picks up the telephone to call for help and finds even that resource unavailable: the elderly Mendelbright sisters, Maude and Cora, have tied up the town's only telephone line for a languorous weekly chat about bad circulation.

Tucker wheels on Andy and vents his spleen. "You people are living in another world! This is the twentieth century. Don't you realize that? The whole world is living in a desperate space age. Men are orbiting the earth. International television has been developed. And here, a whole town is standing still because two old women's feet fall asleep."

Griffith never more closely resembled Rod Serling's *Twilight Zone*, a contemporary program that plunged its guest stars into surreal dreamscapes as a way to render some life lesson.

Tucker is about to learn his. Unable to do anything, he paces back and forth on Andy's front porch. Barney is there, nodding off; Andy is sitting in his rocker with his guitar, singing the hymn "Little Brown Church in the Vale." Barney joins in. They sing and strum and rock; slowly, the soothing music softens Tucker's face. His eyes fix on some distant point, perhaps a cherished moment from a lost childhood. Finally, Tucker lifts his voice and joins Andy and Barney in song.

The scene plays for two full minutes, a remarkable span of tranquility for prime-time television. Gomer finally breaks it up by tromping onto the set and announcing that his cousin Goober has arrived to fix Tucker's car. Tucker snaps back to his old, fretful self. He resumes pacing, while Andy and Barney unfurl a routine that will become a classic. The sketch invokes Don's childhood memories of long, languid evenings back on the farm.

"Ya know what I think I'm gonna do?" Barney says, breaking the silence on Andy's front porch.

"What?" Andy replies.

"I'm gonna go home, have me a little nap, then go over to Thelma Lou's and watch a little TV."

"Mmm-hmm."

"Yeah, I believe that's what I'll do: go home . . . have a nap . . . head over to Thelma Lou's for TV."

"Mmm-hmm."

"Yep, that's the plan: ride home . . . a little nap—"

The prattle drives Tucker over the brink. He explodes, "For the love of Mike, do it! Do it! Just do it! Go take a nap. Go to Thelma Lou's for TV. Just do it!"

Barney glares at Tucker. "What's the hurry?"

The episode was a masterpiece, and it

ensconced Jim Nabors alongside Andy and Don as a star of *The Andy Griffith Show*.

"Man in a Hurry" and the episodes to come represented *The Andy Griffith Show* at its creative zenith. It was a magical time. The program's best writers churned out classic stories at a steady pace. Its finest director, Bob Sweeney, brought the teleplays to life with exquisite camera shots and wrung every drop of pathos from the performers. Andy and Don played their roles with mastery and depth; the fatigue of consecutive thirty-episode seasons had not yet set in. Their comedic partner-ship was now the centerpiece of nearly every episode, even those that ostensibly show-ased others. In the contest for Andy's affections, Barney had no true rival.

But that was about to change.

In the episode "Andy Discovers America," broadcast March 4, 1963, Opie comes home from school and avows displeasure with his new teacher, "old lady Crump." She wants Opie to learn history. Andy thinks she's starting him a bit young.

Andy and Barney assume Opie's new teacher is "one of 'em old witches." But then, Ms. Crump strides into the sheriff's office to confront Andy. She is icy and regal and beautiful.

Aneta Louise Corsaut was born on November 3, 1933, near the salt mines of Hutchinson, Kansas. Her father was a plant scientist, her mother a schoolteacher, her name a misspelling on a Reno County birth certificate. She claimed, years later, to have been a tomboy and said her perfect nose had been broken three times in baseball games. Aneta drew suitors like flies. "She had more dates than any girl in her class," recalled Jesse Corsaut, Aneta's brother. "The boys came around in relays."

But there was only one man in young Aneta's life: Jesse Sr., her father. He bore a faint resemblance to Clark Gable, and Aneta adored him. When he died in her late teens, "I lost my boyfriend," she said. For the rest of her life, she dated a great many men but married none.

Aneta went to New York for acting lessons. She lived on K rations donated by army boyfriends and studied under Lee Strasberg, the reputed father of Method acting. In 1958 she won a role in the independent film *The Blob*, opposite Steve McQueen. She moved to Hollywood in 1960 and broke into television. Soon she was dating the writer Jim Fritzell. Jim introduced her to *Griffith* director Bob Sweeney.

By the time Aneta was cast on the *Griffith Show*, the quest for an Andy Taylor love interest had been abandoned. Aneta was signed for a one-shot part. Had the producers harbored any real hope of kindling romance, surely they would have given the character a more alluring name than Helen Crump.

The *Griffith* writers, all of them men, struggled with any script that called for Andy to interact with a potential inamorata. No one knew this better than Aneta. "[They] admitted that they could write for little girls and older women, but anything in between always came out sort of sweet and bland," she recalled. "And actually, they were not predisposed to listen to us."

Aneta's first encounter with Andy on the Mayberry set swiftly curdled into a heated argument. "We were out on location, standing nose to nose in the middle of a road, yelling at each other," she recounted. "I don't recall exactly what started it, or just what it was about, but it had something to do with feminism."

Andy was smitten. By 1963, the Desilu set was filled with obsequious sycophants who would say anything they thought Andy wanted to hear. He didn't like that, and he was fascinated by this sharp-tongued beauty who seemed intent on driving him away. "I think he respected the fact that I stood up for what I believed," she recalled.

They fought on-screen, as well. In their first meeting on celluloid, Ms. Crump storms into the sheriff's office in a rage. "Sheriff," she fumes, "did you or did you not tell Opie that he needn't do his history?" Andy hems and haws. Helen glowers. Finally she instructs the sheriff, "Would you please do me just one favor? Just stay out of my business, please!" She slams down her purse, wheels around, and storms out.

Aneta possessed "that feminism that comes naturally to intelligent women," a native aversion to being subjugated and controlled by men, recalled her niece, Jennifer Scarlott. In Helen Crump, Aneta would fashion one of the great proto-feminist television characters of her era. Like Laura Petrie on *Dick Van Dyke*, Helen was an equal romantic partner to her man. Like Ann Marie on *That Girl*, Helen supported herself, a single young woman living away from her parents.

Fan mail poured in. Viewers loved Helen Crump, although some questioned whether she had to be quite so hard on Andy. Producers quickly signed Aneta for further episodes.

With Andy and Barney dominating most *Griffith* scripts, other cast members had to wait weeks for their spots to come up on Aaron Ruben's story rotation. Ronny Howard, the child star, felt palpable relief at retreating into a supporting role. Frances Bavier, on the other hand, resented being upstaged—not just by Andy and Don, but by an eight-year-old boy. "I've had to take a backseat and watch others get the laughs," she told *TV Guide*, "and it hasn't been easy."

There was no more enigmatic presence on the Desilu set than Frances, who turned sixty on the third season of *Griffith*. She had perhaps the longest résumé of anyone in the cast. Her romantic résumé was shorter: she was married to a businessman for five years before deciding career took precedence. By the time of her most memorable role, Frances was living alone in a rented duplex in Hollywood. She told an interviewer, "I know that our house at the studio—the set, with the kitchen and living room—isn't home, but . . ." Perhaps, to Frances, it was.

Frances was a singular, sobering presence on the *Griffith* set. She wouldn't dance and sing and laugh with the others. She didn't like coarse language or practical jokes. She could be prickly. Her rapport with Andy was particularly cool, a mutual disapprobation that Andy expressed mostly in the absence of his usual, voluble warmth. He "seemed to bear some kind of resentment toward Frances," recalled Rance Howard, Ronny's father. "I think she was Sheldon Leonard's choice . . . and she may not have been Andy's choice."

Jim Nabors, on the other hand, counted Frances as a dear friend. One day on the set, Andy muttered something under his breath about Frances. "And I remember we were walking back from a table reading on our way to the soundstage," Rance recalled, "and I heard Jim say, not loudly, but he said, 'Andy, she's a good actress. You be nice to her.' And Andy had no reply for that."

Because Aunt Bee has no man in her life, pop-culture mythology suggests she might be gay.

Scholar Alexander Doty pegged her as a "queer cult lesbian" character, along with Alice, the housekeeper on *The Brady Bunch*, and Sally Rogers, the comedy writer on *Dick Van Dyke*. Many people likewise assume Frances Bavier was herself lesbian, although no one seems to know where the rumor began. "Absolutely not," said Jim Nabors, who is himself gay, and who knew Frances as well as anyone. They went antiquing together on weekends.

When the writers built stories around Aunt Bee, they sometimes mined the mystery surrounding the character's romantic life, perhaps because they themselves were curious about Frances. In the spring 1963 story "Aunt Bee's Medicine Man," Bee arrives at the sheriff's office feeling faint.

"Uh, I'll get you a glass of water," Barney cries. "Maybe I'll . . . maybe we better—better loosen something." Then he surveys Aunt Bee, unsure which part of her to touch. "You got something we can loosen?"

Later in the episode, Bee is swept off her feet by a traveling salesman and his medicinal brew, Colonel Harvey's Indian Elixir. Andy and Barney return home to find her at the piano, leading Opie in a jaunty rendition of "Toot, Toot, Tootsie!" She spins on the piano stool. Then she lurches straight into the camera, almost tumbling into viewers' laps, nearly breaking the fourth wall.

"Aunt Bee sure is feelin' good, huh, Paw?" Opie observes.

"Andy, I don't like to say this," Barney offers. "It was anybody else, I'd say she was tiddly."

As the third season of *Griffith* drew to a close, the series seemed to be gaining momentum rather than losing it. Andy and Don couldn't wait to get to the studio each day. Their enthusiasm was contagious: idle cast members would wander in on their days off just to watch Andy and Barney perform.

"Barney's First Car," broadcast on April 1, earned the program its second Writers Guild Award for television comedy. The script, from the celebrated writing team of Jim Fritzell and Everett Greenbaum, reads like a father-son story about life lessons learned, with Andy cast as the father and Barney as the son.

Andy takes Barney out to buy his first automobile, an amusing thought in itself, given that Barney is nearing middle age. He packs Andy, Opie, Aunt Bee, Gomer, and Thelma Lou in for a ceremonial first ride, bobbing his head with smug pride. Tragedy slowly descends: first a tapping sound, then a drumbeat, then a loud clang. Then the steering column begins to float up toward Barney's widening eyes, a worthy sight gag. As the car heaves in its death throes, Barney shrinks into a deflated heap.

Andy and Barney had been padding their

scripts with aimless filler skits for three years. First, the producers resisted them. Then, they embraced them. Now, the writers were contributing skits of their own, invoking folksy stories from their own pasts. The best of these was an exchange scripted for Andy and Barney as the two awaited the new car.

"Last big buy I made was my mom's and dad's anniversary present," Barney says.

"What'd ya get 'em?"

"A septic tank."

Andy stops peeling his apple, turns to Barney, and considers for a long, sober moment, allowing the line to sink in. "For their anniversary?"

"Yeah. Well, they're really hard to buy for. Besides, it was something they could use. They were really thrilled. Two tons of concrete, all steel reinforced."

Andy takes another long, stern look at his deputy. "You're a fine son, Barn."

"I try."

Season three ended with "The Big House." It replayed a well-worn theme: Andy putting crooks in jail and Barney letting them out. But the execution was a comic symphony, a perfection of the absurd little dance between Andy and Barney.

Two hardened criminals arrive at the Mayberry jail for holding. Andy need only keep them locked up for a few hours. He beseeches Barney not to go near them. But Barney becomes swept up in delusion, hell-bent on showing the cons his jail is no "small-town, two-bit lockup." Barney struts up to the inmates, puffs out his chest, and delivers a shrill speech, as if he were addressing an entire cellblock.

"Now, here at the Rock we have two basic rules. Memorize them so that you can say them in your sleep. The first rule is, obey all rules. Secondly, do not write on the walls, as it takes a lot of work to erase writing off of walls. As we tell all men when these gates shut behind them, you are starting a new life. If you're wise, you'll begin rehabilitation."

Andy's face is mostly hidden from the camera, presumably because he cannot keep his composure. Gomer watches Barney in reverential awe, a mesmerized child.

Andy departs. The crooks promptly trick Barney into opening the cell door. They escape. Andy marches them back to the cell. This pattern proceeds until, by the episode's end, Barney has replaced the inmates inside the cell. Andy recaptures the bad guys and releases Barney. "Great work, Barn," Andy exclaims. "Your scheme worked."

"The Big House" was the last *Griffith* episode for director Bob Sweeney, who seemed to understand the program like no director before or after. Sween wanted to try new things. He would go on to help launch the hit series *That Girl.*

Five days after the finale, Andy, Don, and Ronny Howard frolicked together on the cover of *TV Guide*. The accompanying article gushed about the program's 36 million viewers and "unexpected" fans, including Frank Sinatra and *Twilight Zone* creator Rod Serling, who cited *Griffith* as "one of the few genuinely funny comedies in the medium."

On May 26, Don earned his third Emmy, besting Tim Conway in *McHale's Navy*. Most news reports devoted only a single sentence to his achievement. Yet, he was only the second actor in Hollywood—after Jane Wyatt of *Father Knows Best*—to have won three straight Emmys for playing the same character on the same program. Clutching the now-familiar award, Don told the Hollywood Palladium audience, "This is too much."

Hollywood sophisticates no longer dismissed *Griffith* as a provincial knee-slapper.

9.

A Date for Gomer

Summer of 1963 surely marked the peak of Andy Griffith's professional career. The fickle stars of fame, fortune, and artistry had aligned perfectly in his favor, a moment of celestial harmony that would not come again.

Andy's home life was another story. And now, over the summer hiatus between seasons three and four of *The Andy Griffith Show*, a prototypical supermarket tabloid pounced on the fissures in the Griffith marriage. For a piece titled "The Secret Life of a Married Man," a reporter from *TV Radio Mirror* persuaded Barbara to open up about the burden she bore as spouse to a self-absorbed Hollywood icon.

"A comedian's wife has a hard job," Barbara told her interviewer. "It's a constant state of giving. A continual satisfying of the other's needs, because a comic is like a child. Everything must revolve around him." Andy, she said, dwelt in a world "so completely surrounded by himself that he often doesn't even hear me."

Had Andy declined to comment on his wife's missives, the damage might have ended there. But when the reporter telephoned, Andy talked . . .

and talked . . . and talked, giving the writer enough fodder for a seven-page spread, with ironic photos of the Griffith family frolicking at the Carolina shore.

"I'll give you a direct answer," Andy said, a response rendered partly in his Carolina patois. "And that is that I guess I am somewhat arrogant sometimes, sure. But so's everybody. And I do have a purty violent temper. Ah sure do. Both at work and at home."

Andy recounted the time he had splintered a door in the Griffith home. He chuckled. "Guess maybe there's some difficulty in handling me —or anybody successful, for that matter. But there's less with us, because I married Barbara before I became a star."

Perhaps sensing opportunity to sow further domestic dissent, the reporter asked whether Andy would mind if his wife returned to show business. The same question had been posed by another astute interviewer, Edward R. Murrow, in the previous decade.

Andy replied with injudicious candor: "Certainly not. Of course, I don't have a whole lot to worry about, on account of she's not about to do that."

Andy evidently intended that his wife should never perform again. Perhaps Barbara knew that and accepted it.

Andy and Barbara would remain married for another nine years, but his eye was wandering.

When nephew Robert King visited the Griffiths in Toluca Lake around this time, Andy took Robert for a ride in one of his antique cars. As they drove, he pointed out a small bungalow on a quiet street, said it was his, and boasted that a young starlet had just come calling there.

"Three things made Andy Griffith what he was," recalled Dick Linke, Andy's manager. One was "his work, his acting. He was one of the greatest actors I've ever seen. Number two, he loved to drink. . . . The third thing, with his drinking, he loved sex." By the 1960s, Andy was searching for partners outside his marriage.

As season four of the *Griffith Show* approached, the CBS network assembled its roster of stars for an hour-long variety special to promote the fall lineup. The cast included Andy, Jack Benny, Lucille Ball, Danny Thomas, Dick Van Dyke, and Phil Silvers.

As the ensemble broke for lunch one day during the production, Lucille Ball approached Andy, who was eating a sandwich and reading his script. She asked, "You play golf, Andy?" Andy shook his head. "You should," Lucy said. "It would do you good." She paused. "But you don't do anything you don't do well, do you?" Then she walked off. Andy's homespun naïveté was a front, and the queen of comedy knew it.

Jim Nabors, by contrast, radiated an innocence that seemed endearingly real. Thanksgiving week of 1963 brought "A Date for Gomer," a story featuring the newest star in the *Griffith* firmament.

Backstage at the Desilu lot one day, Don asked, "Jim, has anybody recognized you out in public yet?" Jim replied, "At the supermarket the other day, a lady asked me, 'Aren't you the guy on *The Andy Griffith Show*?' And I took fifteen minutes to sign that autograph, because I wanted everyone to see me sign my first autograph." Over the next year, Jim Nabors would become one of the biggest names in Hollywood.

Jim's sexual orientation was no secret to Andy or Don or to others in the *Griffith* cast and crew. Jim maintains he neither hid nor advertised his sexuality. "I've always been out," he recalled, "but I never made a big deal out of it." But homosexuality did not fall within the comfort zone of the mainstream media in the middle 1960s, so news accounts danced around Jim's private life. "We kept quiet about that for a long time," recalled Dick Linke, who managed both Andy and Jim.[*]

A *TV Guide* cover story in March 1964 reported that Jim lived "the life of a bachelor in a pleasant home in North Hollywood with a roommate (not an actor, an engineer), and, more recently, with his mother, who has been visiting in California

---

[*]In the early 1970s, when rampant rumor suggested Jim was to marry cinema star Rock Hudson, Jim dismissed the story as "horrible" and its authors as "sick."

following his father's death last fall. 'Never been married, but I've been engaged a few times,' Jim says, and Andy adds, 'I don't think he wants to undertake all that there just now.' "

Andy and Don adored Jim, but they also resented his abilities. Perfectionist Andy and obsessive Don prepared meticulously for their performances. Jim, by contrast, seemed to rely on talent alone, and he got away with it, and that annoyed Don and Andy to no end. Andy would stop speaking to Jim several years later, when Jim fired Dick Linke and Andy sensed a certain dearth of humility. Don and Jim remained friends, but Don confessed to his psychiatrist that he felt threatened by Gomer's gifts. In later life, Don would dismiss Jim privately, perhaps defensively, as "a one-joke guy."

Jim's effect on the viewing audience was immediate and profound, in a pop-culture sort of way. Within a few months, Gomer had elevated the exclamations "Sha-zayam!" and "Gaw-aw-lee!" to national prominence. And it was apparently he who seeded the *Griffith* tradition of uttering an exuberant "Hey!" as a greeting. William Morris agents raked in offers for Jim to star in various prospective pilots. One was a sitcom treatment of the old Andy Griffith film *No Time for Sergeants*. Jim approached Andy one day and told him of the *Sergeants* offer. Andy replied, "You're shittin' me."

Andy had previously pestered Aaron Ruben, producer of the *Griffith Show*, to find a star vehicle for his ascendant costar. Now, Andy marched into Aaron's office, sat down, put his feet up on Aaron's desk, and announced, "I ain't leavin' until we come up with something for Jim."

Aaron told Andy, "Well, Jim—Gomer—is such an easygoing, peace-loving, sweet guy, I'd like to see him thrust into a situation where he comes up against everything diametrically opposite to his character. Something almost violent. Something that's just like . . . the Marines."

The next day, Andy approached Jim and said, "You need some experience. Why don't you stay on our show another year and we'll do a pilot with you, and you can be one of the owners."

Jim was out of his depth. "I didn't know what the hell that meant," he recalled of Andy's offer. "I was just looking for a job."

Andy's impulse to boost Jim's career might have been pure altruism; more likely, it recognized the inevitability of Jim's departure, with or without Andy's blessing. If Andy took Jim under his wing, then he, Dick Linke, and the rest of the *Griffith* patriarchs could profit along with Jim from his ascent.

The negotiations would spawn *Gomer Pyle, U.S.M.C.*, a series built upon the same premise that had launched Andy's *No Time for Sergeants* franchise, with Jim Nabors starring and the *Griffith* team producing.

With Jim juggling network offers, perhaps Don Knotts felt it was time that he, too, be recognized. After three Emmys, the comic backbone of the *Griffith Show* was finally being treated as an a-list actor. In January 1964, Hollywood columnist Hedda Hopper announced that Don would soon be ready for a television series of his own.

"I have a tough decision to make," Don told Hedda. "I've had several offers to do my own show when I'm free, but I don't know where to jump." Don was contractually obliged to complete five seasons with the *Griffith Show*. After that, he was torn. His ultimate ambition was to make films. But "film offers don't always come in at the right time," he said.

Ominously, Don hinted that the creative surge that had fueled the *Griffith* machine for three and a half years might soon burn out. "We have good writers," he told Hedda, "but it's a grind working on the same thing. We do a mammoth amount of work in a day. . . . You grow skilled at inventing fast, memorizing fast, moving fast, to get the job done; I worry that perhaps it's sacrificing some creative instinct and may hurt eventually."

Every week, Andy and Don and their costars had to learn parts in a swiftly paced two-act play. "When one episode was finished," Elinor

Donahue recalled, "you just had to erase it, totally erase it." The cast termed the skill *forgettery.*

Three years in, *The Andy Griffith Show* still soared atop its creative arc. But at some imperceptible point in the 1963–64 season, the peak was past. Spring of 1964 would bring several more beloved episodes, with a handful of classic stories after that. But henceforth, they would be fewer and farther between.

Some episodes from season four feel almost valedictory in their acknowledgment of the lengthening partnership between Andy and Barney.

"Citizen's Arrest," broadcast on December 16, spotlights Barney's devotion to Andy and to his job, and it plays almost as a real-life tribute to their work as a comedy team.

"I owe you a lot, Barn. I really do," Andy says, noting that Barney has completed ten years on the job. "We've been through a lot together. You've been a fine deputy. A true public servant. You can feel right proud of yourself, you know that?"

"Well, a man does with what he's got," Barney mumbles in reply, moved to the verge of tears.

The new year brought "Barney and the Cave Rescue," one of the more elaborate shoots in a series that seldom lavished money on location. Andy and Helen wander off from the town picnic and become trapped inside an old mining cave.

Barney heroically organizes a rescue party, unaware that Andy and Helen have already found their way out of the cavern. When Andy learns of the rescue effort, he has no choice but to hustle Helen and himself back inside the cavern so that Barney will have someone to save.

The episode teaches another powerful lesson on friendship: Andy cares so much about his deputy's feelings that he risks his life to protect them. When Barney breaks through the rockslide and finds Andy and Helen behind it, he is a hero. Only Andy and Helen know how far the sheriff has gone to stage this moment.

But Andy Griffith was not Andy Taylor, a point underscored in a sprawling article published in a January 1964 issue of the *Saturday Evening Post.* "Where Sheriff Taylor is gregarious, Griffith, something of a loner, holds to an unconscionably suspicious nature," the writer mused. " 'It takes Andy eight months to decide if he likes you,' says a former associate on the show. Set against Taylor's benign self-assurance, Griffith is a fearsome worrier, so petrified by social situations that he avoids most big Hollywood functions." Andy himself observed, "I wish I could be like Andy Taylor. He's nicer than I am—more out-going and easygoing. I get awful mad awful easy."

Andy was again being painted as a maniac: "Griffith does harbor one of the most ferocious tempers extant, his low boiling point—along with his otherwise gracious manners—being parcel to the tradition of the hot-blooded Southerner."

Television viewers were afforded a brief glimpse of those passions two months later, in the episode "Andy's Vacation." Week after week, Sheriff Taylor had patiently maneuvered around the bumbling miscues of his deputy, had disentangled Barney from one proverbial briar patch after another, reuniting farmers with goats, delivering medicine to widows, protecting towns-folk from feral hillbillies and hillbillies from themselves. Now, the sheriff had had enough.

Barney hauls an agrarian couple in front of the sheriff for fighting. He finds Andy in a cheerless state. Andy barks at the couple, "Won't you people ever learn?" Gone is the simpering, saccharine Andy of the *Danny Thomas* pilot. The sheriff fines the couple ten dollars and orders them out. "I'm tired of coddling these people," he tells Barney. "From now on when they break the law, we either fine 'em or jail 'em. Time to make things easy on ourselves around here."

Barney asks Andy what's bothering him.

"I've had it. I'm sick of sheriffin'; I'm sick of this room; I'm sick of this town."

Barney hazards to ask, "Are you sick of me?"

"Well, in a friendly sort of hopin'-you'll-understand way, yes, I am."

Barney tells Andy what he needs is a vacation: "Catch the Sunburst Special to that Miami Beach!"

Don himself took a trip to Florida for the January 17 premiere of *The Incredible Mr. Limpet,* his first starring film role. Warner Bros. brought 250 members of the international press corps to Weeki Wachee, the famed underwater park with its mermaid showgirls. The film was screened in the attraction's million-dollar underwater theater, an event billed as the world's first underwater premiere.

The reviews were good. *Life* magazine said Don had been "perfectly cast." But Don was disconsolate. "Warner Bros. released the picture rather carelessly, and it was not marketed well," he recalled later. The film did a middling business. At Karen Knotts's junior high school, other children called her "fish lips" in cruel homage to her father's animated alter ego.

In spring 1964, as the fourth season of the *Griffith Show* neared its end and Jim Nabors prepared to depart, a new character named Goober was introduced as Gomer Pyle's witless cousin, a man much discussed in previous episodes but never seen. Goober was cast essentially as a simulacrum of Gomer, but with a bit more mechanical skill.

"The Fun Girls," broadcast April 13, plays very much like an orientation film for Gomer's replacement, played by George Lindsey. George had won the part of Gomer in the first place, only to lose it to Jim. A year later, George had not forgiven him. "Jim and I didn't have a lot of interaction off camera during the filming of that episode," George recalled.

In the opening scene, Gomer walks into the sheriff's office with Goober and demands that Andy listen to his cousin's Cary Grant impression. Andy beholds Goober with palpable distaste, looking not remotely pleased to meet him. Apparently it was not an act.

"The bad news about my first *Griffith* episode was that Andy didn't like it, and the producers told me so," George recalled. "Of course, I could easily see that for myself, because if Andy liked your work, he was very friendly to you. If he didn't, he wasn't. It wasn't so much what he said; it's what he didn't say. The silence would just kill you."

A few weeks later, "The Rumor" brought Howard McNear back to Mayberry as Floyd the barber after a sixteen-month absence recuperating from a crippling stroke.

Toiling on a script at the Desilu studio, producer Aaron Ruben had lamented to Andy, "Boy, do I wish we had Howard." Someone replied, "Why don't we see if we can get him." A call was placed, and Howard was back, to the palpable delight of cast and crew.

Andy recalled, "He was paralyzed all down his left side, and so we couldn't show him walking. We had him sitting or we built a stand that supported him. He could then stand behind the barber chair and use one hand. Most of the time, however, we had him sitting. His mind was not affected at all."

Andy and his producers could easily have written Howard off the show and hired a replacement. Instead, Andy labored to accommodate the stricken actor. Andy felt deep loyalty toward those who stuck by him, an impulse just as powerful as his repudiation of anyone who abandoned him. On the *Griffith* set and off, Andy's act was viewed as an extraordinary gesture, the impulse of a television icon at his most benevolent.

"Andy Griffith had a big heart and knew that my mom had never really worked and that I had gone to school and we didn't have a lot of money," recalled Kit McNear, Howard's son. "And he brought my dad back. He didn't have to. That is a really, really rare thing in Hollywood."

Even as the ensemble celebrated Howard's return, they bid adieu to Jim Nabors with a season-ending pilot, "Gomer Pyle, U.S.M.C.," for his spin-off. Aaron Ruben, founding producer of *The Andy Griffith Show*, would follow Jim to *Gomer Pyle*.

Though Gomer was gone, money was yet to be made. In spring 1964, Andy, Don, and Jim traveled together to William Harrah's Lake Tahoe nightclub for a celebrated one-week stand. The three men deeply admired one another's talents and loved working together. Andy trotted out his old country monologues. Don revived his Nervous Man. The two replayed favorite scenes from the *Griffith Show*. Jim walked onstage as Gomer Pyle, then burst into the aria "Vesti la giubba" from *Pagliacci*. That brought down the house. Jim drew the biggest applause of the night. Andy would walk back onstage to a chorus of boos from an audience that wanted more Jim. "Gomer'll be back," Andy would tell the crowd, looking vaguely annoyed. Rumor had it he felt upstaged.

As the fourth season of *Griffith* concluded, its two stars seeded rumors that the next season might be the last. "One of TV's more highly rated and hardy perennials, *The Andy Griffith Show*, is showing signs of breaking up," a *TV Guide* columnist announced on June 20. "The program is set definitely for its fifth season next fall, but the one after that remains questionable." Don hinted he was poised to exit: "I have some offers to do my own show, but things are vague at the moment." As for Andy, manager Dick Linke said motion pictures might lie in his future, but he allowed, "If a television sponsor waves a lot of money at him, this could have an effect."

As far as Don knew, Andy had every intention of rolling up the Mayberry sidewalks the following spring; they had always talked of

Griffith as a five-year project. Perhaps Don felt fatigue creeping in, as well. The cast and crew had completed 127 episodes in four years, and Don yearned for something bigger.

The show seemed to get better every year. Yet, when the 1964 Emmys were handed out, *The Andy Griffith Show* received not a single award. Don, the three-time winner, wasn't even nominated. Perhaps voters had tired of Barney Fife. Or maybe the arrival of Jim Nabors had blunted Barney's impact on viewers. By the end of his one full season on the *Griffith Show*, Jim was involved in most of the comedy right alongside Don. Barney was funnier, but Gomer was sweeter. And now he was gone.

10.

Andy and Barney, Phfftt

The Andy Griffith Show continued to imitate life. Season five opened with a batch of story lines mining themes of reflection, restlessness, and departure, amid persistent chatter around Hollywood that the program might be drawing to a close.

The *Griffith* writers presumed they were producing an ephemeral product and thus didn't trouble themselves much with narrative continuity. Consider: The episode "Citizen's Arrest," in season four, had opened with Andy and Barney reminiscing about the deputy's ten years on the job. Now, in season five, "Barney's Physical" opened with Barney chagrined that Andy had forgotten his anniversary—his fifth. "Spend five years in a place," he fumes, "it's like nobody even noticed."

The season's seventh episode, "Man in the Middle," explored how much easier Andy and Barney found it to navigate their own friendship than to consort with the opposite sex, a lesson surely inspired by their real-life relationships with increasingly estranged spouses. The story opens with Thelma Lou and Barney having a fight. They patch things up, but the dispute spawns more arguments. Thelma Lou winds up angry at Andy, and then at Helen. Andy feels compelled to side with Helen—and that puts him in conflict with Barney, his best friend. Reflecting on their contretemps, Barney recites an adage borrowed from the Gospel of John, one that neatly captures the spirit of his off-camera friendship with Andy: "So deep a friendship hath one man for another that no female caress shall ever tear it asunder." Then Barney deadpans, "Boy, the guy that wrote that must've been some kind of a nut."

Aneta Corsaut, Andy's on-screen girlfriend, owed her presence on the *Griffith Show* at least partly to Jim Fritzell. He was a respected writer in Sheldon Leonard's stable and was dating Aneta when she auditioned for the role of Helen Crump. Jim was a wordsmith, and Aneta would often sit with him as he worked. With his goatee, Coke-bottle glasses, and close-shaved head, Jim would never be mistaken for an actor. And now, his beautiful girlfriend was dwelling among actors. Before long, one of them began spending more and more time with Jim and Aneta in the writing room.

Soon, Andy was paying regular visits to Aneta's bungalow after work. Andy "was coming over every other day and hanging around with her in the late afternoon," recalled Jesse Corsaut,

Aneta's brother, who would drive down from Monterey Bay to visit. "He'd come in, have a drink, and just sit around and chitchat," acting "exactly the way he appeared on the screen, except that he wasn't silly."

Now Aneta had two boyfriends, Andy and Jim, and she seemed unable to choose between them. Instead, Jesse recalled, "She kept them both going."

It wasn't Andy's first affair with a *Griffith* costar. He had told Don of at least one other: Joanna Moore, the Georgia beauty and future mother of Tatum O'Neal, cast in four episodes at the start of season three as a potential girlfriend for the television sheriff.

On-screen, Andy's double dates at the diner with Helen, Barney, and Thelma Lou had become routine on the *Griffith Show*. Offscreen, Andy and Don would make excuses to their spouses and head out for a considerably more upscale double date at some Hollywood bistro with their real-life girlfriends, Andy with Aneta, Don with Lynn Paul, a fiery brunette who worked for Dick Linke.*

Aneta admired Don's work, but the two never grew close, and Aneta later conceded she never felt entirely comfortable around him. In a sense,

---

*Don consistently described Lynn as Dick Linke's assistant. Fifty years later, Dick remembered Lynn but could not recall if she was his employee.

Aneta competed with Don for Andy's affections.

One evening, members of the *Griffith* crew unleashed a practical joke on Andy and Aneta: a young crewman donned a waiter's uniform and delivered dinner to the couple's love nest at a Hollywood hotel. Andy was furious. "They were trying to really keep it on the down low and they didn't think anybody knew—but everybody knew," said Bridget Sweeney, daughter of director Bob Sweeney.

Aneta was a Greenwich Village bohemian at heart. Her home "was always a horrible mess," brother Jesse recalled, not least because of the injudicious quantity of dogs and cats with which the young actress surrounded herself. "She would never clean it up. Aneta would stay up until two or three every night reading mystery stories, and then she'd sleep till noon. And then she'd spend two or three hours putting on makeup, and then she'd look great."

Andy couldn't get enough of Aneta. Eventually, he proposed, even though he was already married. He popped the question at least once and possibly two or three times, as Aneta hinted in later years. She turned him down. Her outlook on marriage seemed to mirror that of Helen Crump, who prized career over domestic bliss. "She didn't want to marry anyone," Jesse recalled. "She wanted to keep her personal freedom. And then [Andy] became pretty sore at her."

Andy would have to settle for marrying Helen Crump, in the glare of studio lights, on a spin-off of the *Griffith Show*. But he and Aneta would remain a couple for years, and friends for life. "That was true love," recalled Ronnie Schell, Andy's longtime friend. "They were closer than anyone knew."

Themes of impermanence and departure surface again in "Good-bye, Sheriff Taylor," broadcast November 23. The story has Andy contemplating leaving Mayberry for a job in the big city.

Barney is incredulous. "Leave Mayberry?" he cries. "Partners all these years, then just like that, phfftt?"

Andy replies, "I told you there might come a time when I'd be movin' on."

"Yeah, but I didn't think you meant anything like quittin'. I thought you just meant dyin'."

Andy labors to explain. "I've been sheriff for twelve years. Twelve years. Ev'rybody needs a change."

By fall of 1964, after four years on the *Griffith Show*, Don Knotts was looking for a change. His stock as an entertainer stood at an all-time high. He was a three-time Emmy winner—the only member of the *Griffith* cast to have even been nominated for an Emmy—and probably the most celebrated television sidekick since Art Carney in *The Honeymooners*. (The parallel didn't end there. Art, like Don, took home Emmy after

Emmy for his supporting role, while Jackie Gleason, like Andy, was overlooked in his starring role.) Almost everyone on the Desilu lot concurred in that view—with one notable exception. Sheldon Leonard, executive producer of *Griffith*, tended to speak of Don as if he were expendable, an interchangeable piece in an ensemble puzzle.

Don earned not quite $100,000 a year, chump change for a television icon. Once, early in his tenure, Don had approached the producers for a raise. They had bristled: *Who the f—do you think you are? Do you think you're the star of the show or something?* Andy wasn't present at the negotiation and may never have learned what transpired.

But everyone knew Don deserved a better deal. As the fifth season began, Don began quietly negotiating an exit from Mayberry.

Andy had no intention of continuing his namesake show beyond the fifth year, despite its soaring ratings. But one Sunday evening, midway through season five, Dick Linke arranged a meeting with leaders of the William Morris Agency. He told them, "I have an idea how to keep Andy Griffith." Dick encouraged the skeptical agents: "Anytime you want to make it so palatable they can't turn it down, get 'em a huge sum of money." Abe Lastfogel asked Dick what kind of sum he had in mind. Dick replied, "a million dollars. I can tell you right now, he's gonna take

it." Abe told Dick the figure sounded "very ambitious." Dick replied, "Well, if you want to keep
him on the air, that's the only way I can think of."

The network agreed. Dick called Andy into his
office. "Andy, I know you don't want to go
beyond five years. But I don't think you're gonna
want to turn this down."

Andy perked up. "What is it, Dick?"

Dick asked, "How would you like to make a
million dollars a year to stay on the show?" As
Andy pondered that thought, Dick told him he
had also negotiated to raise his client's ownership interest in the *Griffith Show* from 50 to 70
percent, giving him a majority stake.

Andy paused. "My goodness," he exhaled
finally. "A man can't turn that down."

The next step was to approach Don. Both
friends had always treated the show as a five-
year endeavor, and Andy knew Don was casting
about for other work.

By this time Don had met with various studio
heads and had collected "some pretty attractive
television offers," he recalled. But his dearest
hope was to progress from television into film.
Don always sought to make his mother happy.
Elsie loved to collect movie-star autographs.
Perhaps one day she would ask for his.

Don met with Lew Wasserman, head of
Universal Studios. Wasserman had seen *The
Incredible Mr. Limpet* and "was very impressed

with the picture," Don recalled. "He told me that if Disney had made it and promoted it the way they do, it would have been a blockbuster."

Wasserman offered Don a five-picture contract. "He said he wanted to build my name in family motion-picture comedies. He offered me free rein. He said I could pick my own screenwriters and decide on my own pictures."

Shortly after that meeting, Andy approached Don and told him he had decided to carry on with *The Andy Griffith Show*. Don was shocked. He hadn't yet signed a contract with Universal, but he and Lew Wasserman had made a verbal agree-ment, and to Don, a deal was a deal.

Andy told Don, "We've got a new deal to offer you," and tendered his friend a small stake in the *Griffith Show*—probably a few percent.* Andy and Dick Linke, by contrast, owned more than half the show between them. "What do you think?"

"Sorry, Andy. I've already committed."

And that is the end of the story, as Andy and Don told it.

But according to Sherwin Bash, Don's manager, the full account is more nuanced.

Sherwin never doubted the *Griffith Show* would continue past five years. Even as press reports forecast its impending demise, Sherwin assumed

---

*In a 1966 interview, Don claimed he'd been offered a 10 percent stake in the series. Privately, he cited a much smaller figure.

fate—or, more likely, sponsors—would intervene.

"When it got down to the fifth year, Andy was playing the game," Sherwin recalled. "Nobody ever believed that *The Andy Griffith Show* wouldn't continue."

Sherwin knew Don wanted to make movies. Television operated on a fall-to-spring calendar, which left Don free in the summer; low-budget comedies, in that era, took only a month to shoot. "So, we negotiated a tentative deal with Universal to make movies," he recalled.

Sherwin planned to approach the *Griffith* producers about extending Don's tenure, but they preemptively approached him, offering a new contract and "a big raise," probably to $5,000 an episode, or about $150,000 a year. Sherwin relayed the offer to Don, who said, "I want to talk to Andy personally."

Don later reported back to Sherwin: he and Andy had talked, and Don didn't want Sherwin to proceed.

Don never elaborated. Then again, Don and Andy operated differently from most television actors. "In the fifty years I was in the business, I don't think I was ever involved with another performer who had that kind of a relationship with somebody he was working for," Sherwin recalled. Don "was really an employee of the show, but he had a different feeling about Andy. Don was older, but Andy was like his older brother. It was much closer than I realized all those years. I don't think that Don and Andy quote 'had a meeting.' They didn't have that kind of relationship."

Sherwin says he finally learned what had transpired four decades later, at Don's 2006 memorial service. There, Sherwin told Andy of his disappointment that Don had rebuffed the offer to continue on the show.

Andy told Sherwin it wasn't quite so simple. At the fateful meeting, Don had told Andy he was ready to continue on the *Griffith Show*—if he could be Andy's partner.

"What's wrong with that?" Sherwin asked.

Andy replied, "I wasn't going to share the ownership of the show fifty-fifty with him. It was my show."

Sherwin was stunned. "Did Don ever say fifty-fifty, or did he say he wanted a share? Did you ever explore that he might have been thrilled to have ten percent, or some other small amount?"

Andy shook his head.

According to Sherwin, the negotiation failed out of simple miscommunication. When Don asked to be Andy's partner, Andy assumed Don wanted half of Andy's share, or a quarter stake in the show. Sherwin believes what Don really wanted was a fair share: something larger than 3 or 4 percent, surely, but smaller than 25. With the help of a negotiator, such as Sherwin, the two men might have settled the math. But Andy and Don wanted to handle the negotiations between themselves, as friends.

In an interview late in life, Andy seemed to corroborate Sherwin's account, but with a significant variation. Andy said Don came to his home and told him, "Andy, if you'll be partners with me, I'll stay." But in this version, Don proposed a theatrical partnership, like that of Dean Martin and Jerry Lewis. Andy said he turned it down: "Don, I'm afraid, because people become partners and they lose their friendship a lot of times, and I'm afraid that might happen to us."

Perhaps Andy confused one conversation with another. Late in life, Don recalled that he indeed asked Andy around this time to consider forming a permanent comedy partnership. "I had asked Andy if we could team up for good," Don once told Larry King, "but he was too good an actor to want to do that. And he shouldn't have, and he didn't."

It's stirring to imagine what might have come of that partnership.

"If they'd been twenty years earlier," Ron Howard mused, "they would've been Abbott and Costello or something. They would've been Laurel and Hardy."

As news leaked of Don's impending departure, no one sounded entirely sanguine about the *Griffith Show*'s future. *The New York Times* opined, "Just where the *Griffith Show* goes from here is not certain." Andy seemed to agree, telling the *Times* columnist, "The character I play is not one who gets into trouble by himself. So the show must introduce some new characters who either get themselves into trouble or get me in trouble—or else we won't have any story."

Betty Lynn, who played Barney's on-screen girlfriend, was on the back lot in Culver City when Andy walked up and told her Don was leaving the show. "Whaddaya mean, he's leaving?" she gasped.

"I was really stunned," Betty recalled, "because I knew that would be the end of me, too." The *Griffith* producers suggested various ways Thelma Lou might remain in a Mayberry without Barney: Perhaps she could open a beauty shop and be a hairdresser. "But I didn't see that," Betty recalled. "My whole life was for Barney."

To others on the set, Don's departure seemed a natural move. "There was no rancor," Ron Howard recalled. "It was just a decision that [Don] had to make and that Andy understood. It always kind of felt more like an inevitable graduation than any kind of abandonment and betrayal."

Andy himself greeted the development with customary candor. "It's entirely impossible to replace Don," he told columnist Vernon Scott. "I really dread the day when we make our last show together."

Peter Baldwin, a handsome former Paramount contract player, arrived at the Desilu studios that winter to direct some memorable episodes. One of the few *Griffith* directors who remain alive, Peter remembers endless peals of laughter during script readings.

"Andy would get a huge laugh on some line," Peter recalled, "and as we were going through the script on the second reading . . . he'd say, 'Wait a minute, why don't you give that line to Don? He'll kill that line.' Because Andy wanted to remain the only sane person in Mayberry. He chose to give away the big laughs, often—not just once or twice a script, but often. And it was really generous of him, because as a comic, you don't give away the big ones."

Andy was thinking like a producer. He knew that if he gave a funny line to Don, Don would make it funnier. And then the camera could catch a reaction from Andy, a deadpan nod or subtle furrowing of the brow, and that would get another laugh—all to the ultimate enrichment of his show.

But that relationship was about to end, and the writers on *The Andy Griffith Show* continued to foreshadow the parting. The episode "Barney Runs for Sheriff," broadcast February 8, 1965, again contemplates the dissolution of Mayberry. Andy entertains another job offer, this one from a company that might take him to a place called

South America. "Well, what about Aunt Bee and Opie?" Barney cries. "You know they don't speak a word of South American.

". . . And what about *her?*" Barney asks, referring to Andy's on- and off-screen girlfriend.

"Who's her?"

"You know who's her!"

"Now, Barney, you know how things stand between Helen and me, and if they keep going the way they have been, I expect I'd send for her."

"Oh, you're gonna send for her."

"Yeah, I'm gonna send for her."

"You gonna send for me, too?"

Barney finally persuades Andy to stay. Off-screen, Don was less successful in making the same case to his wife. The February 20 *Los Angeles Times* announced, in Hedda Hopper's column, that Don and Kay Knotts had split.

"It's not easy to keep a secret in this town," Hedda wrote, "but Don Knotts has managed to keep the news quiet that he and his wife of fifteen years have been living under separate roofs for the past six months." Don "blamed 'personal problems' for the rift but wouldn't name them."

Don had always been faithful to Kay. But sometime after the family's arrival in California, he began seeing other women. Don told Kay of the affairs. This was Hollywood in the 1960s; perhaps he thought she would accept them. "He wanted me to understand it," she recalled, "but I didn't."

By 1965, Don was deeply involved with Lynn Paul, assistant to Dick Linke, Andy's manager. The tryst was the principal cause for the split. Through it all, Don and Kay never fought in front of the children. "So I never saw my parents mad at each other," Tom Knotts recalled. "That was one of the good things."

Kay decamped to an apartment in Westwood with the children, leaving Don in the Glendale family home. Their relationship remained civil, even tender. "I remember once, she was crying all night, and he came over and comforted her," Tom recalled. "I think he really hated to leave, because he was giving up a lot. But he had issues he had to deal with."

Meanwhile, back in Mayberry, the strain of Don's impending exit seemed to be taking a toll.

"The Case of the Punch in the Nose," a spring 1965 teleplay, neatly contrasts Andy's philosophy of policing to Barney's. Andy is Mayberry's fixer, a man who steers every problem to its most sensible solution—even if the remedy falls outside the fine print of the law. Barney is the ultimate doctrinarian, following every regulation to the letter and oblivious to practical concerns.

In this narrative, Barney stumbles upon a minor assault case from two decades earlier and notes it is unsolved. Over Andy's strenuous objections, Barney reopens the case. He approaches the men involved, Floyd the barber and a neighboring shopkeeper named Charlie. Charlie says Floyd punched him in the nose. Floyd denies it. Barney rushes off to investigate further. His interrogations begin to stir things up; soon, noses are being punched all over Mayberry. Barney tells Andy the nose punching is "not our fault." Andy hollers back, "No, it's not our fault. It's your fault! You started the whole blamed thing."

Barney protests, "You mean because I was trying to get to the bottom of a case? Because I was pursuing my duty as a police officer? Because I was trying to be neat and orderly—"

"Aww, shut up," Andy yells—and for the first time in all his dealings with the deputy, his voice rings with real hostility.

The April 24 issue of *TV Guide* served notice to the broader viewing public of the coming changes on the *Griffith Show*. The story, headlined "Trouble in Mayberry," hypothesized that the program's very success had begun "to unravel the close-knit world of Mayberry." First, Gomer Pyle had jumped ship to the Marines. Now the magazine was eulogizing Barney Fife.

"There was good old pie-bakin' Aunt Bee, and Taylor's all-American son Opie," the story said. "But the real humor derived to a large extent from the relationship between solid, twinkly-eyed old Andy and his overly efficient, slightly paranoid deputy . . ." Clearly, a powerful friendship informed that on-screen rapport, imbuing every Andy-Barney scene with sparkle and warmth. As one colleague observed, "It's hard to tell, even on the show, where one stops and the other begins."

The report theorized that Don took displeasure in seeing Jim Nabors decamp to his own series while Don remained in Mayberry. Don denied it. Yet, now Don was leaving, and Andy was staying. The *TV Guide* reporter tracked Andy down in his Desilu lair. He found the actor scowling over a script in his dressing room. Why, he asked, was Andy carrying on with the show? Andy replied without lifting his head from the page. "Didn't get any good film offers, that's why."

Andy wanted to do movies, just as Don did; but he wanted to do serious movies, movies like *A Face in the Crowd*; and in 1965, no such roles were forthcoming.

Griffith producers cast around for a potential replacement for Don. A series of talented comedians paraded through Mayberry in the final weeks of season five, including Don Rickles as a traveling salesman and Jerry Van Dyke, brother of the famous Dick, as the "Banjo-Playing Deputy." Jerry's character tells Andy he was born in Morgantown, a gentle nod to Don.

Don's final appearance on the *Griffith Show* came in a comparatively anonymous episode titled "Opie Flunks Arithmetic." Barney is reduced to a fringe character, the same space he'd occupied on his first *Griffith* episode, five years earlier.

It was customary for *Griffith* episodes to end inside the sheriff's office, with Andy and Barney reflecting on the day's events or unfurling a handwritten skit. At the close of this story, as Andy and Barney chat, Helen Crump walks in, seats herself rather provocatively on Andy's desk, and breaks up their conversation. She and Andy exchange glances. With an odd quaver in his voice, the sheriff asks Barney to step into the other room to fetch Helen a cup of coffee. Andy knows it is the last line he will speak to Barney. When Barney returns, Andy and Helen are gone.

Andy stood behind the camera and watched Don shoot his final scene. Then, cast and crew gathered for their customary wrap party on the soundstage. Don was presented with a gold Swiss watch. On the back was a large number 5 and the inscription "See, we thought we'd put 5 on it because you've been here 5 years." Floyd the barber had uttered that line when Barney was presented with a stainless-steel watch by his Mayberry friends at the start of the season, in the episode "Barney's Physical."

After a time, Andy looked up and saw the stage was empty, except for Don. "They're gone," Andy said to Don. "We might as well go, too."

They walked to their cars.

Andy said, "Well, call me sometime."

Don replied, "Okay."

11.

The Color Years

To viewers who tuned in for T*he Andy Griffith Show* on September 13, 1965, it must have seemed as if Mayberry had somehow slipped clear into the next decade during the summer hiatus. Suddenly, the town fishing hole was rendered in full color: green pine trees, white boulders, shimmering olive-black water. Andy's gabardine sheriff's uniform was khaki, just as one might have expected. But Opie's hair was shockingly, almost iridescently orange. The comforting voice-over announcement was gone; and where, just a few months earlier, Opie had stood only as high as the buckle of Andy's belt, now he reached the sheriff's breast pocket.

The season-six opener, "Opie's Job," was surreal. No explanation was offered for Opie's hair color, a revelation with vaguely unsettling genetic implications. And no account was given for the absence of Barney Fife. Viewers had learned, in the final episode of season five, that Andy's deputy was "away"—and that, it seemed, was that. The unexplained departure of such a major figure from a long-established television program would be almost unthinkable today;

imagine Kramer simply vanishing from Seinfeld's apartment building one autumn. But the television industry treated audiences differently in the 1960s. Characters came and went. So, too, did the actors who portrayed them. Good-bye, Dick York; hello, Dick Sargent.

An odd sort of ontological crisis gripped *The Andy Griffith Show* in its sixth season. Characters appeared and disappeared, arriving without introduction and departing without fanfare; the reassuring permanence of Mayberry and its inhabitants was gone. Lost, too, was the magical time-capsule realism of years past. Before, the doings of Floyd the barber and Goober the mechanic had seemed natural; now, they looked forced. Andy's hapless costars would be placed on a sidewalk bench like props, to frame the sheriff and exchange dialogue that now sounded like lines from a script. The jokes were often flaccid, the smiles strained. And the color camera had an odd effect on Mayberry itself, rendering the town eerily, unnaturally clean. The Culver City exteriors now had a depopulated look, while the Desilu interiors looked almost like . . . sets.

The program still had its tender moments, particularly those shared between Andy and Opie; but the "slight thread of insanity" that had set *Griffith* apart was irretrievably gone. Beneath his makeup, Andy Griffith looked grumpy, forlorn, weary, a man performing by rote, mourning an unspoken loss.

The *Griffith* entourage minimized Barney's exit with the press, who viewed it as a potentially fatal blow. Years later, after Don's death, Andy conceded the truth to Larry King: "I missed him. I missed him so dreadfully, I can't begin to tell you. When Don left, the show lost its heart. It stayed on for three more years and was, in fact, number one for the whole year, the last year that it was on. But it really—it really lost its heart and its soul when Don left."

"You didn't replac c him with anyone?" Larry asked.

"We tried. It just didn't work."

Dick Linke, Andy's manager, recalled the search for Barney's replacement: "It worried Andy and me. We could see going into the sixth year and having the ratings plummet. As soon as that happened, your fate was determined. You knew the show would be canceled. . . . The producers were scurrying around, saying, 'We're going to try this person, we're going to try that person.' "

Into the vacuum stepped Jack Burns.

Jack was a Boston native and had gotten his start in a comic partnership with George Carlin, which ended when both men opted for solo careers. Jack did a stint in Chicago's famed Second City comedy troupe, where he worked up a new act with mustachioed comedian Avery

Schreiber. By 1965, Burns and Schreiber had issued an LP titled *In One Head and Out the Other*. One sketch cast Avery as a long-suffering cabbie and Jack as a bigoted conventioneer; here they crafted their signature comedic volleys, rapid-fire exchanges of "Huh?" and "Yeah." In that context, it worked.

"Burns and Schreiber were appearing at a nightclub in San Diego," Dick Linke recalled. "Andy flew down with producer Bob Ross and executive producer Sheldon Leonard with the idea of trying Jack Burns out on *The Andy Griffith Show*. The three liked what they saw, and Jack was hired."

After dispatching Deputy Fife without comment, the *Griffith* producers rolled out his presumptive replacement in like fashion, without explanation. The stakes were sufficiently high that *Griffith* creator Sheldon Leonard stepped in to direct the episode himself.

"You like that fella you got workin' for ya?" Goober asks Andy in the opening scene of "The Bazaar." The "fella" turns out to be one Warren Ferguson, a man apparently hired as Andy's new deputy between episodes. Deputy Ferguson appears in the next scene, measuring the distance from each car to the curb and picking up bits of litter from the sidewalk, then accosting Aunt Bee and ripping a grocery bag from her hands.

The new character played like an overwrought imitation of Barney. Where Barney invoked pity and poignance, Warren Ferguson merely annoyed. Don had played Barney as an earnest and excitable child; for all his delusions and vainglory, Barney ultimately charmed viewers with his native sweet-ness. Warren Ferguson had much of Barney's manic vigor, but none of his humanity. The overall effect was abrasive, unpalatable, and vaguely menacing; Deputy Ferguson comes off like a deranged Boy Scout, asking Opie, "You're a chip off the old block, aren't ya? Huh? Huh? Huh?" It doesn't help that Deputy Ferguson arrives in Mayberry with a thick Boston brogue.

No one seemed more vexed at Warren's arrival than the sheriff. Andy spends much of his screen time in "The Bazaar" training a withering glare on the new deputy.

"Warren, this is altogether unnecessary," Andy tells Warren as he hauls in Aunt Bee for running a charity bazaar without a permit. He's talking about the permit, but he might as well be appraising the deputy's very presence on the show. Later, Warren returns to place the entire Ladies Auxiliary under arrest. It's classic Barney Fife overreach; the writers even have the gall to assign Barney's trademark "Nip it in the bud" line to Deputy Ferguson. Amid the contrived chaos, Andy shouts, "Will somebody please tell me what's going on?" His pained voice bears no trace of the patriarchal benevolence that had defined Andy's workings with Barney. He looks exasperated, and when he terms Warren "my idiot deputy," he says it without mirth.

CBS suddenly found itself in need of damage control—with the viewing public, who might soon tire of a Barney-less Andy, and with the press, who eyed the program with growing suspicion. A makeshift solution arrived with an hour-long homage to the past—*The Andy Griffith, Don Knotts, Jim Nabors Show*. It aired in October 1965, the same month as the broadcast debut of Barney's replacement.

Andy and Don had remained close since the difficult on-air parting the previous spring, speaking and socializing regularly, neither man harboring resentment or hurt over the circumstances of Don's exit. Nonetheless, Andy probably approached the artistic reunion with mixed feelings. He loved working with Don, but by this time Andy was struggling to carry on the Mayberry brand alone. "This is the last time we'll work together," he told a reporter—a tragic pronouncement, had it proven true.

Written by ex-*Griffith* producer Aaron Ruben, the special exploits the success of the nightclub act in Lake Tahoe the previous year. It presents Andy and Barney in a replica of the Mayberry sheriff's office, singing an old Cole Porter tune titled "Friendship." The comedy duo proceeds into a live reenactment of the judo skit from the "Barney's Uniform" episode, and thence to a demonstration of Barney's skill with firearms. Few things on television in the 1960s were quite so funny as watching Barney Fife attempt judo. But when Andy and Barney reflect on their years together, there is nary a laugh in the house.

"The main reason I keep you around is because you're my friend," Andy says. "I mean it, Barn, you're my closest friend. I don't know what this old office'd be if you weren't in it. You're like a brother to me, you know that?"

Silence falls; Barney, his back to the camera, breaks it by blowing his nose.

"You're not gonna cry, are you?"

"Aw, c'mon," Barney sniffs. "Are you kiddin'?"

The special drew warm reviews, and the sight of Andy and Barney in color was a revelation. "After the laughs from this one, however," the *Los Angeles Times* noted, "a great many viewers probably realized again how much they will miss these two together."

Even as the Warren Ferguson experiment rolled on, the *Griffith* producers cast about for a new on-screen relationship to mine. One of the better season-six stories, "Andy's Rival," plays off the very real chemistry between Andy and his Mayberry girlfriend, Helen Crump. Helen hosts an out-of-town visitor who is male, accomplished, and handsome. This triggers a new emotion in

Andy: jealousy. The writers had finally found a foible in Andy Taylor.

Like many of the better *Griffith* episodes, this one mirrored real life. Aneta Corsaut collected friends, including former lovers. Her life, one article said, was "cluttered with old boyfriends." Now, the *Griffith* writers assigned the same traits to Helen. At the start of the episode, the sheriff moans, "If anybody gets stuck with anybody, Helen always does." Andy eventually confronts Helen about the ambiguous relationship. The resulting argument, heavy by Mayberry standards, was surely inspired by their off-screen liaison.

"You like him, don't you," Andy snaps.

"What?"

"Frank Smith, that's what. You sure finished work early, didn't ya."

"What are you accusing me of?" Helen asks haughtily.

Andy pleads, "I'm just trying to figure out where I stand. I mean, if you want to run with me, you can run with me, and if you want to run with him, you can run with him. Just kinda make up your mind," he says, sounding like a wounded schoolboy.

"Yes"—Helen affirms, veritably shaking with fury—"I will decide with whom I will and will not run. . . . Who I go out with happens to be my own, personal—"

Andy cuts her off with an impassioned kiss.

"—I'll go out with whomever I please—"

Another kiss.

"—and what's more—"

Another kiss. And for one steamy moment, Mayberry is Peyton Place.

A three-week excursion to Hollywood marked another creative peak in the post-Don years. The pretext—that a Hollywood studio had worked up a movie based on Andy's life—was preposterous; yet, writers Sam Bobrick and Bill Idelson milked the journey for considerable laughs. And goodness knows Andy appreciated a three-week reprieve from his new deputy.

"Keep away from those starlets," Helen coos to Andy as he departs in the opening episode, "Off to Hollywood." It's an ironic request, given their off-screen situation. In midflight, Andy realizes he might have forgotten to turn off the gas back home. He raises his head and bellows, "Stewardess, what's the first stop?"

The next episode, "Taylors in Hollywood," brims with Hollywood-insider jokes. On a tour of star homes, the Taylors stop and take a picture of Opie holding Cesar Romero's newspaper, recycling a gag about star worship from the first season. Then Andy's family visits the film set— and is appalled to find the sheriff portrayed by a bald-headed ass. Gavin MacLeod, future captain of *The Love Boat*, just might be the funniest guest star in *Griffith* history. His toupee-clad sheriff is a cross between Marlon Brando and some oily maître d', alternately tossing back his head and stage-punching desperadoes. Aunt Bee protests bitterly—until she learns her part will be played by a glamorous, rifle-toting blonde. "It's a movie, Andy," she then scolds the sheriff. "They have to take liberties in order to make it interesting."

The third episode, "The Hollywood Party," exploits Andy's genuine discomfort with the opposite sex to fine comic effect. Sheriff Taylor is pressured into a photo op with the starlet who plays his girlfriend in the Hollywood film. The starlet, played by real-life glamour queen Ruta Lee, torments Andy playfully when he admits he's "never been in a lady's dressing room before." She sidles over and coos, "You are a big one, aren't you," a rather provocative line for a *Griffith* script. She scoots into his lap, then darts back up and asks, "Ooh, wait a minute, what's that?" For the briefest moment, viewers are left to ponder just what might be protruding from Andy's groin. It turns out to be Opie's autograph book.

Andy winds up in the starlet's apartment that night, on the pretext of taking her out to dinner. Her unabashed flirtation creates the faint impression that Andy might actually bed her. He doesn't, of course. But the sheriff has clearly committed the sin of lust, and Helen Crump treats him to a brutal tongue-lashing afterward. It was all an ironic twist on the reality: Aneta Corsaut was the sexy starlet and Barbara Griffith the gal back home, sulking in her housecoat.

The Taylors returned to Mayberry for a series of mediocre episodes, burdened with unimaginative scripts and a palpably dispirited Andy Griffith. The writers tried to reassign Barney's lines and traits to Warren Ferguson, with jarring results. Artistically, *The Andy Griffith Show* teetered on the brink. "I think *The Andy Griffith Show*, for me, jumped the shark when Don left," recalled Sam Bobrick, one of the show's best writers from its later days. "It became situation comedy, and not at its best."

The cast and crew braced themselves for the ratings decline . . . but none came.

The press was baffled. In *The New York Times*, George Gent wrote, "The series's continued popularity is remarkable because most critics were predicting that the show could not survive the loss of Don Knotts. . . . But in spite of these losses and the dire predictions of the critics, the Griffith show has been in the top 10 all season and was in second place at last count."

Griffith finished fourth in the ratings in the final season with Don and sixth in the first season without him. How did Andy's program remain so popular following the loss of its most beloved character and amid steady artistic decline? The *Griffith Show* was certainly buoyed in the ratings by a relative lack of comedic competition in the 1965–66 season. But there seemed to be more at work.

The interplay between Andy and Don had been central to the program's success as a comedy. "But there was also a very sweet part of *The Andy Griffith Show*," recalled *Griffith* director Peter Baldwin. Viewers seemed to savor the simple pleasures of spending a half hour in Mayberry, even if nothing much happened. Perhaps they simply couldn't bear to leave.

The *Griffith Show* provided Andy steady work and considerable financial reward; yet, the production was beginning to feel like a burden. He missed Don terribly. He envied Don's freedom from the weekly grind, and his movie contract.

Don wasted no time in proceeding from his final *Griffith* episode to his first picture. Casting about for script ideas, Don seized upon an old *Griffith* story, "The Haunted House," a teleplay that placed Barney inside a creaky, old mansion with Gomer and Andy and played off his childlike terror. "I thought to myself, people seem to enjoy the idea of seeing me get scared," Don recalled. He persuaded his favorite *Griffith* writers, Jim Fritzell and Everett Greenbaum, to help him develop a script. Jim harbored a deathly fear of heights, so the first meeting with producer Ed Montagne, scheduled for the ninth floor of the Universal tower, was moved to the basement.

The trio's first outline didn't work. So, Don called Andy. After five years of *Griffith* scripts, Don knew Andy was a gifted constructionist, someone who could assemble the building blocks of a story. Plus, Don missed Andy, and Andy missed Don. Andy read the outline and said, "No, that's not any good." Don replied, "Well, you come over and help us write one."

The group gathered in the basement office at Universal every day for two weeks and sketched the story that would become *The Ghost and Mr. Chicken.* Then Andy returned to Mayberry, and the three remaining writers spent the next month building a script. Don had never laughed so hard in his life. Andy sometimes stopped by to visit. Once, when Everett Greenbaum walked in wearing a handkerchief beneath his glasses in an impression of *The Invisible Man*, Andy laughed so hard that he put his fist through the wall; Andy punched walls when he was happy, too.

The script emerged as a gentle satire of small-town life, much like the *Griffith Show*, with the same slight thread of insanity. Don plays Luther Heggs, a cub reporter assigned to spend a night in a notorious haunted house. He witnesses a series of seemingly supernatural events. His account makes Luther a town hero. Then his story is discredited as the work of an overactive imagination, and Luther is humiliated—until he discovers that the ghostly doings are part of an elaborate plot to get the house torn down. It all sounds very much like a typical Barney Fife story from the old *Griffith Show*, minus the sheriff.

The script's most enduring line came from Andy. He loved the moment when an unseen voice cried, "Attaboy, Luther," as Don delivered a variant of his Nervous Man speech recounting his haunted-house heroics. It reminded him of Juanita, Barney's unseen waitress girlfriend in Mayberry. Andy suggested the writers sprinkle "Attaboy, Luther" throughout the picture as a running gag. It became the film's signature line. Decades later, fans would yell it at Don when they spotted him on the street.

The film was shot in seventeen days that July, a remarkably economical schedule, on a stretch of familiar Universal back lot that invokes déjà vu in cinema buffs. The haunted mansion had seen previous action in the film *Harvey*, while the Munster home and Cleaver residence lay nearby.

The production played a bit like a Mayberry reunion. Don secured *Griffith* director Alan Rafkin. His supporting cast included Reta Shaw, who had played Big Maude Tyler in the *Griffith* episode "Convicts at Large"; Lurene Tuttle, the little old lady from "The Shoplifters"; as well as Hope "Clara" Summers and Al Checco, Don's army buddy. Hal Smith stumbles into the opening shot in a role clearly modeled on Otis.

Don's costar was Joan Staley, a beautiful

Minnesotan with an interesting résumé. Only twenty-five, Joan was a former violin prodigy who had sung backup for pioneer record producer Sam Phillips, posed for *Playboy*, and amassed several dozen television and film credits.

Joan lacked Andy Griffith's comedic discipline as Don's straight man, and she struggled to keep her composure during a diner scene that has hapless Luther labor to eat a bowl of chicken noodle soup while standing up. "He was a master of nuance," she recalled. "He could do just a shift of his eye and just lay you out."

Not everyone was so moved. Skip Homeier, who played one of Luther's bullying coworkers in *Mr. Chicken*, recalled that Don "would come to work and he would work in the scenes and then he would lock himself up in his trailer. . . . He didn't socialize or say 'Good morning' or 'Good night' or 'Let's go to lunch' to anybody." Skip was crestfallen; he had expected Barney Fife.

Don enjoyed the shoot immensely once his customary first-day jitters had subsided. He kept to his trailer to nurse a pulled muscle, an injury sustained while running down the stairs of the haunted mansion, a minor injury that undoubtedly fed his hypochondria. And seventeen straight days of hyperactive performance left Don exhausted.

Mystery leg ailments would vex Don for years to come. Ronnie Schell, a friend and fellow hypochondriac, remembers visiting Don in a hospital around this time. Don had a blood clot in the leg. Andy sat at his bedside. When Andy emerged from the room, Ronnie asked him in a stage whisper, "Have they told him the truth yet?" implying that Don was gravely ill. Don heard, as he was meant to. By the time Ronnie walked in, Don's face was a paper-white mask of fear. Finally, Ronnie broke up. "He never forgave me for that," Ronnie recalled.

When the film was finished, Don sat with his director and producer and watched the final print in an otherwise empty screening room. "The three of us sat there in deafening silence," he recalled. When the screening was over, the men walked outside and stared at one another. Producer Ed Montagne finally said, "I think it's a damn good picture. It just needs an audience." Director Alan Rafkin echoed, "Yeah, that's right, it needs an audience." "Right," Don agreed. But he wasn't so sure, and it would be months before he found out.

In September, Don was shut out of the Emmy Awards for a second consecutive year. The culprit this time was Rod Serling. Vowing "No more horse race," the academy president had narrowed the number of Emmy categories from twenty-seven to four. Don must have assumed his Emmy chances were over.

At year's end, Don returned to the *Griffith* set for a pair of guest-star performances that seemed to put the final nails in Barney's coffin. Don had told Andy he was available, and Andy was over-joyed to have him back, if only for two weeks.

Since Don's departure, nine months earlier, the program had given no account of his absence. Now, the producers tapped their best writers and set about tying up loose ends. In "The Return of Barney Fife," we learn that the fretful deputy has decamped to Raleigh for a job in the fingerprint section of a big-city police department, handling letters *N* through *R*. ("That's the hot section, you know," he tells Andy.) Barney lives in a corner room at the Y; to him, that is the high life.

Barney returns to Mayberry for a high school reunion, wearing a loud Hawaiian shirt that amplifies the jolting transition to color. He and Andy greet with an awkward exchange of shoulder punches.

"How does it look to you?" Andy asks.

"You mean Mayberry?" Barney surveys the Forty Acres lot. "Not bad, Ange. Not bad at all. You know, you people that live in the small towns, you've really got it made."

Barney asks, "How's things going with you?"

"Yeah, you know, same," Andy says, looking pensive.

The real reunion, of course, is between Andy and Don, whose palpable delight at working together again fuels the happiest Mayberry moments since Barney's departure. Don wrings every drop of poignance from the story.

"Well, I heard you got yourself a new deputy," Barney tells Andy, rolling his eyes and pursing his lips as jealousy washes across his face.

"Yeah, yeah." Andy looks a trifle guilty.

"Thelma Lou comin'?"

When Andy informs Barney that Thelma Lou has not been heard from, Barney looks unspeakably pained. Their unresolved relationship becomes the fulcrum of the story.

"You still sweet on her?" Andy asks.

"Oh, no, no. Once it's gone, it's gone, Ange. Can't go back. Course, sometimes a man wonders . . ."

Viewers hadn't been told what became of Thelma Lou after Barney's exit. Now they learned that she had remained in Mayberry, and that Barney had unwittingly broken her heart.

When Thelma Lou finally appears, she has a husband. She introduces him to Andy and Barney, whose face is ashen. Barney retreats to the punch bowl and attempts to get drunk; Andy has to break it to him that the punch is not spiked.

"Sorry, Barn, I know it must've been a shock," Andy says.

"Sure it was a shock. So what?" Barney cries. "It wasn't the first one of my life, won't be the last. That's the way life is, Ange. It's a rough life. Ya can't cry about it." Then, of course, Barney begins to cry. "She was the only girl I ever loved,

Ange. She's the only one I ever will love. I had plans. I had big plans."

The producers try to end things happily by fixing Barney up with another old classmate at the program's end. But the resolution rings hollow. In the denouement, Barney assures Andy he has forgotten all about Thelma Lou. Then he falls silent, his face darkens, as clearly Barney doesn't believe his own words.

The notion of Thelma Lou's forsaking Barney was an unqualified bummer. To get through her scene, actress Betty Lynn convinced herself that her "husband" was actually a friend whom she had persuaded to act the part of a spouse. "I made up this whole little story for myself. But I couldn't help it. I just believed in the relationship so much."

Don's second guest spot, "The Legend of Barney Fife," was a last-ditch effort to shore up support for Jack Burns, who was not panning out. Set on the day after the poignant reunion, the story has Barney collaborate with Warren in apprehending an escaped con. At the close, Barney delivers a speech clearly tailored to persuade viewers it is time for them to accept the new deputy. "I've had my place in the sun here for a lot of years," Barney tells Andy. "It's his town out there, Ange. It's not mine."

Then Barney departs, and Warren returns. "A true living legend, that Barney Fife," Warren tells the sheriff. "I mean, he's something, isn't he, Andy?"

"Yes, he is," Andy says, as if speaking to himself. "He really is."

It was a noble effort. But three weeks later, Warren Ferguson was gone.

"It was our fault," Andy told *New York Times* columnist Val Adams. "We tried to force Jack to do those wild, peculiar things that [Don] did— and he was willing to try—but we made a mistake." Jack's exit reopened the question, the writer mused, of "who Sheriff Andy will talk to for a greater part of the show."

There would be no more attempts to replace Don. No one, it seemed, wanted to see Andy engage with a new buddy, least of all Andy.

Don's second film, *The Ghost and Mr. Chicken*, was released in January. The reviews were mostly encouraging; the *Los Angeles Times* termed it "an appealing piece of Americana," though *The New York Times* found the story stretched a bit thin, even at ninety minutes. Yet, half a century later, *The Ghost and Mr. Chicken* is arguably the most celebrated of Don's films, cherished by film buffs and Mayberry denizens. In a sense, *Mr. Chicken* stands as one of the final bursts of artistry by the community of writers and actors who produced *The Andy Griffith Show*.

Flush with movie cash, Don spent $10,500 on a new home for his mother, back in Morgantown.

Elsie Knotts, now entering her eighties, had never shown much interest in leaving West Virginia. Don was Elsie's baby. He telephoned once a week and returned to Morgantown every year or two, usually during the summer hiatus from filming. When he came home, Don typically stayed not with Elsie but with Jarvie Eldred, his old school chum, receiving guests in Jarvie's living room, heading out to the old Cosmopolitan Restaurant for hot dogs, and otherwise keeping a low profile.

When Elsie came to visit Don and Kay, she always felt a bit out of place. Elsie had an eighth-grade education. She felt uneasy around Kay, the college girl. When Don's illustrious friends came to visit, Elsie would sneak off to dine with the housekeeper.

Don also purchased a new house in Brentwood. Though Don and Kay were separated, their relationship remained warm, and he hoped this new investment might help them reunite.

"We talked about it," Kay Knotts recalled. "Every Thursday, we had a date."

But by this time, Don was firmly ensconced with Lynn Paul, and it was she who accompanied him on his publicity tour for *Mr. Chicken*. During that trip, Don learned from a news account that Kay had filed for divorce. She agreed to a $338,400 settlement, finalized in March, and decamped with Tom and Karen to the Brentwood home. Don moved into the Sunset Marquis, a haven for actors in West Hollywood. He got the kids on weekends.

"He would take us out on Saturday to the movies," son Tom recalled. "We would play charades; he was really good at charades." For Sunday dinner, Don would take the kids to Ships Coffee Shop in Westwood; Don hated the place, Tom recalled, but the children loved it.

Don would travel to Toluca Lake periodically to visit Andy, whose children were close in age to Don's own. "They would sit there as grown-ups, talking, while we were swimming," Tom Knotts recalled. "And they talked a lot on the phone. And he'd call him Ange, I remember that."

Andy and Don still loved to navigate Hollywood together. In early 1966, they guest-starred on the short-lived *Sammy Davis Jr. Show*. Each day on the set, Andy recalled, Sammy would gather his entourage and head out to lunch. "Don and I would just go off by ourselves." One day, Sammy returned from lunch with his retinue and found the two friends. He told them, "I think I get it. You guys don't need anybody else. You've got each other."

Now approaching its seventh season, *The Andy Griffith Show* marched on. The acting remained professional, the writing capable, the direction consistent, and the program never fell from Nielsen's top ten; yet, few in the ensemble could escape the feeling that Mayberry was merely going through the motions.

"I think, for Andy, the show was never the same after Don left," Ron Howard recalled. "He didn't have that partner. The absolute foundation of the show, and why it endures, is Andy-Barney. And, yes, the feeling of what Mayberry was. But without the comedy that they generated, I don't think the show ever would have endured."

The Desilu set remained a familial place. Andy still played music with Lee Greenway, his makeup man, and he still staged elaborate practical jokes, taking particular delight in harassing his costars during nap time. Once Andy had played these pranks on Don. Now, he targeted poor George Lindsey, a man far more sensitive than his on-screen character, and less indulgent. Once, Andy and loyal accomplice Lee sneaked into George's dressing room while he was sleeping and filled it with duck entrails from one of their hunting trips. "I didn't laugh at all," George recalled, "which naturally made it all the funnier for them."

But Andy's mood darkened perceptibly in the final years of the *Griffith Show*. Without Don there to buoy his spirits, Andy laughed less. And when he wasn't laughing, he was often brooding. The cast and crew didn't fear Andy's temper—it never flared, at least not when he was at work. But they came to fear his silence.

"Most of us were deathly afraid of Andy," George Lindsey recalled. "We were all scared to make a move. If Andy thought something was funny, then it was funny to us. He literally controlled every aspect of that show. So we were always trying to please him, or at least I was. Every Monday night, Andy would call you if he liked the show and your performance. So I waited for the call. If it didn't come, I absolutely dreaded going in to work on Tuesday morning."

On May 22, the *Griffith Show* earned its fourth Emmy Award. The award again went to Don, who had appeared in all of two episodes that season. "Would you believe this?" Don asked the Hollywood Palladium audience. It was hard to tell whether the award was more a salute to Don or a swipe at Andy, whose program had failed to earn even a nomination in any other category. "It must be presumed that Don Knotts himself felt a little awkward," *The Hollywood Reporter* opined.

In spring and summer of 1966, Andy made a series of decisions that would assure him a future beyond his show. He paid a visit to the Mount Airy home of his childhood and arranged to move his parents to California, where he built them a house a few miles from his own. They brought only a few pieces of furniture that Carl Griffith had built with his own hands. A few days after they arrived, Carl telephoned and told Andy his mother was crying. She wanted her old bed from Mount Airy. Andy had it shipped.

In July, Andy got the movie deal he had always wanted. He and manager Dick Linke signed a five-year, ten-picture contract with Universal, the same studio that employed Don. Andy's contract called for twice as many movies as Don's, with the first reportedly set for the very next year. In August, a squib in the *Los Angeles Times* announced Andy had also signed a lucrative deal with CBS, extending his *Griffith Show* for two more seasons and promising annual specials for three years after that. In interviews, Andy began mapping out an exit from Mayberry.

"Eight years is long enough," Andy told the *Chicago Tribune* in November. "People might get tired watching it, for one thing. Another is that stories get awfully hard to find, and I'm afraid we might start to compromise."

They already had. Though the *Griffith Show* still reached 31 million Americans, the writers were running short of ideas, and it showed. In one season-seven story, the townspeople are shocked when Aunt Bee purchases a blonde wig. One week in season eight, Andy gets the flu. Would viewers soon be watching him mow his lawn?

Andy had dropped hints that the *Griffith Show* might introduce a new character to Mayberry; not another deputy, but someone to join the gang of feckless goofs outside the barbershop and to pester Andy at the sheriff's office.

One night, Andy and Barbara saw a Eugene O'Neill play called *Hughie*. Andy went backstage after the performance and "just raved about it," recalled Jack Dodson, a mild-mannered Pennsylvanian who had performed the two-man play alongside Jason Robards. Encouraged, Jack went to meet with the *Griffith* casting director, Ruth Burch. She swiftly showed him the door. Puzzled, Jack had his agent call the studio and recount Jack's meeting with Andy. Someone relayed the story to Andy, who replied, "I don't know who the hell you're talking about." Jack urged his agent to try again. An assistant again approached Andy, who repeated, "I've never heard of the son of a bitch."

That night, Andy and Barbara attended the Julie Christie picture, *Darling*. On the way home, Andy grumbled, "You know, that picture stank. The best acting we've seen in a long time was that play with those two guys in it." Then it hit him: "Oh, jeez, that's who that was." Andy made it up to Jack by hiring him.

Jack Dodson joined the *Griffith* company as Howard Sprague, a mustachioed milquetoast who lives with his mother. Developmentally stunted, like Barney, Howard nonetheless possesses an ensemble of neuroses all his own. He is a prototypical nerd—bookish, intelligent, and sufficiently responsible to carry out the duties of county clerk, yet emotionally inept and uneasy both with women and manly men. Whereas Don had played Barney like a nine- or ten-year-old boy, Jack Dodson drew upon memories of himself as a gawky adolescent in creating Howard Sprague. He was the most entertaining character to enter Mayberry since Gomer Pyle, with the possible exception of Goober, who forever dwelt in the shadow of his more successful cousin.

Like other *Griffith* regulars before him, Jack Dodson had to earn a permanent place in Mayberry. "My first year on the show, I didn't have a parking space," he recalled. "It was the number one show on the air, and I had to go out every two hours and put money in the meter."

Howard won the hearts of Mayberry devotees with the November 1966 episode "Big Fish in a Small Town," one of the strongest stories of the program's final years. Andy and his friends mobilize for an annual fishing contest, dreaming of hooking Old Sam, a giant silver carp that has become town legend. Howard has never fished but yearns to join the outing. When no one will have him, Andy—ever the protector of his friends—warily consents. Howard shows up at Andy's home looking like a mannequin from a tackle shop. "Are you going to the moon?" Andy asks.

It is Howard, of course, who catches the storied fish. There is talk of serving up Old Sam at a town fish fry. But in the end, it is essential to the fundamental permanence of Mayberry that the venerable ichthyoid be returned to the lake whence he came.

"A fish is a fish, Floyd," Andy protests.

"No, he isn't," Floyd replies sagely. "Not once he's given a name."

With both Barney and Gomer gone, Jack Dodson helped desperate *Griffith* writers create conflicts for Andy. But no one who remained in Mayberry did pathos quite like Don Knotts. So, in January, viewers were treated to "A Visit to Barney Fife," another guest spot for Don. Andy goes to visit Barney, now implausibly ensconced as a detective with the Raleigh police. Barney tries to persuade Andy he is one of the guys, but the spell is broken when another detective hollers, "Fife! We're out of paper towels in the men's room!" Once again, Barney has been subjugated by bullies; his desk is a repurposed telephone booth. Domestically, Barney has graduated from living at the Y to rooming in a grim boardinghouse, a nod, perhaps, to Don's threadbare childhood.

"Barn," Andy asks, "did you ever think about maybe coming back to Mayberry? . . . I mean, your job's still—open."

Barney replies, "Well, that's awful nice of you, Ange. But I've got everything going for me here. I mean I've got a big job. I got a terrific future. Great social life."

"You mean sitting here on the porch, listening to the radio?"

A second guest spot followed, titled "Barney Comes to Mayberry." In its denouement, Andy and Aunt Bee sit on the porch Andy once shared with Barney.

"You know, I miss Barney," Bee muses.

"I do, too," Andy replies. "I guess there's just the one Barney Fife."

If there was one lesson the *Griffith Show* producers had learned since Don's departure, that was it.

Fortunately, television viewers could see Andy and Barney together again the very next month, paired with country crooner Tennessee Ernie Ford on the CBS special *Andy Griffith's Uptown-Downtown Show*. It was still jarring to see the sheriff and his deputy shuffling across a stage in tuxedos, looking a bit like Bugs Bunny and Daffy Duck in a Looney Tunes cartoon. But variety shows were a lucrative business in the late 1960s. Once again, the program's most successful moments reprised scenes from *The Andy Griffith Show*. In one skit, Andy and Don sit on the front porch and revive the lawman's code skit, with Don laboring to recite the opening of the Gettysburg Address.

Spring of 1967 brought the release of *The Reluctant Astronaut*, Don's second feature for Universal. *The Ghost and Mr. Chicken* had returned more than $3 million on a $750,000 investment. This time, Don's shoot was lengthened to a luxurious twenty-three days. The film's premise—Don plays an astronaut who is afraid of heights—was lifted straight from the life of Jim Fritzell, the writer who could not board an elevator to the ninth floor at Universal. Don again collaborated with Jim and partner Everett Greenbaum, who again elevated a fairly ludicrous B-movie story with clever dialogue and subtle wit. NASA threw open its doors to the crew, allowing them full access to its facilities in Houston and Cape Canaveral on the promise of free publicity. Don, again complaining of a mysterious leg ailment, refused to perform the modestly acrobatic "weightless" scenes at the last moment. They were shot with harnesses, strings, and an anemic stuntman.

Sadly, few sparks flew between Don and his *Reluctant Astronaut* love interest, played by Joan Freeman, a former child star and Elvis Presley moll. The film's best bits paired Don with two other costars: Leslie Nielsen, a washed-out leading man whose autumnal comic genius had not yet flowered; and Arthur O'Connell, a seasoned character actor who played the astronaut's delusional father. It was a family movie, but adults could titter at a priceless bit with Don attempting to cut a grotesquely phallic, rocket-shaped cake.

Leslie later recalled dining with Don and his

girlfriend, Lynn Paul, who ruled their relationship with such a firm hand that Leslie assumed they were married. "People kept coming up to the booth where we were dining and bothering [Don] to talk to them," Leslie recounted. Lynn "just put out her hand and rested it on Don's arm and pushed it down so he couldn't do anything with it, and she said, 'We are very busy eating. Would you mind? We'll see you after dinner.' And Don was just laughing."

Don and Lynn remained a couple for about three years. It was a volatile romance. Lynn once ran over Don's suitcases with her car when he returned from a trip. Another time, during a vicious argument, she eyed Don's perpetually wounded leg with predatory glee, as if she were contemplating a kick. "If you do that to me," Don hissed, "you're stepping over the line," and she backed down. Lynn thoroughly dominated Don in social settings. He later quipped, "She was living with me. Well, it felt that way."

One morning, Jim Nabors ran into Don at Du-par's restaurant in Studio City. They grabbed a booth and spent a few minutes catching up.

"Are you still going with Lynn?" Jim asked.

"No. We broke up."

"What happened?"

"She kept asking me and asking me if I was going to marry her, and I said no. And the other night, we went to a play, and we're walking across the parking lot and she just grabbed me and said, 'Are you gonna marry me?' And I told her, 'No, I'm not.' "

"What happened?"

"She beat the crap out of me!"

Jim exploded in laughter, but then he looked at Don. "And he was damn serious," Jim recalled.

For Lynn, it wasn't over. She continued to show up at the Universal studio, demanding an audience. Don had her barred from the set.

The Reluctant Astronaut premiered in Houston on January 25, 1967. Two days later, en route to Dallas, Don learned NASA had lost three astronauts in a training exercise. The picture was quietly pulled and rereleased several weeks later. It was one of Don's best. A *Los Angeles Times* reviewer said Don's characters succeed because they "are never self-pitying no matter how dismaying the defeat."

After three hits, the critics increasingly discussed Don as a potential inheritor to the grand tradition of milquetoast stars, a lineage that included Chaplin, Laurel, and Harold Lloyd. Don and Andy began to drop hints that they might make a movie together one day. "I'd like to start out doing at least one film by myself, sort of for my own ego, then maybe one or two with Don Knotts," Andy told the *Chicago Tribune*, with typical candor.

The seventh season of the *Griffith Show* ended

sadly, as cast and crew bid farewell to Howard McNear. Though only sixty-two, Howard moved and spoke like a much older man, his body racked by successive strokes. By his final episode, the painful "Goober's Contest," Howard could no longer hide the symptoms of neurological decay. He died two years later.

Andy had planned to fold up the *Griffith Show* after season five, only to be lured back with the promise of money and ratings. As season seven wound down, he again mulled departing. The magic—and the fun—seemed to have evaporated along with Don. Now he fantasized about walking away into a film career, if only to show up the people who chalked up his continued success "to some nonsense that I was only playing myself." But the network offered another $1 million, and Andy halfheartedly agreed to one more year.*

Toward the end of his eight-year *Griffith* tenure, he confessed later, Andy would "come to work without knowing my lines."

On June 4 at the Century Plaza Hotel in Century City, Don collected his fifth and final Emmy for the role of Barney Fife, honoring his work in season seven. This time, the award was clearly no

---

*This deal seems to conflict with the two-year contract Andy had reportedly signed a year earlier. Fifty years later, manager Dick Linke recalled that he and Andy likely signed two contract extensions, one for seasons six and seven and another for season eight.

slap in the face to the *Griffith Show*. The program itself reaped a nomination—for the first time since 1962—as Outstanding Comedy Series. And for the first time, another cast member took home an Emmy: Frances Bavier, for her regal efforts as Aunt Bee.

Don's Emmys were the one subject Andy would not broach with his old friend. In all their years together on the *Griffith Show*, Don later recalled, Andy never acknowledged Don's trophies or offered congratulations. It was too painful a topic.

As cast and crew reconvened to film the last season of the *Griffith Show*, the program seemed as popular as ever; *Griffith* would finish the 1967–68 season at No. 1 in the Nielsens for the first time. Pundits predicted Andy would be television's first star to leave his own series at the top. But Andy was finding it increasingly difficult to shield Mayberry from the changing world outside.

In May 1967, the black-owned *Los Angeles Sentinel* ran a story beneath the headline "Andy Griffith Explains No Negro Policy." The NAACP had approached CBS to note the paucity of black citizens in Mayberry. The network responded in March by featuring the program's first credited black actor, Rockne Tarkington, as Opie's football coach in the otherwise forgettable episode "Opie's Piano Lesson."

The damage control deployed, Andy answered

his critics. "The problem we face is simple," he told the *Sentinel*. "We have to remain honest to the types of people depicted in the small, rural town of Mayberry. . . . Put a Negro doctor in a town like Mayberry and the people most probably wouldn't go to him. A story like ours, which is set in a small Southern town, just naturally leaves itself open for problems—especially when the show is a comedy."

Virtually all of Andy's supporting players were deeply flawed human beings, and much of the fun came from poking fun at the flaws. Otis, the lovable drunk; Floyd, the doddering barber; Goober, the dim-witted mechanic—the program could mock all of those characters partly because they were all white men.

In October, Don and Andy reunited for Don's first TV special, broadcast on CBS. The skits retold fictional events in Don's life. One cast his Nervous Man as a high school valedictory speaker: "Mr. Principal, faculty, fellow students, parents, and guests," Don intones, trembling and twitching, "the theme of my address today is 'Facing the Future without Fear.' " In the touching final sketch, Andy and Don are two old men recounting bygone times. "You're like a brother to me," Andy tells Don. "And I don't know what I'd do if I ever lost you as a friend. 'Cause you're the best friend I've ever had, too."

Behind the scenes, producers of *The Andy*

Griffith Show brokered a deal with its powerful sponsor, General Foods, whose principals were none too pleased to be losing a top-ten show. Word leaked in fall 1967 that *Griffith* would spawn a spin-off.

"The show has a simple premise," Andy told the *Chicago Tribune*. "It's an exploration of what happens when a group of people with enormous love and enthusiasm for life come up against a staid sort of existence." The operative word was *staid*.

The concept for *Mayberry R.F.D.* (the letters are a postal acronym for "rural free delivery") came from Bob Ross, who had replaced Aaron Ruben as *Griffith* producer in season six. The star, Ken Berry, was furnished by Dick Linke, ever eager to find work for his small stable of clients. In another sweet deal, Dick and Andy would own part of the spin-off. But it was a risky move nonetheless, one of the few instances in network history that a series essentially rebooted with a new central character.

Ken Berry, a song-and-dance man turned actor from Moline, Illinois, had made a name for himself on *F Troop*, a short-lived but effective sitcom set on a remote army outpost. Dick had signed him after seeing him perform sketch comedy on a Carol Burnett special. Ken joined the *Griffith* cast late in its final season as Sam Jones, a previously unseen Mayberry resident who happened to be—what a coincidence!—a lovable widower with a young son. Clearly, Mayberry could not carry on with two winsome widowers.

Andy, Opie, and Aunt Bee were gradually reduced to bit players in the final *Griffith* episodes, as the dramatic weight shifted to Ken's shoulders.

Amid the emotional final days of the *Griffith Show*, Andy and Barbara Griffith entertained a houseguest: Mike King, Barbara's nephew, now twenty-four and back from Vietnam in his navy lieutenant uniform. Mike greeted Barbara at a Beverly Hills hotel, where she was sipping cocktails with Margaret Linke, the wife of Andy's manager. "They were well into their drinks," he recalled. When Mike and Barbara returned to the Griffith home, Mike found Andy at his wet bar. "He was smoking one Marlboro after another. He had definitely changed. He was not the guy I remembered from back in Manteo."

When Mike had visited Andy and Barbara in the summer of 1962 on the Griffith estate, "they had their fights, but they still had fun together, and they were still pleasant to be around." Now, it seemed to Mike that the distance between his aunt and uncle had widened considerably; whatever spark had ignited their marriage was gone. "Andy was just gloomy all the time, and there was this meanness. I'm sure they were fighting. I'm not sure it was physical. Barbara would break down and cry a lot. The alcohol was really much greater, and they were just not a happy couple."

Later that year, Mike saw Barbara again at a beach house his parents owned at Salter Path, North Carolina. Everyone was drinking, he recalled, but Barbara was barely coherent. She kept disappearing into the kitchen. Curious, Mike followed her. He watched as she pulled out a valise and opened it, revealing two bottles of Canadian Club. She poured several ounces of the whiskey into a tumbler and knocked it back. Then, she repacked the valise and wobbled back to the party.

Barbara maintained her regal air, always reminding Andy's actor friends that she considered herself their equal. "We did the *Joey Bishop Show* one night," recalled Ronnie Schell, Don's friend. "In those days, you did the show and you'd see the tape later that night. We went to the Villa Capri. And when we got there, I said to Barbara, who was in her cups, I said, 'Barbara, when you see Andy tonight, you're going to be so proud of him.' And she looked at me and said, 'Do you mind if I watch and judge for myself, Mr. Showbiz?'"

Andy, too, was a prodigious drinker. During one of his dustups with Barbara, he put his hand through the windshield of one of his classic cars. Another time, as the two bickered in the food line at Lakeside Country Club, Andy suddenly seized the tablecloth beneath the food and ripped it away, sending food flying and pans clattering. "And nobody said anything," Ronnie recalled. "He was Andy Griffith."

It was a rare lapse. Andy was "a very big drinker," Dick Linke recalled, but he almost never drank to excess when he was working. He had a volcanic temper—but it almost never erupted in public.

"He had two personalities," Dick recalled. "One was laughable and affable. It was a joy. He was a joy. And the other side—he had a dark side that was unbearable. The worst. But you had to be there to know it."

February 21, 1968, was the last day of shooting at the *Griffith Show*. The story, "A Girl for Goober," was the 249th episode filmed. It was not the last broadcast; that honor would go to a listless story titled "Mayberry R.F.D.," devoted almost entirely to farmer Sam.

"I felt strange this morning," Andy told the reporters who dropped by to capture the moment. "It was the same when Don left, three years ago." Each of the cast and crew looked "as if he had just finished running a thousand miles," a reporter observed. Ronny Howard would return to the Burbank public schools the following Monday. Andy mused, "I don't know what I'll do next week."

Just after four o'clock, the *Griffith* company filmed its final scene. "For one last time," *TV Guide* reported, "Sheriff Andy Taylor stood silhouetted against the jail-cell mock-up on Stage 1 at the Desilu Studios, a six-pointed silver star pinned to the left breast of his gabardine uniform."

The mood was wistful, and Andy struggled to stay in character. The crew needed just one take to capture his final line, a question posed to Goober about his date: "Are you gonna see her again?"

Then, Andy retreated to his dressing room and removed his badge.

That night, 251 guests converged on Andy's golf club in Toluca Lake for a wrap party. Don was there, along with Jim Nabors, Danny Thomas, and Sheldon Leonard, who took the stage and recounted the 1959 midnight meeting in New York where the program had taken shape. Dick Linke, Andy's manager, had organized the party and played master of ceremonies. Cast and crew presented Andy with an $800 twelve-gauge Beretta shotgun for his hunting trips and a silver cigarette case engraved with their signatures. An ad agency gave him a music box, its cover inscribed with the program's Nielsen ratings. It played the Earle Hagen theme song when you opened the lid. Guests arrived to the sounds of Les Brown's seventeen-piece orchestra and departed with key chains shaped like miniature Mayberry sheriff badges.

At fourteen, Ronny Howard had lived more than half his life on the *Griffith* set. "When we got to that wrap party," he recalled, "here I was fourteen, had gone through puberty, and the last thing I wanted to do was cry in front of these people, and I was weeping openly."

Andy was uncomfortable with good-byes. He kept his speech short. "Well, it's been awfully good," he said, tears welling in his eyes. "It's been the best eight years of my life. I'll see ya again."

Andy and Don clown with Jim Nabors, the Alabama boy Andy discovered singing arias at a Santa Monica nightclub. For all his renown, Gomer Pyle would remain on the *Griffith Show* for just twenty-three episodes before striking out on his own.

Andy with Aneta Corsaut, one in a parade of love interests written into the Griffith Show in a tireless quest to spark chemistry with Andy. This time, it worked all too well. Offscreen, Andy and Aneta fell in love.

Don in *The Incredible Mr. Limpet,* his first lead role in a film. Though best-known for television work, Don wanted nothing so much as to make it in the movies to impress Elsie, his mother.

Don bags his fifth and final Emmy for his work on the *Griffith Show.* And for once, he has company: Frances Bavier, the only other Mayberry actor to be honored by the academy.

Andy and Don with Jack Dodson and George Lindsey, their *Griffith Show* costars and Andy's drinking buddies. Don seldom joined in their binges.

319

Don with his second wife, Loralee Czuchna. Don and Loralee kept a low profile, much like Andy and his second wife. They divorced in 1983.

Andy with his second wife, Solica Capsuto, a Greek American actress. Solica was sweet and funny but something of a flower child; to Andy's old friends, they seemed an odd match.

Don with his *Three's Company* costars. His 1979 television comeback capped a mostly successful decade for Don, who rebounded from a disastrous variety show with a run of hit Disney films and a part on the storied ABC sitcom.

Andy with third wife Cindi Knight, a dancer and high school teacher. They met at a volleyball game one summer in Manteo. His career would become her life.

Andy and Don at a Hollywood party in 1981. Though they mostly worked apart after *Griffith*, Andy and Don never missed a chance to stoke their friendship.

Don with actress Francey Yarborough, who became his third wife. They met on the set of the short-lived sitcom *What a Country!* Like Andy and Cindi, Don and Francey were soul mates, together till the end.

Don and Andy on the set of *Return to Mayberry*, the 1986 reunion. They had talked of reprising their most famous roles since the early 1970s.

Andy with guest star Dick Van Dyke in an early episode of *Matlock*, Andy's hard-earned autumnal television comeback. With a nine-year run, *Matlock* outdistanced even *The Andy Griffith Show*.

Don and Andy in the Mayberry-esque kitchen of *Matlock*. Don reunited with Andy as a guest star in seventeen episodes; it was the most fun either man had had since the old days.

Andy poses with Don at the unveiling of Don's star on the Walk of Fame. Andy had earned his two decades earlier.

Andy sent this card to Don on his eightieth birthday, invoking Jack Benny, Bobby Benson, and other memories of days gone by. Two years later, Andy would be the final visitor at Don's deathbed.

July 21, 2004

Dear Jess,

Here are some radio shows of Jack Benny, Fred Allen, Vic and Sade, AN Bobby Benson and the B-Bar E

It was Jack Benny's Birthday and Rochester called on the phone saying he had made him a cake!

Rochester: "How many p's are in happy?"
JB : "2"

Rochester: "UH OH"

JB : "You gotta add one?"

Rochester: "I gotta take one off!"
WE GOT 3

So, my dear friend,
Jessie Donald Knotts

HAPPPY BIRTHDAY!

324

Don's gravestone at Westwood Village Memorial Park. Widow Francey Yarborough Knotts penned the inscription: *He saw the poignancy in people's pride and pain and turned it into something hilarious and endearing.*

Andy's statue in Mount Airy, adorned with flowers and flags on July 4, 2012. Andy had died on the previous day.

12.

The Death of Andy Taylor

Summer of 1968 brought the release of *Wheels of Fire*, a psychedelic blues album by the British supergroup Cream with a swirling foil cover; *Rosemary's Baby*, a film about a woman impregnated by Satan; and *The Electric Kool-Aid Acid Test*, Tom Wolfe's breathless new-journalism portrait of acid guru Ken Kesey. And for those content to dwell in the past, there was a new Don Knotts movie, *The Shakiest Gun in the West*.

As the 1960s drew to a close, Don, Andy, and much of the Hollywood establishment found themselves suddenly struggling for currency. In the 1967 Emmys, *The Andy Griffith Show* had been bested by a virtually plotless, marijuana-fueled free-for-all called *The Monkees*. In 1968, the hot new show was *Rowan & Martin's Laugh-In*, a sexually and politically charged romp that took its title from hippie culture.

For Don's third Universal project, the studio wanted a remake of *Paleface*, a Bob Hope hit from twenty years earlier about a jumpy frontier dentist who winds up wed to a lady gunslinger. But Don sat down with writers Jim Fritzell and

Everett Greenbaum and "wrote an entirely different picture."

At forty-two, Don found himself acting opposite Barbara Rhoades, a tall, voluptuous redhead who had just turned twenty and had amassed only one Hollywood credit, a forgotten Robert Wagner film called *Don't Just Stand There*. Don pressured the studio to fire her, thinking her inexperienced. But the studio refused, and Don made nice.

"The first night he came to pick me up, he took me out to dinner," she recalled. "Of course he was hysterical. I always had tears running down my face, because I was undisciplined at that age."

Barbara was touched at how Don attended to her welfare. He didn't like to see her anywhere near a horse or wagon, a tall order on the set of a western. Don himself was terrified of stunts and mistrustful of directors. He walked up to Barbara on the set once and hissed, "Get . . . out . . . of . . . that . . . buckboard! Are you crazy? You're gonna get hurt!"

Slackening social mores permitted Don and the writers a bit more latitude in scripting the film's seduction scene. Barbara slinks into Don's chamber and coos, "I'm sorry to bother you like this, but I have a terrible toothache," as Don's gaze drifts down toward her cleavage. "Is it in your mouth?" he stammers.

Don stumbles and fumbles around his patient, dropping his dental mirror down her dress.

She grabs his wrists and pulls his face toward hers. "You know what I think?" she purrs.

"Mmm-mmm," he replies in a tiny voice.

"I think you're very nice."

"You know what I think?" he sputters weakly. "I think I might faint."

The Shakiest Gun was ignominiously paired in a double feature with the disaster film *King Kong Escapes*. The *Los Angeles Times* detected an inferior script. "However, Knotts himself is so good it's a delight to watch him work even when he doesn't have as much to work with as he usually does," the reviewer concluded.

The film was a hit, Don's third in a row. But when the time came for the next picture, Don and his studio decided it was time to update his image. They seized upon Jim Fritzell's concept for a spoof of Hugh Hefner and *Playboy*. Sadly, Jim and his partner weren't available to write Don's script; they were probably busy writing Andy's. (Andy's first Universal feature, *Angel in My Pocket*, was also in the works.)

To replace them, Don recruited Nat Hiken, the writer-producer behind *The Phil Silvers Show* and *Car 54, Where Are You?* Nat rivaled Don as a perfectionist and workaholic. He wrote and rewrote scenes so many times that Don found there was no point in reviewing them until the screenplay was finished.

Nat's script for *The Love God?* strays far from

the classic Americana of Fritzell and Greenbaum. The story is a farcical commentary on the hormonal hysteria of Beatlemania and the hypocrisy of the sexual revolution. Don portrays the provocatively named Abner Peacock, publisher of a bird magazine, *Peacock*. The script seizes every opportunity to profit on the double entendre through such lines as "I'm sure that after our efforts here tonight, *Peacock* will remain safely in Abner's hands."

A Larry Flynt–styled pornographer dupes poor Abner into retooling *Peacock* as smut, and Don's character evolves into a velvet-sleeved Hefner parody. For Don, that wasn't much of a stretch. In the years after his separation from Kay, Don would squire a number of glamorous women around Hollywood, including the occasional costar. "It was sort of an industry joke that Don had become the big lothario," recalled Sherwin Bash, his manager. Once, while Don dined at the Villa Capri on Yucca Street in Hollywood, Marilyn Monroe sidled up and cooed, "Ooh, you're so cute." Dean Martin reportedly once said of Don, "Frank and I get all the publicity, but this little guy gets all the girls."

The Love God? pays faint homage to Don's *Griffith Show* past. As the camera pans across Abner's hometown near the start of the film, the choir at Peacock City Community Church sings "Juanita," the song Barney Fife once warbled

329

over the telephone line to his unseen waitress paramour. As Abner squires scantily clad women around the big city, the preacher's daughter sits back home in Peacock City, awaiting his return on a front porch that looks very much like Andy Taylor's. That role went to Maggie Peterson, a wide-eyed Coloradan who had played hillbilly daughter Charlene Darling on the *Griffith Show*. Maggie was part of Dick Linke's stable of stars and not-quite-stars. Don doted on her. "I came out of the dressing room one day and there was an extra sitting in my chair," Maggie recalled. "So, Don went up to the person who was sitting in my chair and told him to get out so I could sit in my chair."

Now with five films under his belt as leading man, Don Knotts seemed poised to join the top tier of Hollywood comedians.

Andy Griffith, too, found himself at a professional peak, albeit one of a more pecuniary sort. In the previous year, manager Dick Linke had secured Andy $1 million for three CBS variety shows and another million for the final season of *Griffith*. Looking ahead, Andy's film deal with Universal would generate two films a year for five years and a minimum paycheck of $2 million, plus a third of the net profits. "This is big business," Dick told *TV Guide*.

Andy Griffith sat at the center of a Dick Linke empire that now encompassed nearly everyone and everything Andy knew—with the notable exception of Don. According to a *New York Times* account, Don had once asked Dick to manage him, back on the set of *No Time for Sergeants*, and Dick had turned him down. Decades later, Dick recalled no such episode. In any case, Don and Dick apparently enjoyed a cordial relationship throughout the *Griffith* and post-*Griffith* years.

Dick managed ten clients. Andy, the "big A," sat atop the heap, followed, in rough order of marketability, by Jim Nabors, Ken Berry, Bobby Vinton, Jerry Van Dyke, and the rest. Three of them, including Andy, lived within a short drive of Dick's North Hollywood home. Dick found his clients housing, helped them purchase birthday presents and life insurance policies and write wills, procured cars and jewelry and furs, and oversaw a cottage industry of side businesses launched in the late 1960s and early 1970s, including a chain of Andy Griffith Barbecue stands and "Friends and Nabors" mobile homes. Dick managed just one female client, Maggie Peterson. "Who wants to worry about their hair, or carry fifteen suitcases?" he told an interviewer.

As an overcaffeinated Hollywood manager, Dick seemed straight out of central casting. "I remember him crying at his father's funeral," recalled Ronnie Schell, one of Dick's clients. "And as he was crying, he was checking his watch to see how long the ceremony was going to last."

TV Guide detailed the workings of "The Wondrous Andy Griffith TV Machine" in a July 1968 cover story: "Day-by-day operations of a complex structure involving six separate corporations are conducted behind the poker face of Linke, a former publicity man whose thinning hair is trimmed each week by a shapely female barber. He hunches in a Naugahyde judge's chair, responding to incessant jarring buzzes which signal incoming phone calls—the fuel that fires the machine. They are relayed by either of his two secretaries to any one of 11 extensions illuminating his desk-side console."

Dick and his chauffeur drove the reporter to Andy's Toluca Lake estate, where they discussed casting plans for the maiden project of Andy Griffith Productions, Inc., a film titled *Angel in My Pocket*.

"Right down the middle for the masses," Dick told the reporter, channeling Lonesome Rhodes. "Give me the rest of the country, the mashed-potato belt. You can have New York and Los Angeles."

Andy gathered his Mayberry entourage around him for his first Universal feature, using much the same formula—and many of the same people— Don had tapped for *his* first Universal feature, three years earlier. He employed *Griffith* director Alan Rafkin, *Griffith* writers Jim Fritzell and Everett Greenbaum, and *Griffith* actors Jack

Dodson, Maggie Peterson, and Al Checco. He also used Don's producer, Ed Montagne. For comic relief, Andy retained Jerry Van Dyke, his Dick Linke stablemate. For a love interest, he found Lee Meriwether, a lovely former Miss America who had played the villainous, leather-clad Catwoman in the first *Batman* movie.

Lee had first met Andy on Coldwater Canyon Drive, where she found him one day, standing beside his car, seemingly lost in thought. "He was parked on the side of the road and there was a drop-off. It was very strange; I thought, 'That's Andy Griffith!' " She parked and walked over to greet him. "I'm sorry to bother you," she said, although she couldn't discern precisely what she was interrupting. They spoke for a few minutes, then Lee departed. Now, a year later, Lee was summoned to meet with Al Rafkin to read for a part in *Angel in My Pocket*. "It's so nice to see you again," she told Andy. She was rewarded with a blank stare.

Andy plays Samuel Whitehead, a new minister assigned to a parish in a small town filled with mean spirits, small minds, pettiness, and hypocrisy. In many ways, Wood Falls, Kansas, is the antithesis of Mayberry, where small-town Americana is idealized and celebrated. In this film, it is scorned. Sam labors to rebuild the dilapidated church and, by extension, the town itself, but he is thwarted at every turn. Only when the church burns to the ground do the townsfolk embrace him.

The film is shot in the harsh, vérité style of its era; young marrieds Andy and Lee look sweaty, and Lee wobbles around with a prosthetic baby bump. ("Well," Andy consoled the actress, "at least you'll get a seat in the commissary.") Still, they emanate a gentle chemistry.

After eight years on *The Andy Griffith Show*, Andy wanted to do drama. But the studio wanted *Angel in My Pocket* to replicate the gentle comedy of *Griffith*. The result was a gentle satire, capably acted and deftly written—but hardly a bold artistic statement.

Back at CBS, there were signs that the Wondrous Andy Griffith TV Machine was beginning to misfire. As the filming date neared for the first episode of *Mayberry R.F.D.*, CBS executives grew restless over the artistic direction of the spin-off. The plan called for the network to simply rebroadcast the final episode of the *Griffith Show* as a pilot for *R.F.D.* In that episode, farmer Sam welcomed a quirky family of Italians onto his Mayberry farm, setting the stage for rural Italo-Carolinian high jinks.

But now the network was having second thoughts about retiring the familiar ensemble of Mayberry characters to make way for the Italians. With lovely Letícia Román strutting around the kitchen of the Jones farm, there would hardly be room for Aunt Bee. In an about-face, "the network now demanded a carbon copy of the *Griffith Show* that would enable viewers to identify with their old Mayberry favorites," *TV Guide* reported in July 1968.

CBS unceremoniously dumped the Italians. *Mayberry R.F.D.* would be populated with as many Mayberry regulars as could be rounded up. No one bothered to mention the changes to Ken Berry, the star of *Mayberry R.F.D.* "I talked to [Letícia Román] over the phone one day because I hadn't heard from her," Ken recalled. "And she was very quiet."

The pilot of *Mayberry R.F.D.*, when it finally aired, played more like a lost final episode of *The Andy Griffith Show*. The script neatly settled the affairs of Andy, Barney, Helen, and Aunt Bee, all of whom gamely returned for the episode. The main event was the long-awaited wedding of Andy to Helen.

In the opening scene, Andy coughs up a characteristically unromantic toast to his bride: "If I know the lady I'm marrying, and I should, then the years ahead should be no letdown." From there, the pilot settles into a retread of the *Andy Griffith* premiere from eight years earlier. Widower Sam invites Aunt Bee out to the farm to help him raise his son, who is clearly being groomed to replace the pubescent Opie. Aunt Bee threatens to flee, but she finally succumbs to the charms of the widower and his towheaded lad.

The episode is polished, professional, and unremarkable—until Andy is reunited with Don, and then some of the old magic returns. When the preacher asks the assembled to speak now or forever hold their peace, best man Don unwittingly clears his throat, bringing the ceremony to an awkward pause. When the preacher asks the couple to join hands, Barney thinks the instruction is meant for him. Then, he cannot locate the ring. He rips at his pockets, bug-eyed, as Andy and Aneta struggle to maintain their composure. When the newlyweds retreat down the aisle, Barney rushes forward to join them, clasping Andy's shoulder and waving to the audience. Helen is aghast; Andy just smiles.

In the final scene, Andy serenades Helen on his guitar. Then, a second voice chimes in, and the camera pulls back to reveal Barney, who has joined the newlyweds in their honeymoon suite.

Viewers loved it. Yet, casting the beloved comedy partners in the *R.F.D.* pilot "may not have been too smart," a *Los Angeles Times* reviewer noted. Seeing Andy and Don together again only reminded viewers of "the perfect comedy chemistry existing between these two," who wouldn't visit Mayberry together again for another eighteen years.

Ron Howard would move on to a short-lived series called *The Smith Family*, opposite Henry

Fonda, and thence to *American Graffiti* and *Happy Days*. Aneta Corsaut would return for one more *R.F.D.* episode, "Andy's Baby." Jim Nabors was through with Mayberry; but George "Goober" Lindsey, Jack "Howard" Dodson, and Frances "Bee" Bavier all would make a career of *Mayberry R.F.D.*, remaining as regulars more or less until its cancellation in 1971.

These years were uncharacteristically slow for both Andy and Don, and they spent many idle hours together, alone and with their children. Andy grumbled about the new *Mayberry*. "We saw a lot of him during this period," Tom Knotts recalled. "And I remember him talking about how much he just hated that show. Hated it."

Nonetheless, Andy became close friends with his Mayberry successor. He and Ken Berry lived in the same neighborhood, within easy reach of their mutual manager, Dick Linke. One night, Andy and Ken ventured out with George Lindsey and Jack Dodson to see Merle Haggard perform at the Shrine Auditorium in Los Angeles. "Each of us had a quart of whiskey and a quart of chaser," George Lindsey recalled. "I went out and bought everybody aviator caps, with goggles, and we all wore those. We had a big, white limousine take us to the theater, and then we just raised hell. Before it was over, we got onstage with Merle, and I bet he just wanted to kill us. Andy was always bigger than life and always laughed longer and screamed louder than anybody I've ever known, and this time he wasn't alone."

Suddenly liberated from the punishing schedule of television and halfway through his forties, Andy finally had time for the classic trappings of a midlife crisis. He purchased a beige-carpeted motor home and a small fleet of dirt bikes. Thus equipped, Andy would summon Ken, Jack Dodson, and Lee Greenway (the banjo-playing makeup man) and head for the desert. "We'd go out to those many thousands of acres out by Palmdale, and they would go hunting," Ken recalled. "And I'd sit in the camper because I don't like to hunt. And afterwards, we'd get on these motorcycles and ride all over the place and laugh and have a great time."

Don did not join the excursions. Andy liked to whoop and holler and get wild. Don wasn't about to climb on a dirt bike. "Andy's more of a man's man," he would say.

The desert provided a fitting metaphor for Andy's career prospects in fall 1968. Even before his first Universal film hit theaters, the studio showed signs of panic. A squib in the October 10 *Los Angeles Times* announced that Andy would be reuniting with Don in a forthcoming Universal picture titled *Me and My Shadow*, with the winning team of Fritzell and Greenbaum supplying the screenplay. Just a few months earlier, the

Universal executives had promised to make Andy into another Jimmy Stewart. Now, they seemed to think Andy could not carry a movie by himself. They wanted to revive the comedy duo, a proven hit.

Andy told Dick Linke he wanted out. His five-year, ten-picture deal with Universal would end after a single film.

January 1969 found Don back in Morgantown, where Elsie Knotts, his mother, lay in a hospital ward. The front page of the *Dominion-News* daily paper from January 23 pictures Don, Elsie, and Don's daughter, Karen, joined by Sid Knotts, Don's rough-hewn older brother, all smiling for the camera. Don patted his mother on the hand and said, "Here's the gal who got me started."

Don was summoned back to Morgantown in spring; Elsie was dying. The thought of her passing was more than Don could bear. He found her comatose and sat at her bedside, calling, "Mother? Mother?" over and over, until finally she voiced a faint "Mmm-hmm." She knew he was there. Don lingered for a few moments, then rose and bolted from the hospital room, never to return.

Elsie died on April 3. Don could not summon the strength to attend his mother's funeral.

Elsie had been Don's first fan, his greatest supporter during the long, hard journey from West Virginia to New York. Elsie had protected

Don from his demon father, his bellicose brothers, and all the other perils lurking in the dark corners of his Morgantown home. After Don had found fame on *The Andy Griffith Show*, Elsie would sometimes furrow her brows and tell her son, "Everybody wants to know why you don't do your ventriloquism anymore." Don would spend the rest of his days looking for someone to replace her.

Spring 1969 saw the release of Andy's *Angel in My Pocket*, and summer brought Don's *The Love God?* Both garnered mostly positive reviews; the *Los Angeles Times* called Don's film one of the "funniest and most pertinent pictures to come out of Universal in years," and the same critic hailed Andy's movie as the best Fritzell-Greenbaum story to date. Yet, neither feature did much at the box office. That was particularly bad news for Andy, who hadn't had a hit film since *No Time for Sergeants*, two decades earlier.

The Love God? received an M rating, for mature content, under the new MPAA system, an ill omen. "Even though the sexual revolution was in full swing and people were taking their clothes off right and left in movies, people apparently didn't want to see me in anything but clean family pictures," Don recalled. Universal struggled to book *The Love God?*

"I went to the theater with him," son Tom Knotts recalled. "And we went in and the manager took us back to his office. And we looked, and there were, like, three people. And he was so embarrassed to have to tell Dad that practically no one was going."

Don, exhausted from work and grief-stricken at the passing of his mother, traveled alone to Waikiki and fell in with a group of hippies, who deemed him a loser and thus sufficiently anti-establishment to merit their respect. He swam with them in the ocean, according to a *TV Guide* account, hacking off the pant legs of a $300 suit; when he emerged, a girl cried, "Who needs pot? I can blow my mind just looking at his shins!"

Don's personal life had become decidedly more complex. In 1968, Kay Knotts relocated to Round Mountain, a lumber town in Northern California. Their son, Tom, moved north with Kay. Karen, thirteen at the time, remained with her father. Don rented a house in the swanky coastal enclave of Pacific Palisades. The next year, he rented another home in Beverly Hills, where he remained until a windfall enabled him to buy one.

Sunni Walton, a singer-actress-impressionist from San Francisco, was Don's major romantic companion in the years after Lynn Paul. Sunni sang in nine languages and did voice-overs in commercials and animated films. She landed a bit part in *The Love God?* The romance lasted two years and was a much calmer relationship than Don had known with the fiery Lynn. He thought

Sunni beautiful, and he loved her red hair. But they had little in common.

CBS offered Don a chance to bounce back from *The Love God?* with a one-hour variety special, *Don Knotts' Nice Clean, Decent, Wholesome Hour.* The special aired on April 3, 1970, with a guest appearance from Andy. It was a hit, and network producers took note.

Don started work on his fifth and final Universal movie, *How to Frame a Figg.* He collaborated with producer Ed Montagne and several writers on the script, which cast Don as Hollis Figg, a dim-witted town accountant who "flunked French because it hurt his sinuses"; Don himself was plagued by sinus trouble. When Hollis discovers money is missing, corrupt town officials try to pin their misdeeds on him. Hollis sets things right with the aid of a room-size computer named LEO, in homage to HAL from Stanley Kubrick's *2001* film of two years past.

Once again, Don is surrounded by a bevy of beauties. Yvonne Craig, a voluptuous dancer-actress who played Batgirl in the 1960s *Batman* series, is dispatched by the crooks to seduce Hollis. For the obligatory nice-girl counterpoint, the producers chose Elaine Joyce, a Hungarian-American beauty who was married to Broadway star Bobby Van.

Elaine Joyce Pinchot began her career as a teenage actress. She did one episode of the

Griffith Show—as a "fast" girl, sought out by Andy for a revenge date after a fight with Helen. "I just had this scene with Andy in the car where I tried to kiss him," she recalled; later, in the town diner, her character asks for a root beer float and coos, "They make me bubbly all over." Elaine was twenty-one and Andy was forty; the whole thing struck her as unsavory.

Elaine knew Don only from his characters. "The guy smoked, he drank, he was into women," she recalled. "And I was, like, 'Wow, this is amazing.' I thought he was really the character he played, this terrified, self-conscious guy."

The two became close. Bobby Van, Elaine's husband, "was doing movies someplace. I was always free," she recalled. "We would go, and we would talk, and he would tell me about his life, his family, his mother, who he adored."

Don told Elaine about his past girlfriends, and about his housekeeper, who looked after daughter Karen as if she were her own; and about his daily ritual of eating half a cantaloupe, "because his mother told him he'd live to be ninety-five if he did that." He told her about his children, particularly Karen, who was gently pressing him to help her become an actress. "He was worried about Karen all the time," Elaine recalled, "worried that she would always be a recovering actress."

And Don told Elaine of his current girlfriend:

Loralee Czuchna, a young USC student he'd met on a blind date.

Don liked women, and not just for romance. He often seemed more at ease with female than male costars—Andy was the notable exception. After enduring years of abuse from men in his youth, Don "picked his male friends very carefully and sparsely," Loralee recalled. Friendship came more easily with women "because he just felt more comfortable. Women liked him, and he could talk to them." From romantic partners, Don craved emotional support. He wanted to be loved; he also wanted to be mothered. He wanted another Elsie.

Shortly after Don completed work on *Figg*, he got a call from his manager, Sherwin Bash. Mort Werner, programming chief at NBC, wanted to talk to Don about launching a variety series on the momentum generated by his CBS special. Don was reluctant. "Look," he told Werner over drinks, "I spent six months gathering the material for that show. Coming up with a script for a variety hour every week is an entirely different story." But Werner persisted, offering Don an unfathomable $5.5 million for a single season. It was the biggest deal of Don's life.

At the close of the 1960s, Andy Griffith's telephone wasn't ringing. He did some TV guest spots and spent three months with his family at his Manteo estate, bored and brooding. "I'm not a fisherman, I'm not a carpenter, I'm not a hunter. There was nothing to do," he told a *Chicago Tribune* columnist. "I am emotionally not a person who can be unemployed."

In spring 1970, without Andy's knowledge, manager Dick Linke met with CBS executives and told them Andy might be ready to return to television. "I knew he was unhappy," Dick confided later to a *TV Guide* reporter. "And I knew a completely new series, different from the old image, would be like plasma for him." The CBS brass were suspicious: Would Andy really come back? Dick assured them, "Nobody knows Andy Griffith better than Dick Linke. For a million dollars, he'll reconsider."

The executives "were so enthralled at the idea of getting Andy back," Dick boasted later, "that they offered us one of the most fantastic deals in the history of television. They signed us for a half-hour weekly series even though we had no script, not even a format in mind. They were willing to take Andy in *anything*. We could have given them a dirty picture if we'd wanted to. And with not one word on paper, we got a contract for five years at three and a half million dollars a year."

Dick conveyed the offer to Andy. "I don't want you to be a family-picture star," he told Dick. "No money in that anymore." Soon, Andy was meeting with his old writer-producer, Aaron Ruben, to map out a return to television. "School is where it is today," Aaron told Andy, and Andy agreed. They plotted a series that would posit Andy as headmaster of a small private school. Andy would reshape his Lincolnesque sheriff persona into that of a sage educator, more articulate than Andy Taylor, and more outspoken.

Now, both Andy and Don had sweet television deals. Both would soon run aground.

The premise for *Headmaster* fed Andy's fantasy of reinventing himself as a Southern Henry Fonda. He would populate his new program with noble speeches on America's Vietnam-era moral crisis. Neither he nor his entourage seemed to comprehend that Andy had already done this, far more effectively, as the soft-spoken Andy Taylor.

To give Andy's new character more gravitas, the producers looked for a woman of East Coast refinement to play his wife. They found Claudette Nevins, a Broadway actress with Shakespearean elocution.

"Andy was interested in broadening his scope and changing his image," she recalled. "He wanted to be known for something other than comedy. *A Face in the Crowd* was a spectacular piece of work; I think he wanted to get back to something like that."

Andy's show would be swept up in a sea change at CBS that ultimately closed the curtain on

Mayberry. Ratings were down. Fred Silverman, the new programming chief, shifted the network's focus to younger viewers, who were thought more likely to buy sponsors' products. In spring 1970, he began a systematic purge of programs that skewed toward older viewers. In their place would come new programs to "deal with the now scene," a vice president explained to *Time* magazine. Mary Tyler Moore, the outspoken spouse from *The Dick Van Dyke Show*, would be brought back to play a single career woman at a television station. Andy Griffith would return in *Headmaster*, bridging the generation gap. "I think CBS is using us to do a little face-lifting," Andy bragged to a *Chicago Tribune* columnist that summer.

Sadly, CBS and Andy Griffith did not see eye to eye on *Headmaster*. Andy wanted to make important television. CBS wanted laughs. Would Andy's new program be a comedy, a comedy-drama, or a drama with a bit of comedy thrown in? "Griffith seems none too sure himself," one columnist concluded.

Headmaster took to the air on September 15 with big ambitions, with writing contributions from future Hollywood icon Rob Reiner and a theme song sung by Linda Ronstadt. "We're gonna try and deal with many of the situations that young people come up against these days," Andy drawled in a CBS preview.

The pilot drew scathing reviews. "Modern TV waste," *The New York Times* opined. Critics noted that Andy seemed inserted into the scripts almost as an afterthought, and then only for pompous, Fonda-esque soliloquies on substance abuse and civil liberties. Some whispered, too, that Andy himself was becoming a bit haughty. A visiting reporter watched him wrap a scene and bark, "Print it," without bothering to consult the director. By week three, *Headmaster* had fallen from the top forty.

When it became clear *Headmaster* could not be saved, a conference call was hastily arranged. Dick Linke brokered a solution: Andy would be his own "midseason replacement," quietly scuttling *Headmaster* in January and returning the following week in an entirely different series. New series were getting clobbered in the 1970–71 season, including the sublime *Mary Tyler Moore Show*. The network wanted something old, something proven. So *The New Andy Griffith Show* was born.

Andy would return to the air "as a kindly authority figure in a small Southern town—this time as a mayor instead of a sheriff, and with a wife (Lee Meriwether) and two children, instead of a widower with one son and an Aunt Bee," *TV Guide* explained. "With these slight differences, it was the old *Andy Griffith Show* all over again."

Andy, forthright as ever, took full blame for

the *Headmaster* debacle, which became known across the industry as the $3.5 Million Misunderstanding. "The truth, plain and simple, is that I was lousy," he said. "I wasn't comfortable playing a sophisticated educator. I couldn't identify with him. I realize now that every time I played a successful character in the past, the character always had the same roots. First, he was a Southerner. Second, he was based on things I knew in my dumb little town in North Carolina."

Andy and Dick traveled to New York to meet with William Paley, the CBS chief, to discuss the transition. The two men shared a lavish suite at the Warwick Hotel. They talked and drank until midnight, when Dick went to bed. Sometime later, he was awakened by "this goddamn commotion. It was like a hurricane." Dick emerged from the bedroom to find that Andy had demolished the adjoining living room. "Glass was all over," Dick recalled. "He broke a credenza. It was a shambles." Dick turned to Andy and growled, "What the hell's the matter with you?" Andy just shrugged his shoulders and laughed.

Andy's new *Griffith Show* had much of the same talent as the old one. Aaron Ruben wrote the pilot, *Griffith* alumnus Lee Philips directed it, Earle Hagen crafted the theme song, and Mayberry regulars George Lindsey and Paul Hartman came on as guest stars. Andy even tapped ever-loyal Don, the friend with whom he had refused to collaborate on a film just a year earlier.

The goal was nostalgia, but *The New Andy Griffith Show* emerged as a surreal muddle of Mayberry memories. Andy is cast as the mayor of a fictional town called Greenwood. (Dick Linke helpfully apprised reporters, in all seriousness, that Greenwood was "about fifteen or twenty miles" from the equally fictitious Mayberry.) His name is now Andy Sawyer. He has a wife and two children, and he seems to bear no relation to Andy Taylor. But several of the sheriff's old friends are on hand, pestering Andy to exercise his mayoral influence in rezoning some land. What are Goober and Barney doing in Greenwood? And if this is a different Andy, then why are they his friends?

Don drives up to Andy's curb, wearing Barney's familiar salt-and-pepper suit. "It can't be," Andy gasps. Don and Andy never utter each other's name, perhaps out of sheer confusion. Instead, they punch each other desperately on the shoulder, crying, "You son of a gun!" "You're a son of a gun yourself!"

The pilot drew better ratings than the debut of *Headmaster*, proving the enduring strength of the *Griffith Show* brand. Reviews ranged from sympathetic to savage. *The New York Times* termed it "a situation without the comedy." The very name of the new series, the critic wrote, betrayed the conceit of its creators that "there are millions of Andy Griffith fans across the country who would watch Mr. Griffith brush his teeth for 30 minutes."

By the second episode, the Mayberry gang was gone and *The New Andy Griffith Show* began to find its way. Lee Meriwether and Ann Morgan Guilbert, who played Andy's wife and his sister-in-law, procured sweatshirts for the cast and crew that had the show's title printed on the front and HEADMASTER crossed out on the back.

But ratings lagged, and the series was canceled at the season's end.

Just as his television world was crumbling around him, Andy Griffith found himself a surprise guest on the March 25, 1971, broadcast of *This Is Your Life*. Faithful Dick Linke had helped arrange the affair, which reunited Andy with a bewildering array of loved ones and long-lost friends: the Reverend Edward T. Mickey, the Mount Airy minister who'd taught Andy the trombone; members of the glee club he'd led at Goldsboro High School; director Elia Kazan, who gave Andy his greatest film role; Sheldon Leonard, Jim Nabors, and Ron Howard from *The Andy Griffith Show*; Ken Berry, his Mayberry replacement; and Andy's parents and children. Andy was furious. He liked to control his projects, not be blindsided by them.

The one curious omission was Don Knotts,

Andy's dearest friend. Was this an intentional act by Dick Linke, part of a campaign to dissociate his greatest client from the former partner? Decades later, Dick maintains he never intentionally excluded Don from the broadcast. Perhaps Don was simply too busy with his variety show.

Meanwhile, Andy Griffith's lovable second banana increasingly resembled a star.

"Don Knotts and his life style have changed drastically since the days when he drove the Plymouth in from Glendale," *TV Guide* reported in fall 1970. "Today, Don lives in Beverly Hills and drives a Cadillac. His clothes, far from the Barney Fife image of *The Andy Griffith Show*, are smartly tailored to his slight frame. He sports sideburns, and onstage he hides his spreading bald spot with a hair piece."

Don was proud of the new show, and of the variety special that had spawned it. He marked the occasion by purchasing a new house from reclusive actress Barbara Stanwyck in Beverly Hills. But deep down, Don knew he wasn't cut out to headline a full-blown variety series. He was an actor, not a stand-up comic, and he seemed to function best when deputized to other actors. Even in his films, Don played a deceptively submissive leading man, a perpetual underdog, always taking orders or enduring abuse from some alpha-male costar. Only when the credits rolled did Don gain the upper hand.

Now, Don was about to headline twenty-two consecutive variety shows. "For the first time in my career," he recalled, "I felt I was up against something I could not handle. For openers, I couldn't deal with writers firing that many sketches at me every week. I couldn't seem to make decisions on material that fast." On the day when Don was to meet the press and talk up his new variety show, he awakened with a mystery ailment and begged off. Poor Bill Dana, Don's head writer, was forced to fill in.

Don was expected to serve as producer, director, and star, overseeing a regular cast that included former *Figg* costars Elaine Joyce and Frank Welker, a dozen writers, and a parade of guest stars, from Bill Cosby and Bob Newhart to Jimmy Durante and Steve Allen.

"That's the hardest I ever remember seeing him work," recalled Tom Knotts, Don's son. "He worked day and night under such pressure. He was stressed-out."

Like Andy, Don felt he had no choice but to return to television. "Frankly, I've gotten a bit confused with what's going on in the movie world," Don told a *Chicago Tribune* reporter in spring 1970.

Alas, Don wasn't the only Hollywood star head-lining a song-and-dance series. That transitional

1970–71 season offered a glut of "variety." Don's former costar Jim Nabors had a show. So did fellow *Steve Allen* alumnus Tim Conway. And Red Skelton, Carol Burnett, Glen Campbell, Johnny Cash, Dean Martin, Flip Wilson, Tom Jones, Andy Williams, and Lawrence Welk.

The Don Knotts Show debuted on September 15, 1970. The first episode built a thin narrative around Don's vying for control of his own show with guest star Anthony Newley. It was all too close to the truth. At one point, Anthony comes onstage and commands, "Finish the joke!" "I've finished it," Don stammers. Another lantern-jawed alpha male was dominating him.

"It was funny," wrote Cleveland Amory in *TV Guide*. "And so was Don *trying* to be a host. But Mr. Knotts actually as a host?"

"He never throws his weight around, what little weight there is," noted a *TV Guide* reporter who visited the set. "He speaks softly and diffidently. ('Do you want me to stand here? Unfortunately, I can't see the cue cards.') If he has a suggestion to make to a guest star about the reading of a line or a piece of stage business, he takes the star aside and gives his advice gently and privately."

Don's stock was high enough to attract A-list guest stars. In one pantomime sketch, Bill Cosby brought the house down simply by picking a chess piece off the board and eating it; he had asked the prop department to make one of the pawns out of chocolate.

But *The Don Knotts Show* was getting creamed in the ratings by *Mod Squad*, ABC's hip new cop show, just as *Headmaster* and *The New Andy Griffith Show* were being bested by ABC's bubblegum sitcom *The Partridge Family*. Former *Griffith* director Bob Sweeney was brought in to Don's series at midseason to shore up creative decline. Sween imported new writers and future *M*A*S*H* star Gary Burghoff and a weekly segment that invoked front-porch memories of Mayberry, all to no avail.

"He suffered so much through that," recalled Elaine Joyce, who gave up a spot on *The Carol Burnett Show* to join Don's ill-fated project. "Every week, the ratings weren't good and the material wasn't good enough. He suffered through it. We all did. You just wanted to abandon ship." The show was canceled at season's end. Don, exhausted, flew to Hawaii and spent a week asleep in a hotel bed.

Andy, too, was having a bad year. Still smarting from the failure of not one but two programs in the 1970–71 season, he and Dick Linke suffered further financial loss with the axing of *Mayberry R.F.D.* in the infamous "rural purge."

The purge was particularly brutal for Dick. "CBS canceled all three of our shows on the same day," he recalled later. *The New Andy Griffith*

Show, *The Jim Nabors Hour*, and *Mayberry R.F.D.* all had been Dick Linke productions.

Don's final Universal film, *How to Frame a Figg*, opened in February 1971 to modest returns but warm reviews. The *Los Angeles Times* theorized that, in a rapidly changing cinema universe, Don Knotts was "the last American film comedian to sustain a consistently developed screen characterization in a series of films dictated by that personality." Ironically, Don would effectively retire the Nervous Man with *Figg*—for a few years, at least.

In summer 1971, both Andy Griffith and Don Knotts found themselves unemployed for the first time in more than a decade. Andy returned to the nightclub stage. He drove his camper bus to Las Vegas for an engagement at Caesars Palace, the second-biggest room in town. Three years earlier, buoyed by the *Griffith Show*, Andy had drawn capacity crowds. Now, "you could have shot a cannon in there without hurting anybody," he recalled. Worse, the hotel staff kept mistaking him for Andy Williams, the singer, who sometimes played the same venue.

After every show, Andy would retreat into the desert with his camper and his motorbikes, beyond the reach of telephones, until the next night's performance.

"I'm cursing the day you got that bus," Dick Linke growled, as a *TV Guide* reporter listened.

Andy replied, "We're putting a phone on that bus."

"Can I have the number?"

"No."

"What if somebody offers you a picture?"

"Take it."

Andy dispatched Barbara and the children to Manteo for the summer. Then he sat around the Toluca Lake house, alone, thumbing through scripts. "What we're trying to do now is turn me around," he told *TV Guide*. "It's like starting all over again. I want to become an actor and play character parts. It'll be a long time before I play the lead."

At a party at Don's house one night, Andy struck up a conversation with another invitee. Talk turned to their mutual admiration for Don's work. "He's won five Emmys," Andy said. The two men turned to admire the awards on Don's mantel. Then the other man turned to Andy and asked, "Say, didn't you work with Don once?"

Andy wondered if the fickle American public was beginning to forget him.

For Don, the transition from employment to unemployment was just as abrupt in 1971 as in 1955. The failure of *The Don Knotts Show* "had put my name on the back burner," Don recalled, "and it was a good three months before my phone rang again. . . . I began to wonder if my career was really over."

Then, Jim Burrows, an ascendant director who later oversaw hundreds of episodes of *Taxi* and *Cheers*, persuaded Don to return to the theater for the first time since his run in *No Time*, two decades earlier. Don drove down to San Diego to examine the venue, and to swallow his pride. "It was a tiny house called the Off-Broadway Theatre, and it didn't pay much money, but I decided to give it a whirl," he recalled. "Hey, I wasn't working!"

Don jotted down a note, in his choppy script, inside his dog-eared personal copy of the script for *Last of the Red Hot Lovers*: "Property of Don Knotts, who performed this play at the Off-Broadway Theatre for 6 weeks during Oct. + Nov. 1971 in San Diego."

Encouraged by the sellout crowds, Don moved the production north to Hollywood as a showcase, hoping to leverage a return to television or cinema. It didn't work; Don wouldn't land another major role for three more years.

But regional theater opened up a new chapter in Don's career. In the months that followed, Don would populate the blank pages of his script with a running diary of his travels as Barney Cashman, a middle-aged married man who yearns to join the sexual revolution before it's too late: two and a half weeks at the Marquee Theatre in El Paso, March 1972; sixteen days at the Huntington Hartford Theater in Hollywood in

April and May; and parts of June and July at the Arlington Park Theatre outside Chicago.

He formed a lifelong friendship with Sandra Giles, an understudy in the *Lovers* ensemble. Sandra "had found a niche in Hollywood where she would become friends with stars and she would figure out what they wanted in their lives," one friend recalled. "He wanted to throw parties—just to kind of meet people. He was kind of shy. He had this big new house in Beverly Hills. She knew how to put it together."

The span between Don's final Universal film and his next film project was a sort of *Lost Weekend*. Don threw parties at his Beverly Hills home and hung out with other comedians, including Bill Cosby and Flip Wilson. Though he was idle— perhaps *because* he was idle—Don remained prone to deep wells of anxiety.

He became increasingly dependent on Dick Renneker, his therapist and guru, who was again prescribing sedatives for Don after successfully weaning him off them. If Andy served as surrogate brother to Don, Dick had become Don's ersatz father, providing all the counsel and comfort that Jesse Sr. could not. Dick, in turn, savored the trappings of Don's fame, accompanying him to parties and sometimes offering unsolicited advice to his writers, who were not amused. One such overture nearly landed Dick in a fistfight with Everett Greenbaum.

Don had been in therapy continuously since his arrival in Hollywood. He was still haunted by the fire-and-brimstone nightmares of his fundamentalist childhood. Someone had told Don, decades earlier, that people who didn't sleep were going to die. He worried about that story, and it made him lose sleep, and the sleeplessness made him worry more. The pills helped him find sleep.

Andy and Barbara Griffith finally separated in fall 1971, after twenty-two years of marriage. In subsequent interviews, Andy hinted that the implosion of his career was what finally drove her away. "Barbara wasn't thick-skinned enough for show business," Andy said. "You've got to be able to fail and stand it."

By this time, Barbara was sober. Perhaps a year before the split, Barbara had gone on a bender that left her bedridden. She and Andy were so estranged that it fell to the housekeeper to summon a doctor. Barbara was dispatched to the hospital, "and that's when she dried out and went to AA," nephew Mike King recalled.

Barbara would sue for divorce the following June. Andy got custody of fourteen-year-old Sam, their son, and Barbara took twelve-year-old Dixie. This was a loose arrangement, though, as the children would continue spending their summers with Andy on the Carolina shore. Dick

Linke found a temporary rental for Andy near the family home in Toluca Lake. The settlement awarded Andy an easement off the back of Barbara's home so Andy could continue to tinker with his beloved antique cars.

A year after the divorce, in 1973, Andy bought a new home: the old Bing Crosby residence, a six-bedroom colonial estate in Toluca Lake with a swimming pool and tennis court. Andy's new home lay just blocks from the old one, where Barbara remained; Andy's former rental house was purchased by none other than his manager, Dick Linke.

Andy spent that summer and the next in Manteo with his now-teenaged children, Sam and Dixie. The younger Griffiths worked at *The Lost Colony*, the historic pageant that had once employed their parents, singing in the chorus and carrying banners on and off stage.

"It was an idyllic summer camp, and they would pay us one hundred dollars a week," recalled Craig Fincannon, a family friend who spent summer 1974 at Manteo. "All of us were actors, and we all had dreams of being Dustin Hoffman." Andy would occasionally slip into the choir unnoticed and join his children in song. Sam and Craig became close, and Craig soon found himself invited to the Griffith estate for dinner.

"I remember the very first time I ever saw Andy

Griffith," Craig recalled. "We were standing in the kitchen, and Andy walked in, and he was in long pants and a short-sleeved shirt, and he was barefooted. That, to me, was what Manteo was for him."

Craig remembers Sam as "a California kid with long blond hair. He was exotic. The fact that his dad was Andy Griffith made him even more interesting to me. . . . But I guess I could tell that it was not easy to be the kid of a big star. I could feel, even in those days, that he was not an outwardly optimistic, gregarious kid."

Andy took the boys out on his boat, tubing and water-skiing. They would anchor at one of the Tom Sawyer islands that dotted the sound and indulge in "the kind of fun that we had in the seventies," Craig recalled. When Craig's college girlfriend came to visit, Andy had the couple over for dinner. After they'd dined, Andy invited Craig's companion to join him on the couch. "He pulled out a photo album and showed her all these pictures of his travels. And I remember thinking, 'Andy Griffith is flirting with my girl-friend.' "

The 1970s would serve up a second adolescence for Andy; finally, this Carolina country boy was free to climb trees, skin knees, and indulge all the boyish urges his overprotective mother and hectic career had thwarted. With fewer projects to distract him, Andy began spending longer stretches in Manteo, hunting and fishing, boating, riding his red Honda motorcycle, and drinking with a band of merry pranksters, some local, some imported. Andy sometimes turned up with Lee Greenway, his makeup artist; or Jack Dodson, a far more festive spirit than the milquetoast he'd played in Mayberry.

Andy "had a big pontoon boat. He would take people out water-skiing and raising hell," recalled Quentin Bell, a Manteo neighbor who was perhaps Andy's closest Manteo friend during this time. "We'd meet out here and play volley-ball on the sand. . . . He liked to party; he liked to drink; he liked everything we did here."

Quentin took Andy duck hunting. "I loaned Andy my gun and I said, 'Now, when you jump a ditch to get a dead bird, make sure the barrel of the gun doesn't go in the dirt, because dirt will lodge in the end of the barrel, and when you shoot, it will blow the end of the gun off,' " he recalled. "And damned if he didn't do that, and he came up to me and the barrel of the gun looked like a flower."

Quentin knew how close Andy remained to Don, and they spoke often of Andy's Mayberry deputy. "But darned if he ever came to Manteo," Quentin recalled.

Another friend recalled that Don did pay at least one brief visit to Andy in Manteo, one summer in the mid-1960s, shortly after his exit from the *Griffith Show.* Don came alone. He, Andy, and Barbara spent long hours on Andy's boat, joined by the family dogs and local friends, drinking to excess, telling stories, and laughing into the night.

In a television interview in 1972, Andy waxed nostalgic for the old comedy partnership: "I don't think anybody works together quite like we do, and I'd like to try that again."

Andy and Don were seeing a lot of each other at the time, and they came quite close to reuniting on a film, a development that would surely have brought great acclaim to the old *Griffith Show* duo. "Andy and I are making a movie," Don announced to a reporter in summer 1972; he said he was working on the screenplay. According to Loralee, Don's girlfriend at the time, the two friends were planning a cinematic reunion of *The Andy Griffith Show*. But nothing would come of these ruminations for another fourteen years.

Andy would spend the remainder of the 1970s largely on his own, headlining a procession of television movies, some good, some bad, nearly all forgotten. He deliberately chose roles that would shatter the benevolent image of his Mayberry sheriff. After all his success on *The Andy Griffith Show*, Andy seemed now to be trapped in the sheriff's role. He wanted out.

The first project was *The Strangers in 7A*, a CBS Tuesday Night Movie that paired Andy with screen veteran Ida Lupino. Movies of the week had a cachet in 1970s Hollywood. Andy plays a decidedly uninspiring antihero as the meek superintendent of a Manhattan apartment building. A beautiful young woman lures him into the snare of a gang of thugs, who use his building as the base for a bold bank robbery. Andy spends most of the movie perspiring and looking licked; only in the final minutes does he find his courage and gain the upper hand. It was bold and different, and that was just what Andy wanted. A *Los Angeles Times* review declared the movie "a good vehicle for Andy Griffith's straight dramatic ability." He was off to a solid start.

Next came *Go Ask Alice*, a teensploitation film based on the blockbuster novel and falsely marketed as the diary of a real teenage girl whose prim life spirals into drugs, sex, homelessness, and Mackenzie Phillips. Andy plays a priest who operates a shelter for recovering addicts. He faces off with Alice in one long, overwrought scene, shot in a church.

"Do you want an opinion, or do you want an alibi?" the priest asks.

"Don't hassle me," Alice cries.

"You're looking for magic."

"I'm looking for *help!*"

The film "was a big deal" in its day and endures as a modest cult classic, said Jamie Smith-Jackson, the blue-eyed, long-tressed actress cast as Alice. Andy, she recalled, "was just an angel. He was just so real. He cared so much about that scene in the church. He really was trying hard to become a serious actor."

The next year, Andy retreated to the desert for a pair of roles that he hoped would shatter the Sheriff Taylor image forever.

The first was *Pray for the Wildcats*, an ABC Movie of the Week broadcast in January 1974 and ripe for rediscovery as camp. Andy plays Sam Farragut, a wealthy industrialist who stages a dirt-bike trek through Baja as a means to torment three admen who manage his account. The agency is desperate for his business, so the men indulge Sam's every whim. Imagine a midseventies *Mad Men* on motorcycles.

The picture surrounds Andy with big-name actors awaiting better roles: William Shatner, five years shy of the *Star Trek* revival; Robert Reed, in the waning days of *The Brady Bunch*; and Angie Dickinson, slumming as Mike Brady's unfaithful wife.

The men set out wearing ridiculous matching leather jackets over colored tunics that look suspiciously like cast-off Starfleet uniforms. They pull up to a cantina, where Andy's character drunkenly accosts a lovely young hippie, his eyes all menace and lust. "Now we're gettin' it on, baby," he cries. When her boyfriend refuses Sam's offer of one hundred dollars for a few minutes with the girl, Andy disables his truck, leaving the young couple to die in the desert. Captain Kirk takes him to task; Andy tries to run Kirk down with his motorbike, but it is he who hurtles spectacularly off a cliff.

The night before he shot the cantina scene, Andy dreamed that he murdered Don, his best friend. "I dreamed I hit his head and kept hitting him and killed him," he recalled later. "And I woke up and my conscience was killing me and I tried to call Don [to see if he was all right] and I couldn't find him. It was driving me crazy!"

Later, Andy asked a psychiatrist friend about the dream. The shrink told Andy, to his infinite relief, that the dream wasn't really about killing Don. It was about killing Andy Taylor. Andy and Don laughed about it later.

Andy completed his cycle of terror that fall with another made-for-TV absurdity, *Savages*. This time, he plays a wealthy lawyer who accidentally shoots a man during a desert hunting trip, then spends the balance of the movie hunting down the young guide who saw it all. Andy's quarry is Sam Bottoms, a blond-maned actor in the Peter Frampton mold. The story devolves into a tiresome retelling of "The Most Dangerous Game," with amusing David-and-Goliath imagery; shirtless Sam eventually overpowers his pursuer with an actual slingshot.

Andy's other venture of 1974 was *Winter Kill*,

another ABC Movie of the Week, which cast him in a more familiar setting. Andy plays a small-town police chief investigating a string of murders at a sleepy—and chilly—ski resort. Andy and Dick Linke pitched it as a pilot for another series, something Andy dearly wanted. But the locale proved a poor choice. The production company endured 60 mph winds in California's San Bernardino Mountains, wearing ski masks and dragging gear up a steep slope. One wonders, too, whether this tiny town could possibly have yielded enough murders to sustain a weekly series. It was a moot point; *Winter Kill* was not picked up.

It would be another dozen years before Andy scored again.

13.

Second Chances, Second Wives

Don Knotts was in Chicago, playing in the middle-class satire *The Mind with the Dirty Man* at Arlington Park, when he got a call from Sherwin Bash, his agent. "Disney wants you to do a movie," Sherwin said. Until that moment, in summer 1974, Don had every reason to believe his film career was over. Don hadn't headlined in three years. His telephone wasn't ringing. The family-comedy genre that had spawned *The Shakiest Gun in the West* and *How to Frame a Figg* was played out.

Disney seemed a natural move. The studio was almost single-handedly sustaining the family genre. "I had always thought I was Disney material," Don recalled.

It wasn't Disney that wanted Don so much as Norman Tokar, who was about to direct a screen adaptation of a Jack Bickham novel called *The Apple Dumpling Gang*. The story ostensibly concerns a trio of orphaned children who are taken in by a reluctant gambler in the Old West; but much of the comedy centers on two bumbling robbers who play off the urchins. For these parts, Norman Tokar envisioned a new comedic partnership between Don and Tim Conway.

A Cleveland native, Tim Conway established himself in radio and won a part on *The Steve Allen Plymouth Show* just as Don was leaving. He became one of television's *other* great second bananas of the 1960s, working opposite Ernest Borgnine on the hit ABC series *McHale's Navy*. By the time of his Disney casting, Tim had become an established player on the smash *Carol Burnett Show*.

Don was one of Tim's idols, but until their Disney pairing, the two had never worked together.* "If I'm in the business," Tim once said, "it's because of Don Knotts."

Don hadn't worked with a real partner since he left *The Andy Griffith Show*, nearly ten years earlier. Tim Conway was a far cry from Andy Griffith. He was the resident maniac on *Carol Burnett*; equally adept as a doddering old man or a man-boy in a beanie, he seemed to delight in reducing Harvey Korman and his other castmates to paralytic laughter with his ad-libbed insanity. Don was nearly a decade older than Tim and, at fifty, just a touch slower on the draw than in his Barney Fife heyday. Now, for the first time in his

---

*This, at least, was Don's contention. Tim, in his 2013 memoir, suggests that the two briefly worked together on *Steve Allen*.

career, Don would be working with a comedian more highly caffeinated than himself.

The Apple Dumpling Gang is a capable family western, shot on an idealized Old West set that looks lifted straight from Disney World and featuring the estimable talents of Bill Bixby, Slim Pickens, and Harry Morgan. But it is Don and Tim and their dust cloud of comedic entropy that render the film memorable.

In October, when shooting was done, Don flew to Hawaii with his son, Tom, and wed Loralee Czuchna, the former USC student who had become his more-or-less-exclusive girlfriend since their first blind date, three years earlier. Andy could not attend the remote ceremony.

Don and Loralee had grown close in the dark days that followed the cancellation of Don's variety show. "His career had just gone up," she recalled. "The studios didn't return his calls. He was not only modest and humble, but, remember, underneath, every actor thinks he's never gonna work again. Don was up sometimes, but there were a lot of times he wasn't." Loralee buoyed his spirits: "You had to keep reminding him, every day, how great he was."

By this time, Don had grown dependent on an ever-changing menu of sleeping aids prescribed by his psychiatrist, Dick Renneker, Loralee recalled. Don smoked and drank, as well, although Loralee does not remember seeing him frequently drunk. He suffered relentless sinus problems and leg ailments, and he would grow nauseated if Loralee put too much food on his plate. He sometimes seemed to sleepwalk through his days. After dark, though, Don would come to life. "The funny part of being with Don," Loralee recalled, "was late at night, when he would cut loose. I would laugh until I ached."

They married in an open-air church near the Diamond Head crater. At the reception, someone kicked Don's bad leg on the dance floor. It turned red. "We left the next day," Loralee recalled, "and it was my parents who went on our honeymoon for us."

Released on July 4, 1975, *The Apple Dumpling Gang* would earn $37 million, making it one of Disney's top-grossing films of the era. *The New York Times* termed the film "as cheerful and indistinguishable as rice pudding."

Don and Tim were ready for more films. But Disney passed on the script Tim wrote for their second project, tentatively titled *They Went That-a-Way and That-a-Way*.

Instead, Don's next Disney film, *No Deposit, No Return*, teamed him with David Niven, Darren McGavin, and Vic Tayback. In best Disney tradition, the four seasoned actors lent their talents in support of two children and a pet skunk.

In *Gus*, his next feature, Don acted opposite a mule. In *Herbie Goes to Monte Carlo*, he was reduced to warbling his lines to a car. Both were hits.

Disney finally reunited Don with Tim Conway for a 1979 sequel to *The Apple Dumpling Gang*. Don loved working with Tim, who seemed to understand Don's many quirks as well as Andy. When he wasn't gently eviscerating Don's neuroses, Tim would simply talk, unfurling a manic travelogue on the passing scenery. Don would laugh himself sore.

Parts of the *Dumpling* sequel were shot in Northern California, and other parts in hundred-degree Fort Kanab, Utah. The sets were hot, the dressing rooms cold. The script for *The Apple Dumpling Gang Rides Again* called for Tim and Don to spend a fair amount of the film in drag, disguised as showgirls. Once the shoot commenced, Don complained that he was freezing to death during the costume changes in the ice-cold wardrobe room. Tim suggested Don dress in his motel room and ride to the set in costume.

Later that week, Tim drove Don back from the set and dropped him off to change, while Tim waited in a nearby saloon. A few minutes later, Don walked into the bar still wearing his dress. "And it's up in Northern California," Tim recalled, "where they really hate performers. They would really rather run them over. Nobody was really thrilled about our being there. And I'm sitting there, having a beer, and in comes Don, dressed in this whole rig. And he comes up to me and says, 'Tim, have you got the key to the room?' And I look at him and say, 'Pardon me, sir, shouldn't we talk about price first?' "

Later Don hissed, "We could've been killed."

The sequel turned a cool $21 million. Tim Conway, on a creative high, quickly wrote two more scripts for Conway-Knotts films and sold them as independent features. "Don was my first choice," Tim recalled. "It's gold, what he does, and you don't have to worry about making a movie that's going to offend anybody, because we're not going to offend anybody. We're not bright enough to offend anybody."

The first project was *The Prize Fighter*, a boxing film that became a hit for Roger Corman's New World Pictures. The second was *The Private Eyes*, a mash-up of Sherlock Holmes, Inspector Clouseau, and various haunted-house pictures of yore. Don plays the Holmes-styled Inspector Winship, and Tim is sidekick Dr. Tart. Their interplay here is calmer and slower paced than in their Disney films; the understatement renders the slapstick more explosive, when it comes.

The Private Eyes was shot at the historic Biltmore House in North Carolina. Tim would pick Don up for the twenty-minute drive from town. His passenger was a tireless complainer. "Don would get in the car in the morning and he would say, 'You know, that damn air-conditioning last night, that was blowin' all over me. I'm gonna tell those people to put some cardboard over it or something. I can't take that much longer,' " Tim recalled. "Then we'd go by some houses, and he'd say, 'Look at that. Brick houses. I hate brick houses.' And we'd get almost out to the house in the country. And he'd say, 'Look at those cows out there. What the hell do cows do all day?' "

One morning, Tim surreptitiously recorded Don's rants. "So, next day, we got in the car, and Don goes, 'I'll tell you, that meat loaf kind of got to me last night. Boy, that backed up on me.' And I said, 'Don, would you mind very much if we don't talk this morning? Just listen to the radio?' " Tim put on the tape, and Don heard his complaints of the previous day issue forth from the speakers. After that, "we played that thing every morning when we went to work."

By the middle seventies, Andy Griffith's career as a Hollywood leading man seemed to be over. But he was working as hard as ever. Andy spent fall 1974 shooting *Hearts of the West*, a sort of big-budget art film. Director Howard Zieff managed to capture both Andy's dark side and his fundamental warmth, a feat few others had matched.

On January 18, 1975, Barbara Bray Edwards Griffith married Australian-born actor Michael St. Clair. Barbara now had a tidy sum of Andy's money and a new husband.

The very next day, January 19, Andy lost his father, Carl, the wellspring of his laughter. "He was real close to his dad. Not too close to his mom," recalled Quentin Bell, Andy's Manteo friend. "His dad died, and he was really in a funk."

Andy's grief, perhaps coupled with the affront of his former wife's nuptials, may have driven Andy himself into hasty wedlock. That June, Andy married thirty-two-year-old Solica Capsuto,* a Greek American actress of Sephardic Jewish heritage, with olive complexion and dark chestnut hair.

Andy and Don each married three times. Of the six pairings, this was surely the most mysterious. Solica was, by all accounts, delightful, with a sharp sense of humor and a deep well of compassion. "She was funny," recalled Ken Berry, Andy's friend. "But a more unlikely couple you never saw. She looked like a flower child. I don't mean that in a bad way at all. But the image that Andy has—you would just never pick them as a couple."

Don and Loralee attended the wedding. Dick Linke stood as best man. "It was beautiful," Loralee recalled. "They had a harp in the backyard. All the comedians were making jokes— 'Are we in heaven?' " But Don never quite com-

---

*Official documents and press clippings render Solica's maiden name three ways; this spelling seems the most plausible.

prehended the relationship. "He said Andy must have been really lonely," one friend recalled. "They were nothing alike."

Andy and Solica set out for a two-month honeymoon in Manteo, but the couple quickly discovered that Solica disliked the Outer Banks. They returned to Hollywood.

Andy settled into a new domestic routine, inviting his children to dwell with him and Solica within their palatial home. He began spending more social time with Don; they talked of staging a play together. Andy and Solica also spent many evenings in the home of Ken Berry, Solica laughing as she regaled Ken with stories of Andy's peccadilloes.

In 1975, a full twenty years after Andy's television debut in *No Time for Sergeants*, the civic captains of Mount Airy began to rebrand their community as Andy Griffith's hometown. The city leased the old Rockford Street School—Andy's grammar school—to the Surry Arts Council. The council remodeled the structure around the 350-seat auditorium where Andy had given his first performance, back in the third grade. Andy graciously lent his name to the structure, but he was not on hand for the opening. Perhaps he had not yet forgiven his hometown for past wrongs.

Andy resurfaced on television in fall 1976 with another hopeful pilot, this one titled *Street Killing*, a Tarantino-esque mélange of conga drums, wah-wah pedals, wide-lapeled gangsters, and towering Afros. Andy's character is intelligent and refined, hiding his intellect behind a veneer of folksy Southern charm. Andy had been perfecting this act since his arrival in New York, two decades earlier. The character worked; the movie didn't. ABC passed on the series.

The late 1970s were a frustrating time for Andy, who, at fifty, surely thought his best years were behind him. In an ironic moment, Andy reaped a star on the Hollywood Walk of Fame in April 1976, two months shy of the milestone birthday. Don Knotts would have to wait twenty-two more years for his star.

Andy was still trolling for another series. He starred in two NBC television movies in 1977 tailored to set the table for a weekly cop drama, with Andy cast as chief of another small-town police department. They posited Andy as Abel Marsh, a folksy, plainspoken law enforcer. Abel could easily be Andy Taylor, retired now and padding his Mayberry pension.

Sharon Spelman, the actress cast as Chief Abel's girlfriend, remembers Andy talking about Don and laughing, then, about his utter failure to collect so much as a single Emmy nomination to match Don's five awards. "But it was all very good-natured," she recalled, "and Andy was proud of Don." Perhaps Andy's competitive fire was beginning to cool.

Critics praised Andy's performances but mostly panned the films; this was becoming a trend. *Abel Marsh* would not be picked up.

Still desperate for another series, Andy signed on to star in an odd ABC pilot called *Salvage 1*. A product of that *Star Wars* era, *Salvage 1* was a genre-bending mishmash of science fiction, espionage, and Jack London adventure. Andy played Harry Broderick, a junk dealer who dared to dream big. How big? "I wanna build a spaceship, go to the moon, salvage all the junk that's up there, bring it back, and sell it," he pronounces in the two-hour premiere.

Reception was predictably mixed. *The New York Times* termed it "an upscale, white *Sanford & Son*," while the *Los Angeles Times* called it "so unreal, you half expect Don Knotts to come in and take over the controls."

Salvage 1 had already been approved as a series, so twelve more episodes aired in winter and spring of 1979. "I need this series," Andy told an interviewer. "I've got to make it work."

With *Salvage 1*, Andy happily resumed the brisk schedule of his *Andy Griffith Show* days, but with less booze and more sleep. He awakened at five thirty for a Moravian prayer, according to a *People* magazine feature, before turning to his script. He dressed and climbed into his '69 Rolls for the five-minute drive to the Burbank studio, where his RV awaited. Between setups, he snacked on crackers topped with peanut butter and mayonnaise. He sometimes indulged in a vodka gimlet at lunch. After work, he took a swim and worked out on the bedroom treadmill. He was generally in bed by nine o'clock.

With characteristic candor, Andy owned up to the interviewer that the previous decade had been one long dry spell: "I did five pilots that got nowhere, had two series that flopped. I went from pillar to post and became known as a character actor around town. A deep panic set in, mostly when I went down to North Carolina and after two weeks nothing came in the mail—no outlines, no scripts, no phone calls. The idea that the movie community was running along so beautifully without me—man, it drove me up the wall."

Pitted against NBC's endearing *Little House on the Prairie*, Andy's *Salvage 1* did not fare well. The network waffled on a potential second season. Studio heads finally settled on half a season, but then they pulled the plug after six episodes had been filmed. Once more, Andy was out of work.

In summer 1979, Don's manager, Sherwin Bash, called with astonishing news: the producers of *Three's Company*, ABC's smash sitcom, wanted Don to join their cast.

By the late 1970s, coeducational living had spread from college campuses to urban apartments; yet, to many older adults, such domestic arrangements still shocked. *Three's Company* had pushed the boundaries of sexuality and good taste on prime-time television with a story built upon the tension among three platonic, mixed-gender, twentysomething roommates and their landlord, a man of Archie Bunker's generation. For landlord Stanley Roper to accept Jack Tripper as a new roommate for young lovelies Janet Wood and Chrissy Snow, Roper first had to be persuaded, ironically, that Jack was gay. *Three's Company* was otherwise a classic comedy of errors, with much of the humor arising from one character seeing or hearing some innocent exchange and investing it with sexual double entendre.

In the third year, the ABC producers persuaded Norman Fell and Audra Lindley to depart *Three's Company* for a spin-off titled *The Ropers*. The season ended without a landlord, and the producers spent the summer shopping for a replacement. They wrote a new character named Ralph Furley, a sort of anemic Hugh Hefner, a man two or three decades older than Jack Tripper but with all of Jack's romantic ambition. They auditioned hundreds of actors, looking for someone suitably vain, overwrought, and self-delusional—looking, in short, for someone like Don Knotts.

"Every day there would be this line of characters coming in. The line would get smaller, and eventually there would be no line, and no Mr. Furley," recalled Kim Weiskopf, a *Three's*

Company writer. "Finally they said, 'Has anybody called Don Knotts?' "

The producers were so sure of the casting that they did not subject Don to the customary audition. The network simply made him an offer.

In the decade since Don's fifth and final *Griffith Show* Emmy win, his star had only risen within the industry. Still, Don couldn't believe he was being invited to join ABC's hottest show. His new costars couldn't believe it, either.

"He was a legend in his own time," recalled Joyce DeWitt, whose prim Janet was the closest thing to a straight man on *Three's Company*. "The first day he came in, we sat down to the table to read, and John [Ritter] and I are reaching over and pinching each other."

The young actors didn't just know Don, they idolized him. "I was totally aware of the fact that the man had won five Emmys," recalled Richard Kline, who played Jack's sleazy wingman, Larry. "And I had watched him in the old *Steve Allen Show*, so I was very familiar with the Nervous Guy."

For all his accolades, Don was intimidated. He had never done a sitcom taped before a live audience, apart from a few failed pilots and guest appearances. Multicamera comedies demanded a different sort of acting from methodical, single-camera shows such as *Andy Griffith*. Much as the rest of the cast admired him, Don felt it was he who had to measure up. "Everybody was good, and I knew it," Don recalled. "And everybody was a lot younger than me."

He needn't have worried. When Don walked onto the soundstage for the first time, the audience applauded for "what seemed to be about ten minutes," one producer recalled.

Don's first scene in "The New Landlord," broadcast on September 25, 1979, has him enter the Regal Beagle—the neighborhood fern bar that serves as a secondary set on *Three's Company* —wearing a blue, patchwork polyester suit to match his eyes. He orders Scotch and root beer, does his trademark snort, and sips the drink. Then his eyes bug out and he chokes, "Could ya put a little more root beer in there?"

Ralph Furley approaches Janet and Chrissy. He means to introduce himself as their new landlord, but the women assume he is merely hitting on them.

"Guess what I am?" Don crows, after trying and failing to hoist his leg over the back of the chair.

"I don't have to guess what you are," Janet sneers.

"Whatever he is," Chrissy observes, "he's a funny-looking one."

The trio milk the misunderstanding, Don assuring the ladies, "Just think how safe you're gonna feel when you go to bed at night, knowing I'll be sleeping right underneath you."

Mayberry this was not.

Don's nerves subsided after a few episodes. His repertoire of facial tics was tailor-made for a program built upon misapprehension and shock. Don soon found he could keep pace—just—with John Ritter's frenetic, knee-cracking physical humor. "I was doing falls I'd never done before," Don recalled.

Producers outfitted the aging swinger in a kaleidoscope of polyester. His arrival at the tenants' apartment would often be their first glimpse of what Don was wearing that week. "And God forbid you were the one who had to answer that door," Joyce DeWitt recalled. "He would be standing there with absolute innocence on his face, knowing that he was about to kill you."

Behind the macho bluster, Ralph Furley was a prude. In the episode "Chrissy's Hospitality," broadcast November 13, 1979, Jack helps Chrissy install a shower curtain. Furley arrives and over-hears the following exchange inside the closed bathroom, with mounting horror:

Jack: "Okay, Chrissy, I'll get in the tub with you, then we can get it on."

Chrissy: "Get next to me, I'll show you what to do. . . . I don't think it'll reach."

Jack: "Of course not, you've gotta unfold it first."

The two emerge from the bathroom and

encounter Janet, wearing a skimpy nightie. "Hey, what's goin' on?" she asks. "I thought we were all gonna go to bed together."

Furley explodes. "Aha! I knew it! Now, you listen to me. This is a respectable place. No Roman orgies here, or else," he cries, with a sweep of his hand.

Three's Company ended its fourth season ranked second in the Nielsens. Don's star rose further during season five—at the expense of Suzanne Somers, who was gradually being written out of the show. Somers was in a public standoff with the network over pay; she began missing episodes. By season's end, her character was reduced to a humiliating weekly telephone conversation, as if she were in sitcom prison.

"They started writing a little looser for me, a little crazier stuff," Don recalled. "That's when my character began to take off."

Yet, Don empathized with Somers, who was, in his view, being punished for seeking a raise, a scenario Don himself had experienced a decade earlier with the producers of *The Andy Griffith Show*. He didn't like the way the rest of the cast was shunning her. One day, he strode up to John and Joyce and said, "Excuse me, I'm going to go talk to Suzanne." Later, Don traveled to Las Vegas to help Somers launch her solo act.

By the time of *Three's Company*, Don's second marriage was on the wane. Son Tom returned from a trip to Europe in summer 1977 to find that his father had fled to an apartment in Malibu. "I've got a pad at the beach," he explained to his son, sounding like a teenager himself.

Loralee recalled that she and Don had led "a much smaller life than most people would think," keeping mostly to themselves. "Going out in places with the kids and me, that was hard, because he was basically a shy person. He did not like being trapped in public places. People expected him to be funny and tell jokes." At such times, Don would beseech Loralee to fend off the crowds: "I've got a nice-guy complex," he would say, "so you've got to be the bad guy."

Don's neuroses had fed mostly on unfounded fears and phantom ills. Now, well into his fifties, Don faced a real and potentially crippling malady. On a trip to Hawaii around 1980, Don gazed out at the horizon from the hotel patio and told Loralee, "Gee, it's funny how it's so curly." Doctors diagnosed macular degeneration, a deterioration of the retina that causes loss of sight in the center of the field of vision. In time, the disease would compromise Don's ability to read scripts and navigate sets.

For Don's marriage, this was a fatal blow. "When he started to lose his vision, I think he just panicked, and he started to live out some sort of bucket list," Loralee recalled. Don began to stray. In spring 1984, she filed for divorce.

Andy had separated from his own second wife, Solica, well before their 1981 divorce. The parting was bitter; Andy deeply resented handing over assets to Solica. "He never said a kind word [about her] after that," recalled Quentin Bell, Andy's friend.

In 1978, Andy struck up a friendship with a lovely, elfin-featured dancer named Cindi Knight. Cindi was a high school English teacher—a real-life Helen Crump!—from Jacksonville, Florida, and a summer performer in Andy's beloved *Lost Colony* production. Cindi had joined the company in 1976 as a dancer. By 1978, she was an understudy for Eleanor Dare, the same part played by Andy's first wife, Barbara, almost a generation earlier. Cindi and Andy met at a volleyball game. Cindi was twenty-two, nearly three decades younger than Andy, whose age had not yet caught up with him. Over the next five years, Andy and Cindi would become inseparable.

Professionally, the 1970s ended in frustration for Andy with the failure of his *Salvage 1* series, and the next decade began with yet another setback. One day in early 1980, Andy climbed to the roof of the old Bing Crosby home to repair a leak. As he worked, Andy watched his tools slide down the roof. "Then, I started to slide off," he recalled. I made one lunge for a big tree limb, missed, and hit the ground in a sitting position twenty feet later. I felt an extraordinary pain going through my whole body. Then, I passed out."

The impact fractured Andy's back and shaved a quarter inch off his height. Bizarrely, Andy found himself hospitalized in the same wing as Barbara, his ex-wife, who was dying of cancer, according to Bridget Sweeney, daughter of *Griffith* director Bob Sweeney: "He said it was the worst karma he ever felt." Andy visited his former spouse on her deathbed more than once, according to friend Quentin Bell, but Barbara didn't recognize him.

Barbara died on July 23, 1980, at fifty-three, of a brain tumor. It was a "rough death," nephew Robert recalled, and the experience drove her daughter, Dixie, into a career of hospice care. Barbara's will instructed that her former husband not benefit in any material way from her passing, such was her ire for Andy at the end, according to nephew Mike King. The Griffith name does not appear on her tombstone. Yet Andy was grateful that Barbara chose to leave her estate—most of it earned by Andy—to their children, Sam and Dixie.

Don was deeply moved at how Andy, in Don's view, had stuck by Barbara through the years of decline. Andy spoke well of her to the end. "She had some problems with alcohol," Andy told an interviewer, years later. "And anyhow . . ." His voice trailed off.

For nearly two decades, Andy's career had been his life and Barbara's, too. He had lived those years "surrounded by himself," as Barbara put it, and she never found a way back to the man she had married.

Andy spent several months in Manteo recuperating from his injury. When he returned to Hollywood, Cindi Knight followed. Andy and Cindi were now a couple. He helped her get a bit part in his next film.

Andy was cast in the NBC production *Murder in Texas*, a film treatment of a true-crime bestseller about the mysterious deaths of a celebrated Houston plastic surgeon and his wife. In yet another impressive cast, rugged Sam Elliott plays John Hill, the surgeon who discreetly poisons his wife (a ponytailed Farrah Fawcett) and runs off with his mistress (Katharine Ross, a decade past *The Graduate*). Andy portrays the vengeful father, who sacrifices everything to bring his former son-in-law to justice.

For his efforts, Andy earned an Emmy nomination, the only one of his life. Alas, he did not win. Andy told the *Atlanta Journal-Constitution*, "I've never won anything in my life and I don't expect to. I'm not angry about that." He joked, "It would be nice to have one when my mother comes over, or a cousin comes to visit. But I can manage without it."

Andy's run of strong roles continued in 1983

with *Murder in Coweta County*, the true story of a corrupt 1940s Georgia landowner who operates above the law—until he inadvertently kills a man in an adjoining county. The murder pits bad-guy Andy against Johnny Cash, a formidable foil as Sheriff Lamar Potts.

Momentum was building in Andy's moribund career, and he had found true love.

Andy and Cindi married in April 1983. In a modest and impromptu affair, ten guests were summoned to the living room of Andy's Manteo estate, some of them invited that same day. Andy's children, Dixie and Sam, were not among them, nor was Don. After a five-minute ceremony, Andy telephoned a local seafood restaurant and booked a table for lunch, according to the *National Enquirer*. The arrangements were odd, although not by the standards of Hollywood celebrity; Andy's passion for privacy would follow him to the grave.

After the wedding, Andy and Cindi flew to Los Angeles, where Andy contracted a flu. Days passed, and the flu gave way to "terrible, searing pain that ricocheted through my entire body," Andy recalled. On May 7, after watching the Kentucky Derby on television, Andy stood up and fell back down, suddenly unable to control his feet. At the hospital, doctors diagnosed Guillain-Barré syndrome, an inflammatory nerve condition that causes pain and paralysis.

Doctors told him they could do nothing: "You've got to ride it out." Andy found the pain "so consuming that there was nothing else in my life." He spent a month in daily sessions of physical therapy and pain management. Then came a moment, Andy recalled, when "the therapist working on me saw one of my toes move." The paralysis began to lift, and doctors slowly weaned Andy off pain medications.

But it took nearly a year for Andy to recuperate. He couldn't work, and, as a fifty-seven-year-old invalid, he feared he might never work again.

The Griffiths were nearly broke. They put the old Bing Crosby estate up for sale, and Andy thought of selling his beloved antique cars. By the end of 1983, Andy recalled, "I sat in our unsold house with no bank account to speak of, and no work in sight."

14.

The Gentleman Lawyer

In years past, faithful Dick Linke had swept in to rescue Andy Griffith from the occasional bumps in his deeply rutted career. This time, it was Cindi Griffith.

Andy found his professional life at an impasse. He was ready to cut his losses and crawl back to Manteo, presumably for good. Cindi saw past the obstacles in Andy's path. To her it seemed that the setbacks had sapped Andy's self-confidence, a quality he had always been able to tap in the past. Sell his antique cars? That seemed an over-reaction verging on panic. Ever so delicately, Cindi talked her husband off the ledge.

"Maybe it's a good thing we couldn't sell the house," she reasoned. "Maybe it was God showing us grace. If we moved to North Carolina now, you might indeed never work again. What we need to do is stay here and stoke the fire."

Cindi's allusion to God signaled a shift in the couple's beliefs. The protracted illness had set Andy and Cindi to thinking more seriously about their faith. Andy had always been a spiritual man, but after the year of faith-testing pain, religion loomed at the center of his thoughts. Hereafter, Andy was apt to invoke the name of the creator in casual conversation. His religious zeal would set Andy apart from many of his Hollywood peers. Yet, for a new generation of tradition-minded, churchgoing fans of *The Andy Griffith Show*, the change would have quite the opposite effect.

Emboldened by Cindi's pep talk, Andy reached back to the dogged routine that had served both him and Don so well three decades earlier in New York: making the rounds. "That day, and every day for quite a while," Andy recalled, "Cindi and I went over to the William Morris Agency at lunchtime and sat in the lobby. My agent and every agent in the building saw us. Everybody talked to us, invited us to their offices, some to lunch."

Cindi bade farewell to her theatrical career, just as Barbara had to hers. Andy's career became her life.

Andy had reconnected with a wide swath of the American public in the late 1970s as the spokesman for Ritz crackers. ("Mmm-mmm. Good cracker."). In 1984, he resurfaced as the face of AT&T. With stories of paralysis circulating in Hollywood, Andy secured a guest spot on the television drama series *Hotel*, a role that required him to jog. He wore leg braces; the effort was agony, but he hid it, and the resulting scene quashed the rumors.

The journeyman actor had spent a dozen years refining a new character, someone with all of Andy Taylor's gravitas and wit but with other, darker traits thrown in. He had played a tough-love priest in *Go Ask Alice*, a psychopath in *Pray for the Wildcats*, a wary prosecutor in *Street Killing*, a vengeful father in *Murder in Texas*, and, most recently, a gay cattle baron in the Western spoof *Rustlers' Rhapsody*. They weren't all good movies, but thanks to Andy's obsession with craft, they were mostly good performances.

With the 1984 television miniseries *Fatal Vision*, Andy's new persona was complete. He played Victor Worheide, a federal prosecutor assigned to go after a military doctor accused of murdering his family. In Andy's first scene, grieving father Karl Malden walks in to find Andy unceremoniously clipping his toenails. In reply to Karl's desperate entreaties, Andy growls, "So what do we have here? I'll tell you what we don't have. We have no confession. We have no apparent motive. We have no witnesses. And any attempt to convict this man is unlikely to succeed."

Brandon Tartikoff, president of NBC Entertainment, saw Andy's performance and immediately envisioned the character at the center of a television series. The success of *Murder, She Wrote* for aging film star Angela Lansbury had set the networks to wonder what other graying thespians might be ready to pilot their own murder mysteries.

"Andy was a remarkable actor. They had never really given him his due," recalled Dean Hargrove, a television writer and producer who had piloted many successful *Columbo* episodes in the 1970s. Dean was assigned, along with fellow producer Fred Silverman, to create a new show for Andy. They called it *Matlock.*

As a template for Ben Matlock, Dean studied colorful Southern defense attorneys, men such as Percy Foreman, who reputedly handled fifteen hundred death-penalty cases and lost only fifty-three. "He always got his money in advance," Dean says of Foreman. "He once saw a woman in a restaurant who owed him money, and he ripped the necklace off her neck." Dean sketched out the character to an exultant Andy, who hid his leg braces beneath boots. Dick Linke negotiated a sweet deal for his client: $200,000 an episode, or nearly $5 million a year.

Andy's first scene in the pilot, "Diary of a Perfect Murder," places him in a courtroom, wearing a gray seersucker suit and delivering a closing argument. Ben Matlock is defending an accused murderer, and this is his last chance to seed "reasonable doubt." In a bold tack, Matlock announces that the murdered man is in fact alive, and that he is about to enter the courtroom. It's a bluff—but now Matlock has everyone's attention.

"Each and every one of you was staring at that door because you had a reasonable doubt that a crime was even committed," Matlock drawls. "And you must let this man go free. He was staring at that door as hard as you were. And so were they," he says, pointing over to the prosecution table.

Ben Matlock is a venerable Atlanta defense attorney whose just-folks persona conceals a fierce intellect. He hates to lose almost as much as he hates injustice. He's cheap enough to shine his own shoes, and sufficiently mercenary to shake down a client for his last $100,000. "Look at it this way, Steve," Matlock reasons with his client. "If I win, it'll be worth it. If I don't, then they take you to the Georgia Diagnostic Classification Center, over near Jackson, and they electrocute you."

The pilot, broadcast March 3, 1986, set up a formula for 193 episodes to come: Ben Matlock agrees to represent a murder defendant— reluctantly, because he harbors a thinly veiled dislike for the defendant or thinks the case unwinnable. Then he commences his own murder investigation, aided by a small but plucky team that doesn't play by the rules. He identifies and eventually confronts the real murderer, who scoffs; Matlock has no proof. Then, just before the final commercial, Matlock finds the proof, which he unveils dramatically in the epic final court-room scene. The judge releases Matlock's innocent client as the real killer is led from the stand.

The crew traveled to Atlanta to establish *Matlock*'s setting. The fall 1985 trip coincided with the twenty-fifth anniversary of the first episode of *The Andy Griffith Show*. Already, the tenth and twentieth *Griffith* anniversaries had passed with little fanfare. Now, Andy's and Don's crowning achievement was a quarter century old, and no one seemed to care.

But behind the scenes, nostalgia was taking root. In 1979, three fraternity brothers at Vanderbilt University had formed The Andy Griffith Show Rerun Watchers Club as a way to get dibs on the dwelling's lone television set. A decade later, the club would count twenty thousand members in five hundred chapters. In 1981, English professor Richard Kelly published *The Andy Griffith Show*, one of the first serious book-length studies of a television series. In 1984, teenager John Meroney organized the Andy Griffith Show Appreciation Society, whose membership reportedly once included George Herbert Walker Bush. In his youthful zeal, Meroney set out to find a real town that would change its name to Mayberry to mark the coming twenty-fifth anniversary.

Andy swiftly halted John Meroney's plan. "This whole idea of searching for a town to change its name to Mayberry is enormously embarrassing to me," he told the *Winston-Salem Sentinel*.

Slapping down a fourteen-year-old boy was not, perhaps, how Sheriff Taylor would have handled it. But it wasn't the last time Andy would block someone's seemingly benevolent memorial to Mayberry. At such times, he seemed steered by a passionate mix of emotions: proprietary indignation that others might seek to profit from his Mayberry brand, and a powerful impulse to protect the legacy of *The Andy Griffith Show*. Call it quality control, or micromanagement, or simple possessiveness, but nobody was going to celebrate Mayberry without Andy's blessing.

As far back as 1972, Andy and Don had discussed reuniting the *Griffith* cast, but "they both agreed that unless it could be great, they didn't want to do it," recalled Loralee Knotts, Don's second wife. By 1985, Andy had a new incentive. He had waited two decades for another hit series, and with the *Matlock* pilot, he had his best shot yet. A hit reunion show might help persuade NBC executives to green-light *Matlock*. And with *Griffith* nostalgia mounting, a reunion would surely find an audience.

Two surviving *Griffith* writers, Everett Greenbaum and Harvey Bullock, were enlisted to collaborate on a script. Andy himself spent six weeks on rewrites. Beloved Bob Sweeney returned to direct.

In February 1986, the *Griffith* principals traveled to Southern California wine country to begin shooting *Return to Mayberry*. They had little trouble rounding up the surviving cast—including Jim Nabors, with whom Andy had patched things up after a lengthy chill. The exception was Frances Bavier, Aunt Bee. The official explanation was illness, but Frances simply wasn't interested in returning to Mayberry. She refused to record even a few lines to be played, like a voice-over from beyond, in a scene that had Andy visit her grave. She particularly disliked a line that instructed Andy to "always wear clean underwear." She said, "I will not say *underwear*. I have never said *underwear*, and I will not say *underwear* now." Most cast and crew "weren't all that unhappy that she declined," recalled Dean Hargrove, an executive producer of the reunion show.

The Mayberry pecking order had changed in a quarter century. Ron Howard was now the ascendant director of *Splash* and *Cocoon*; he arrived at the *Return to Mayberry* set as head of his own production company. Don Knotts, by contrast, had fallen off the radar since the conclusion of *Three's Company*. His only notable film credit since 1980 had been a minor part in the Burt Reynolds comedy *Cannonball Run II*, a brief but rewarding reunion with Tim Conway and an orangutan.

If not superstars, Andy and Don at least remained visible. Jim Nabors, on the other hand, had retreated into semiretirement in Hawaii. George Lindsey hadn't made much of an impact since his Goober days. "When I got to the location for the first day of shooting of the movie," George recalled, "I went up to the motel room where Andy and his wife, Cindi, were staying. We visited for a little while and then Andy said, 'Well, Cindi and I are going to get a cheeseburger,' and they just left me there. That was about the tone for me on the set for the rest of the shoot."

The others went home with mostly fond memories. Andy and Don shared a dirty joke on the set, and for the first time they told it to Ron, who was finally old enough to hear it. Ron talked for hours with Andy—interviewed him, really, about his memories of running *The Andy Griffith Show*, asking all the questions he had never thought to pose on the old Mayberry set. Andy told Ron he never realized at the time "how personal the show was," how closely Andy Taylor's milieu mirrored his own.

Mayberry fans flocked to Los Olivos for the nineteen-day shoot, along with a throng of journalists—so many that the producers finally closed the set.

Return to Mayberry was part movie, part reunion show—and on those terms, it far exceeded Andy's dim hopes. The writers wisely built the story around the friendship between

Andy and Barney. A quarter century on, the deputy has ascended to acting sheriff of Mayberry, while Andy has left town to be a postal inspector in Cleveland. He returns with thoughts of running for sheriff again, only to find that Don already seeks the vacant seat.

The narrative is sufficiently thin to indulge ample moments of Mayberry nostalgia: Two versions of the old *Griffith* theme song play, one of them jazzed up for the Reagan eighties, and the *Mayberry R.F.D.* theme is tossed in for good measure. Opie now runs the town newspaper; Otis has sobered up and drives an ice cream truck. Andy and Barney escort Helen and Thelma Lou on a double date. Andy spends much of his screen time racing around town trying to protect Barney from harm and from himself, invoking memories of the sheriff at his most noble.

The story concludes with Barney and Thelma Lou marrying at last, setting right the grave injustice of her character's wedding another man twenty years earlier in "The Return of Barney Fife." Rance Howard plays the minister.

At the reception, Andy toasts the couple with words surely meant for Don and his other friends on the *Griffith* cast: "There's something about Mayberry and Mayberry folk that never leaves you. No matter where life takes you, you always carry in your heart the memories of old times and old friends. So here's to all of us. Old friends."

The toast—and the tears—were real. *"Return to Mayberry* was the nicest thing Andy could have done for anybody," recalled Mitch Jayne, of the Dillards, the bluegrass ensemble Andy had discovered and promoted on the *Griffith Show* two decades earlier. "It told people that he had never forgotten the place, or the people who had loved him for creating it. He wanted to say good-bye to it in the best way he could come up with because, like all of us, he was moving on."

As the credits roll, Andy and Barney lower the flag and walk off down the street, side by side.

Broadcast on April 13, 1986, *Return to Mayberry* reached 28 million homes, making it the most watched television movie of the year. Andy Griffith was on a roll. His *Matlock* pilot, "Diary of a Perfect Murder," had aired on March 3 and reached 21 million homes. "We were in," Dean Hargrove recalled.

The celebration was short-lived. A month after the Mayberry reunion, Andy flew back to Hollywood to bury his mother. Geneva Griffith died on May 13, 1986, at age eighty-six, of heart failure.

That summer, production began on *Matlock*, and Andy resumed the grueling weekly schedule of study, rehearsal, and filming that had governed his life on *The Andy Griffith Show* for most of the 1960s. Andy had been thirty-four when *Griffith* went on the air. Now he was sixty, and coming to work in leg braces.

Andy would spend Saturday and Sunday mornings rehearsing his climactic courtroom scene till he had it memorized. He would carry around little prompts scrawled on note cards in his left hand. The scenes were long and taxing; when they were over, and the cameras were off, Andy often reaped a standing ovation.

"The whole set was filled. And I bet you ninety-eight percent of the time, he did it on the first take," recalled Nancy Stafford, Andy's longest-serving *Matlock* costar.

Andy learned the scenes by treating each as an extended monologue, like his *Hamlet* and football sketches of three decades earlier. "That was his secret," Nancy recalled. "He wasn't waiting for somebody to give their reply. If you go back and watch some of the shows after you get that in your head, you can see he steamrolls, sometimes, right through someone's answer."

Joel Steiger, a young television writer, joined *Matlock* as a producer. Like Dean Hargrove, Joel deeply admired Andy, especially for *A Face in the Crowd*, a film that had aged well. "There are those people who believe that Andy's performance in that movie is one of the greatest sustained performances ever given in a movie," Joel said.

Matlock aired at 8:00 p.m. Tuesday nights, opposite ABC's *Who's the Boss?* and *Growing Pains*, both top-ten shows in the 1986–87 season. "Our job was to come in a strong second," Joel recalled. "And we did it, forever. We knew almost immediately that this show was going to be successful and was going to continue."

Andy's new show would end its first season tied for fifteenth in the Nielsen ratings, and it would place fourteenth the following year.

Success on *Matlock* allowed Andy to finally escape the rut of the previous eighteen years, hustling from job to job and enduring lengthy spells of no work at all. Andy credited Dean Hargrove with turning his career around; the producer now found himself the subject of almost unhealthy adoration from his star. "He was enormously appreciative," Dean recalled, "because his career at that point was pretty moribund. This series was really bringing him back to life."

Matlock animated Andy's tired frame. A few months into production, he threw off the leg braces he'd worn for three years. "They squeaked, and the soundmen could hear them," he joked.

Two decades earlier, producers of *The Andy Griffith Show* had labored to find the right love interest for their star. Now, on *Matlock*, they struggled to find Andy's character a suitable daughter. Lori Lethin had played attorney Charlene Matlock in the pilot, only to be replaced by Linda Purl in the next episode. A year later, Linda was gone. Season two of *Matlock* opened in London and featured yet another female lead:

Nancy Stafford, a seasoned actress and former Miss Florida. This time, producers tried a different tack: Nancy's character would be Ben Matlock's protégé, but not his daughter.

"He was always, always singing," Nancy recalled of Andy. "You could hear him walk out of the makeup trailer onto the soundstage, humming. And he'd walk back into his trailer, and he was singing. I think one of the things I learned from him was just a great affection for the work. He was happiest, I think, when he was working."

At first, Andy had little or no say in the *Matlock* scripts. In time, though, Andy's confidence grew and he began to assert himself on the set. Andy's writing had lifted the quality of *The Andy Griffith Show*; here, finally, was a chance for him to flex his artistic ambitions on another character he loved.

But a lot had changed in the two decades since *Griffith*; by the late 1980s, television networks wielded enormous influence on the direction of successful shows. To a much greater extent, script-writing was executed by formula and over-seen by men and women with business degrees.

"When I was doing the *Griffith Show*, the network was only your host," Andy recalled. "They came down once a year to say hello. . . . When the network gained control and they put all these children in these offices, it all went to hell then." He added wistfully, "It was all so easy in the early days. It was just Sheldon and Aaron and me and Don."

On the *Griffith Show*, Andy was accustomed to rewriting lines he didn't like. Now, Andy found that the balance of power had shifted. And he found himself clashing with Dean Hargrove, the man who had rekindled his career.

Dean was a seasoned television mystery writer; Andy was not. Dean was happy to allow his star to tinker with his character's mannerisms and to craft the occasional joke. He would not let Andy alter the course of a story.

"His ideas of comedy were unparalleled," Dean recalled. "When it had to do more with the plot, the mystery, that was when we'd tend to stay with what we had. It would be like trying to pull the threads out of a sweater."

Andy harbored enormous ambitions for *Matlock*, and he shared them with Don. He envisioned Ben Matlock as a sort of antihero, more complex than Andy Taylor, vain, uncultured, cheap, and vaguely unlikable. He imagined Matlock struggling with alcohol addiction, getting thrown out of court, tossed into jail. He wanted Matlock to jam with Atlanta bluesmen.

Andy approached Dean—and later, Joel—with hundreds of ideas for *Matlock*. Some they liked; most they didn't. Andy would always argue his case, and sometimes he would yell. Dean would stand there and take it, the very picture of propriety, until Andy had said his piece. Then Dean would calmly proceed with the show. In one of the more heated exchanges, Dean rejected one of Andy's suggestions with "I don't think that's right for the show." Andy shot back, "That's because you don't know anything about comedy, Dean!"

It was Andy who imbued *Matlock* with humor. Over its nine-year run, *Matlock* became an increasingly whimsical series, with the formality of early episodes giving way to a looser, warmer, more Southern style. The humor was often subtle: a raised eyebrow or gentle groan when Matlock heard something he didn't like, or a drawn-out "Noooo," just like Barney Fife used to do it. Ben Matlock didn't make viewers laugh: He made them smile.

"He loved to invent bits," Nancy Stafford recalled. "The shoe-shining bit was his, and the hot-dog-eating bit was his. And after he'd invented these bits and they'd show up in the script, he'd do this very fake but quite dramatic act of complaining, right as we were shooting a scene: 'Why did I invent this? Why do I have to eat another hot dog?' The very bits that became his character's most lovable quirks—and that Andy created—he would disparage them when he was on the set."

Andy was no prima donna, but he was a man of routine, and his producers knew better than to tamper with it. "Andy was very fond of peanut butter," Dean Hargrove recalled. The crew would set out peanut butter and apples for Andy. "And he would get distressed sometimes because people who were not part of the crew would come on and eat the peanut butter and the apples. Andy was a hawk-eye on it, too."

When he was down, Andy could be dour and petty. But when he was on top, Andy was the picture of magnanimity, lavishing favors—and parts—on his friends. As the *Matlock* franchise prospered, Andy began to import bits of Mayberry into *Matlock*. Betty "Thelma Lou" Lynn turned up as Matlock's secretary. Aneta "Helen Crump" Corsaut, Andy's former paramour, played a judge, as did *Griffith* writer Everett Greenbaum. Bob Sweeney, the beloved *Griffith* director, took the helm on two 1987 episodes. Andy even asked the producers to hire Aaron Ruben, the brilliant writer-producer from *Griffith*, to pen some jokes.

What Andy wanted most of all, though, was to work with his best friend. In 1988, before the start of *Matlock*'s third season, Andy approached Joel Steiger and said, "I'd like to put Don on the show."

Don had been out of movies and television for most of 1985 and 1986. Like Andy, Don was fending off rumors of ill health—in his case, a debilitating case of macular degeneration. His fortunes turned, though, not long after the Mayberry reunion, when Don got a call from a pair of former *Three's Company* writers. They were looking to insert him into another established series.

But *What a Country!* was no *Three's Company*. It was, instead, a modestly successful sitcom, set in a night school for immigrants and staged as a vehicle for Russian comic Yakov Smirnoff, whose catchphrase supplied its title. It was funny but derivative; the ensemble-of-goofballs formula had borne more fruit on *Taxi* and *Night Court*, and the classroom-of-goofballs scenario had worked better on *Welcome Back, Kotter.*

Don entered the production in midseason as the new principal of a school that seems to have only a single classroom, filled with ethnic stereotypes: the fiery Latina, the demure Asian American, the impoverished Indian American, and so forth. "You have something on your head," the Indian student says of Don's toupee as his character enters the class. "It looks like a little cap made of hair."

What a Country! would be canceled after a single season. But the production would launch a more enduring relationship between Don and a production assistant on the show.

Francey Yarborough, a beautiful, kind-hearted actress, had settled in Hollywood to pursue improvisational comedy. In early 1987, she was hired on *What a Country!* Her main job was to help Don learn his lines. She was in her twenties, and he was entering his sixties; yet, they were kindred spirits.

"We had an instant rapport," Francey recalled. "I was living kind of a goofy life, and so was he. We would just talk and talk and talk. He loved hearing stories about my family. He had a crazy family; I had a crazy family. He liked the nuances of people."

Don and Francey started going out to La Scala in Beverly Hills, trading stories and making each other laugh. After a few months, they were a couple. Francey moved into Don's Century City condo, a sort of *Love God*–styled bachelor pad to which Don had decamped after his divorce from Loralee.

"He was like a kid living in a big apartment," Francey recalled. "My first reaction to him was that he was so vulnerable. I'd never met someone so vulnerable."

By the time he met Francey, Don was leading a largely nocturnal existence, drinking too much and eating too little. He smoked to excess, stayed up too late, and found sleep only with the aid of pills. Yet, soon after he met Francey, Don abruptly stopped smoking. "One day he heard a wheeze," Francey recalled, "and he dropped his cigarette and never looked back."

It would take a much bigger scare, several years later, to drive Don away from the other vices.

Don's dimming vision made it hard for him to drive safely, and he found it increasingly difficult to read scripts. With his talents in less demand, Don filled his time with commercials and live theater. He could sell out a regional playhouse with ease. Don was doing *Last of the Red Hot Lovers* in Traverse City, Michigan, when Andy telephoned. "I've been watching the old shows," Andy said, "and I miss you and all the fun we had. It would be so nice if you would come on the show sometime."

Andy had called Don several times before, saying he was thinking of writing him into the show. Don didn't think Andy was serious; usually, it came to naught. But this time, Andy said he wanted to talk business. "And I realized then that he really meant business," Don recalled.

Joel Steiger, who was taking over day-to-day business on *Matlock*, watched the creeping "Mayberry-ization" with growing unease. Andy seemed intent on re-creating his greatest television success on *Matlock*, even if it imperiled the success of his comeback.

"He wanted to put Don on the show," Joel recalled. "I didn't know how we were going to use him, because Don as a character could really only be Andy's friend. So the question became, how do you work him into the script without compromising everything you're doing when you use him? We came to the conclusion that we would not use him in every episode. And we'd use him as a friend who stopped by the office, and stuff like that. . . . I didn't want to rip the show apart just to have Don in it."

NBC called a press conference to announce the reunion. "Don Knotts is the best comic actor I ever met," Andy said, beaming, "and I play straight for him better than any man in America."

Don appears at Ben Matlock's window in the season-three opener, "The Lemon," as Les Calhoun, self-described King of Plastics, a man who found prosperity by making "those little loops on your sneakers."

"There good money in it?" Matlock asks.

"Ate chop suey and wore lizard-skin shoes every day," Les replies.

Les sounded quite a bit like *Jess,* the name Andy called Don when they weren't acting. Don called Andy's character *Benj,* a close cousin of *Ange.*

Andy worked harder on this script than on any of the forty-eight that had preceded it. He leavened it with touches of the gentle country humor that he and Don had brought to the *Griffith Show*: no punch lines, just whimsical exchanges and bits of observational humor. In one memorable line, Matlock tells his graying friend, "You ever notice, when guys our age talk about the war, nobody asks which one?"

Matlock was hard work for Don, too. Rising at dawn was no easy task for a man accustomed to sleeping till noon.

Don's presence strained *Matlock*'s sturdy formula, just as Joel Steiger had predicted. Yet, it was the most fun either Don or Andy had had on a Hollywood set in a good long time.

For the season-four premiere, in fall 1989, Andy indulged another fantasy: bringing the cast and crew of *Matlock* to Manteo.

Andy's relationship with his longtime summer residence had evolved. In the fifties and sixties, he and Barbara had frolicked with other young couples in the sand and surf. In the post-Barbara seventies, Andy had partied with the boys. Now, ensconced with Cindi and slowed by age, Andy mostly kept to himself, walled off within his forest compound, living quietly and privately, though he still popped into Edward Greene's Christmas Shop or the local Ace Hardware from time to time. When autograph seekers appeared, it was usually Cindi who politely shooed them away. Most locals knew better than to approach them.

"We always gave Andy space," Edward Greene recalled. "When Andy wanted to shop on his own, he'd call me and he'd come in at eight o'clock, while my staff was vacuuming the shop and we were preparing to open."

Now, Andy persuaded the *Matlock* producers to film on location in the Outer Banks. Andy hired locals as crew and extras. "Everyone was vying to be cast in something, and a lot of them were," Edward Greene recalled. "It was the biggest thing that ever happened in the town."

"The Hunting Party," a story probably inspired by Andy's own excursions into the Carolina woods, captured scenes at the beach in Nags Head and on *The Lost Colony* grounds. At the end, Andy's real-life friends surround Matlock and demand photos, an ironic moment for all involved.

Toward the end of 1989, Andy took a call from Lee Greenway, his old friend. Lee said Frances Bavier was dying, and she wanted to talk to Andy. Frances had fallen out of touch with most of her old Mayberry colleagues. Ron Howard had once gone so far as to leave a note on the door of her Siler City home, never hearing a reply. Aunt Bee's relationship with Andy had been chilly for years, but they mended it the day Andy telephoned.

"I'm sorry we didn't get along better," she told him. "It was my fault. I wish we had." Frances died in December, the first of the principal *Griffith* actors to perish. She left a house filled with fourteen cats, and a Studebaker with four flat tires. No one from the *Griffith* cast attended her service.

The next year, Tanya Jones of the Surry Arts Council, a nonprofit based in Andy's birthplace, attended an auction of the Bavier estate. A tall man walked up, recognized her Mount Airy name tag, and introduced himself as Jim Clark, leader of The Andy Griffith Show Rerun Watchers Club.

At the dawn of the 1990s, Mayberry nostalgia was a booming business. The *Griffith Show* was airing on more than a hundred stations, including "superstations" WGN and TBS, saturating the nation. The typical fan was a man of Opie's baby-boom generation, earnestly videotaping his favorite childhood show so he could share it with his own children one day.

Jim told Tanya he was assembling a cast reunion in Charlotte to mark the thirtieth anniversary of the first *Griffith* episode. He asked her whether Mount Airy planned a similar observance. "I said that we absolutely were," Tanya recalled. In truth, there was no plan. Tanya returned to Mount Airy and began work on an event. Thus was Mayberry Days born.

The Charlotte cast reunion was set for Saturday, September 29, so Tanya selected Friday, September 28, as Mayberry Day. "We had zero budget—zero budget for an unknown event," she recalled. "We didn't have hotels then. We didn't have tourism support then. The infrastructure was not there." Her expectations were correspondingly low. Then came a story in *The Atlanta Journal-Constitution*, noting the new festival in Andy's hometown. "I started getting phone calls from *The Washington Post*, *The Baltimore Sun*, all these major newspapers."

The Mount Airy of 1990 lay largely untouched

by time or tourism. Shop windows displayed few references to Andy Griffith or his show, and the telephone book held only a modest number of Mayberrys. The Snappy Lunch, one of Andy's teenage haunts, was very nearly the only surviving business that had ever been referenced on *The Andy Griffith Show*. But something in all that was charming, authentic. And in 1990, many still-living Mount Airians had genuine Andy Griffith stories to share.

By the time the press and the public rolled in, shopkeepers had dutifully pasted photographs of Andy and Barney all over the historic downtown, and Russell Hiatt's barbershop had been rechristened as Floyd's. The city paid $1,400 for a vintage 1962 Ford Galaxie and had it detailed to resemble Andy Taylor's squad car.

A couple hundred people gathered outside the old city hall for the opening ceremony, joined by a phalanx of reporters. Mount Airy's mayor arrived gamely dressed as Mayor Stoner, his Mayberry counterpart, and members of the Mount Airy High School chorus sang the *Andy Griffith* theme a cappella while snapping their fingers.

The next day, Jim Clark's fan club hosted twelve hundred Mayberry fans in Charlotte for a cast reunion, billed as the largest public gathering of its sort to date.

Andy attended neither event. "He's not doing any interviews," manager Dick Linke barked to

The Washington Post. "He just can't be there, and he doesn't have time to talk about it."

Tanya Jones and her bluff would spawn an $80 million tourist industry in little Surry County, with 95 percent of it lavished on Mount Airy.

Matlock remained a consistent top-twenty draw through five seasons. NBC's sales department would target the series from time to time because of its graying fan base; the demographic squabbles that had pulled *Mayberry R.F.D.* off the air two decades earlier had not yet subsided. But Dean Hargrove and, later, Joel Steiger managed to fend off the attacks, emboldened by the ratings. *Matlock* was becoming a part of popular culture. For good or ill, Andy and his program became synonymous with the over-sixty crowd, a point frequently noted on the irreverent animated sitcom *The Simpsons.**

In *Matlock*'s fifth season, Andy Griffith began broadcasting his intent to leave the program the following spring. "I'm financially comfortable. I'm in my sixties, and there's no reason to stay around," Andy told *TV Guide.* For anyone old enough to remember, it was a familiar routine. Andy had threatened to leave *The Andy Griffith Show* in season five, and again in season seven,

---

*In one *Simpsons* episode, the mayor of the fictional town of Springfield renames a local thoroughfare the Matlock Expressway to court the elderly vote.

before actually exiting after season eight. Each time, CBS had offered a staggering sum, and Andy had stayed.

Now, NBC executives persuaded Andy to return for another season of *Matlock*, promising him more latitude to break with the courtroom-drama formula and inject his own gentle comedy into the scripts.

But *Matlock* lacked the cachet of *Griffith*. In the spring of 1991, Andy learned his program had been left off the schedule for that fall. *Matlock* had been relegated to the status of a relief pitcher, idling in the bull pen and awaiting a spot in the lineup. Fresh from that insult, fashionista Mr. Blackwell placed Andy on his worst-dressed list. Cindi clipped the article from *TV Guide*, hoping Andy wouldn't see it. By October, two flagging NBC shows were out and *Matlock* was back in. Once again, Andy vowed that the season would be his last, and the complicated dance played on.

Cindi Griffith was a regular and welcome presence on the *Matlock* set, keeping Andy company and fussing about his health. "She was his greatest fan; she adored everything he said," costar Nancy Stafford recalled. "She laughed continuously. I felt he had a little extra lilt in his step when she was around. She protected him, in a wonderful way that you would want your spouse to protect you."

Andy, in turn, fussed over Don. "Don's eyesight

was failing," Dean Hargrove recalled, "and Andy was enormously protective of him. I think we had oversized scripts made." It was the same impulse that had driven Andy, three decades earlier on the *Griffith Show*, to demand that Don have his own seat at the writing table.

Nancy Stafford recalled a "crackle of excitement" when the cast and crew knew Don would be joining Andy for a *Matlock* episode. "That was one of those rare occasions when people from other soundstages, from other shows, would start migrating toward our stage. You had executives coming from the Black Tower at Universal."

Off the soundstage, Andy and Don would fall into their old *Griffith* routines. "Their off-camera antics were just hysterical," Nancy recalled. "They had been together so long. They knew each other's rhythms. They fell into this kind of banter. Nobody could make Andy laugh like Don. They would start singing. They would do these little riffs."

Some of the fun came at Don's expense. Once Andy, in his trailer, took one of *Matlock*'s neckties and whipped it at Don's posterior, over and over, shattering his quiet dignity. Another time, Don's hand accidentally brushed against the hindquarters of a female costar. He swiftly apologized. Andy broke into a devilish grin and said, "Now, Don, you've gotta know the rules around here."

Backstage, Andy would rant to Don about the

simmering conflict with his producers. When Andy would offer rewrites, the producers received them coolly, ever fretful that Andy was trying to turn *Matlock* into *The Andy Griffith Show*. Andy would ask Don, "When did the accountants get control of show business?"

Don and his manic energy had often carried the *Griffith Show*. Andy just as surely carried *Matlock*, appearing in nearly every scene and speaking half the lines. It seemed to Don that Andy had grown more serious, and more grandiose, in his autumn years. Finally, a quarter century after *Griffith*, Andy again dwelled at the center of his own hit show.

At the close of *Matlock*'s sixth season, the character of Les Calhoun was quietly retired. Don and Andy conceded what the producers had thought all along. "It didn't work," Andy recalled. "*Matlock* wasn't like the *Griffith Show*. You couldn't stop for these little comedy scenes that didn't go anywhere."

By the 1990s, Don's habit of medicating himself to sleep had escalated into a ritual that sometimes blurred the lines between night and day: he was sinking into a retread of the cycle of insomnia and pills that had nearly destroyed him before he ever reached Hollywood. One afternoon in spring 1991, Francey came home and found she couldn't awaken Don. He had just changed from one brand of pills to another, more toxic variety. This time, he had inadvertently taken a few too many.

Francey dialed 911. Rescuers rushed Don to the hospital, where he awoke an hour later. Still groggy, Don tried to convince the doctors it was a fluke. Francey persuaded them Don needed an intervention. They marched her into his room to deliver an ultimatum: "I told him that if he didn't stop, that I would go." She expected resistance, even defiance. Instead, Don gazed back with a look of relief and said, "Okay."

"It was the strangest reaction I ever saw in my life," Francey recalled. "My guess is, he needed something to stop him."

Upon his release, Francey said, sixty-six-year-old Don "became a different person. In the morning, instead of being exhausted and not in the best mood, he'd sing—and sing—and sing. Songs I'd never heard. 'The bears went a-huntin' . . .' No more pills. Never touched a drop of alcohol again for the rest of his life."

Don started swimming daily and resumed golfing regularly. He abandoned many of his favorite restaurants after realizing he'd patronized them only for drink; the food wasn't all that good. He broke off his thirty-year association with psychiatrist Dick Renneker, the man responsible for breaking Don's pill addiction three decades earlier. Don never saw a therapist again.

"It was the same guy, but he looked healthier

and ate better," recalled Stella Berrier, a longtime friend. "[Francey] turned his life around. . . . Every time he felt like 'Woe is me,' they'd get in a car and drive to Las Vegas and laugh all the way. She could bring him out of any mood."

Brandon Tartikoff, the NBC executive who had sparked Andy Griffith's television revival, left the network in 1991. His replacement, Warren Littlefield, set about "building for the future." He immediately targeted *Matlock* and *In the Heat of the Night*, both popular crime shows headed by aging stars. *Matlock* ranked fortieth among 123 network series at the time; *Heat*, starring *All in the Family*'s Carroll O'Connor, was tied for twenty-eighth. Warren offered Andy a graceful exit: six two-hour *Matlock* movies over the next three years. "I don't think Warren Littlefield ever liked the show," Andy quipped.

Andy and Cindi had lunch with Fred Silverman, the man who had created *Matlock* along with Dean Hargrove. With little to lose, Andy negotiated to move the production from Hollywood to Wilmington, NC, a short plane ride from his Manteo estate. The series could be produced cheaply within the burgeoning North Carolina film industry, and Andy and Cindi could begin a gradual retirement to Roanoke Island. Andy asked that new characters be added to the cast, reducing his weekly dialogue chores and seeding more comedic subplots. NBC passed, but Fred Silverman easily sold the concept to ABC. *Matlock* was still a top-forty series, after all.

Notably absent from the meeting was Dick Linke.

Andy had once seemed closer to Dick than to his wife Barbara; Dick demanded such intimacy. Now, Andy was going to Cindi for counsel. The brush with mortality at the start of their marriage had forged an intense bond. People on the *Matlock* set felt a palpable tension between Cindi and Dick, who had become a third wheel. "I'd fire him," Andy once told Don, "but it'd be like putting a bullet in his head."

In December 1991, Andy called a meeting with Dick at their beloved Lakeside Golf Club. Dick knew what was coming: he was about to be fired. "Andy," he said, "let me tell you something. I've worked hard in this business. I've been in it longer than you have. Now, at my stage in the business and in my life, I can handle everything. I can handle everything but one thing, Andy: pillow talk."

Andy considered Don his best friend. But for decades of Andy's life, Dick had been his closest confidant. Andy once told an interviewer, "If it hadn't been for Dick Linke, there would be no Andy Griffith."

Back in 1961, the two men were walking along Seventh Avenue in New York when Dick told

Andy their seven-year management contract had lapsed. He asked whether Andy would sign another. "Contract?" Andy replied. "You don't need a contract with me. You have a contract for life."

Now, three decades later, Dick sat across the table from Andy wearing a gold ring on his right hand, a recent present from Andy, with the number 35 etched on its face, for thirty-five years together. None of Andy's wives or girlfriends had ever come between them—until Cindi. "She wanted to take over," Dick recalled. "And that's what happened. And I was crushed."

Andy's world was shrinking. In the twilight of his career, Andy would grow increasingly remote from many of his old friends, and from his children. The relationship between Andy and his adopted son and daughter had played out along the lines drawn in his divorce settlement with Barbara, two decades earlier. Barbara got Dixie; Andy got Sam. The younger Griffith idolized his famous father but chafed at the pressure that came with being his son.

"That's why he drank," said Mike King, Barbara's nephew, of the younger Griffith. "It had to be a rough, contentious relationship, Andy being the dominant guy that he was."

Sam descended into alcoholism. Andy eventually cut off contact, telling friends he had emotionally disinherited his son. In September

1992, a California judge placed thirty-three-year-old Sam on probation after he admitted to beating his pregnant wife, weeks after their wedding. The union was clearly dysfunctional; Sam's wife claimed he had kicked her in the stomach, while Sam alleged her bruises were the result of a car crash. They swiftly divorced.

Andy and Dixie had a loving relationship. But he saw little of Dixie in his grandfather years, largely due to his busy life with Cindi and his hectic schedule on *Matlock*.

By the time filming commenced in Wilmington, in summer 1992, the cast and crew of *Matlock* scarcely resembled the company first assembled six years earlier. One change was the exit of Dean Hargrove. He and Andy had suffered what Dean tactfully termed a "falling out" over Dean's waning attention to Andy and his show. Dean was busy with other projects, and Andy felt "that I had abandoned him," Dean recalled. "He had put me on a very high pedestal to begin with, and when you're on a high pedestal, there's nowhere to go but down."

At the start of 1993, Andy and Don reunited for another round of Mayberry nostalgia. Andy finally seemed to be warming to the thought of honoring his past. The gang gathered at Disney-MGM Studios and then traveled to Wilmington, Andy's *Matlock* home base, to tape *The Andy Griffith Show Reunion*. Broadcast in February on

CBS, it was the first full-blown gathering of *Griffith* principals since *Return to Mayberry* in the previous decade. The show opened with a medley of celebrity Mayberry buffs whistling the theme song, including actor Burt Reynolds, country crooner Randy Travis, and pitcher Nolan Ryan.

Craig Fincannon, Andy's old friend, witnessed a stirring moment in Wilmington that never made it to the screen: "I saw Andy walk over to the sound operator and whisper something to him. And he gathered everybody around, and he said, 'Don, come here.' And Don walked over, and we all crowded around the monitor. And Andy said to the group, 'This is the greatest moment of television comedy ever recorded.' And he told the guy to hit play. And he started to play the Preamble-to-the-Constitution scene with Don," from an old *Griffith* episode. "And Don had to take off his glasses and get about five inches from the monitor to see it. And Barney started, 'We the P—, We the P—,' and everybody in the whole group was absolutely cracking up. And Andy was standing behind Don. And I watched Andy watching Don. And Andy cried. And it was tears of laughter."

As *Matlock* neared its end, Andy filmed a pair of TV movies and joined Leslie Nielsen in the action spoof *Spy Hard*. Otherwise, the latter half of the 1990s would be a quiet time for both Andy and Don, as befits men entering their seventies.

Andy was now a full-time resident of Manteo, tooling around in his Jeep or his pontoon boat and going to bed by eight.

In January 1996, Andy's idyll was shattered. His son, Sam, had been found dead, slumped over a desk in his North Hollywood home. He had drunk himself to death. He was thirty-seven. "Quite honestly, I think his body just gave out on him, after all the years of abuse," attorney James Blatt told the *Los Angeles Daily News*. The obituary described Sam as an out-of-work developer.

When Don called to express condolences, all Andy could say was "It's very, very, very painful." Andy didn't speak of Sam much after that. But he once confessed to Don, "I don't know how good a father I was."

Perhaps those events put Andy in a contemplative mood. He returned to the recording studio that year for the first time since the 1960s to record *I Love to Tell the Story*, a collection of hymns sold over an 800 number flashed on television screens. The idea had come from music producer Steve Tyrell, who'd traveled to Wilmington to record country artist Randy Travis for *Matlock*. "He came into my dressing room, and I played him a cut of an old record I made twenty or thirty years ago," Andy recalled. "I said, 'I'd like to try that again sometime.' The next thing I know, I'm in Nashville."

The recording sold more than 2 million copies

and earned Andy a raft of national publicity—and a Grammy. It would be Andy's first top-shelf artistic award. He must have smiled at the irony of being recognized for his "overbrilliant" baritone. The television industry's failure to note Andy's talent had always haunted him; now, he was being honored for the wrong talent. Nonetheless, the award lifted his spirits and may even have softened him on the decades of past snubs. "I've got it on my mantelpiece," he told an interviewer. "I've never won anything before. It was nice."

Andy sent a copy of the record to Don, his old duet partner. "He sang and sang along with that thing, until he couldn't sing anymore," Francey Yarborough Knotts recalled.

Don spent much of the 1990s on the road, performing regional theater and signing autographs at a seemingly endless series of fan events. At Walt Disney World and in Las Vegas casinos, Don would be mobbed as if he were Elvis; sometimes Francey would summon security, lest she and Don be trampled. Fistfights occasionally broke out in autograph lines. Don, ever gracious toward his fans, would sign stacks of his signature photograph, a head-to-knees shot of Barney Fife holding his pistol. The shading of the black-and-white image left him nowhere to sign but his crotch. Don came to hate that picture.

"They would line up along the hotel, three

blocks, and wait in line to get an autograph from him," recalled Dodie Brown, a stage actress who worked with Don and Francey in that era. "They would come up and say, 'I'm your best fan.' Every single person would say that. Every policeman would bring him bullets." Don never knew what to do with the bullets. Hundreds of them rattled around the drawers of his Century City condo.

For his traveling shows, Don fell back on old favorites: *Last of the Red Hot Lovers*; *Harvey*; *On Golden Pond*; *Norman, Is That You?* Don was usually the big draw, although *I Dream of Jeannie* alumna Barbara Eden joined him on some dates. A stack of Don's old press clippings reveals the breadth of his travels: Jupiter Theatre, Florida, in May 1990; Des Moines Civic Center, Iowa, in April 1993; Stage West Theatre Restaurant, Mississauga, Ontario, June 1995; Claridge Casino Hotel, Atlantic City, February 1998.

Because of his eyesight, "all of the scripts we learned, he had to have orally taught to him by Francey," Dodie Brown recalled. Yet, Don nearly always filled the house, and he could still command an audience. Francey, a talented actress in her own right, often joined Don in the cast.

Don loved the theater. During one of his tours, he and Francey passed through New York. The city brought back such warm memories: Windy Wales and the B-Bar-B Ranch; Andy Griffith and *No Time for Sergeants*. One night, with

Francey in tow, Don unexpectedly glided down the stairs of the Plaza Hotel and broke into song, crooning the Burton Lane standard "How About You?" He strode into the street, still singing, as if he were in a musical. It was after midnight, and men were sleeping on the sidewalk. One by one, they awakened. One cried out, "It's Don Knotts. He's *singing!*" Some of the men rose and began to shamble along behind him. Don popped into a store and got change for a $20. Then he ducked back onto the street and began handing dollar bills to the vagabonds, one by one, singing all the while.

Andy flew to Norfolk in 1993 to see Don in *Last of the Red Hot Lovers*. At dinner later, Cindi dutifully reported that Andy "was a-whoopin' and a-hollerin' " through the performance. Andy and Don spent the rest of the evening breaking each other up by chanting an off-color parody of a school cheer: "We are the girls from Norfolk / We don't drink and we don't smoke / Norfolk, Norfolk, Norfolk!"

In 1996, the celebrated film *Sling Blade* and the ascent of Arkansas wunderkind Billy Bob Thornton brought a new character into the Andy-Don tableau. Both men became obsessed with the movie, which explored a darker Mayberry. Andy telephoned Billy to register his approval. "Then," Billy recalled, "he started calling me all the time."

Born in 1955, Billy Bob Thornton had grown up with *The Andy Griffith Show.* He broke into Hollywood with a hayseed parody of *Othello* inspired by Andy's *Hamlet* monologue. He won a small part in a 1987 episode of *Matlock.* On the set, Billy walked up to Andy and said, "I just wanted to tell you that you're literally the reason I started acting." In reply, Billy recalled, Andy "kind of looked at me strange and then walked away."

Nine years later, Andy didn't remember the meeting, and Billy didn't remind him. The two began to dine together when Andy was in town. Don sometimes joined them. "It was like I was in a dream," recalled Billy, who counted the *Griffith Show* as his favorite program and Don as his favorite actor. More often, though, Andy and Billy dined alone. After a few glasses of wine, those sessions would invariably lead to Andy "crying and putting his arm around me," telling Billy "that I was like a son to him. And he would beg me to quit smoking. And he talked about losing his son. He said, 'I don't want to lose you.' "

Billy became perhaps Andy's closest Hollywood friend in the latter years, apart from Don. Yet, it was "a very difficult relationship," Billy recalled, "because Andy could be very dark and melancholy, and other times he was on top of the world." In darker moments, Andy would brood about diminished artistic currency. "I think he never accepted the idea that he wasn't still someone who they should just jump all over," Billy said. "And I think maybe if he had let go of the past a little bit, it would have changed it for him."

Billy wrote Andy into one of his movies, the quirky Southern comedy *Daddy and Them*. Andy "was pretty cranky at that point," Billy recalled. "His feet hurt him really bad and he didn't like to work really long hours." Moreover, Andy didn't find Billy's script particularly funny. "I think Andy's sense of humor was in a state of arrested development, in some ways," Billy recalled.

Don resurfaced on the national stage in the 1998 film *Pleasantville*. The story cast him as a TV repairman who transports Tobey Maguire and Reese Witherspoon into a 1950s sitcom. It is a perfect role, Don portraying a sort of cathode-ray Oz with the power to sweep the unsuspecting off to Mayberry. Yet something about Don's television repairman is vaguely malevolent; he arrives unbidden, amid thunderclaps, and gently mocks the culture of television addiction that *The Andy Griffith Show* helped to spawn. He earnestly quizzes the boy on bits of *Pleasantville* trivia, just as *Griffith* fans quizzed each other at the annual Mayberry Days festivals.

Like Andy, Don was not entirely comfortable with satirizing his greatest comedic achievement.

"I had a little difficulty doing that one," he recalled later.

As the 1990s drew to a close, *The Andy Griffith Show* migrated to a new home on the cable network TV Land. In three decades of syndication, much had changed: the patchwork of local stations that had saturated the nation with *Griffith* was on the wane. Superstation TBS, which had aired *Griffith* reruns nationwide for twenty-seven years, had relegated the program to 4:30 a.m. It mattered little to hard-core fans, who had long since videotaped their favorite episodes and would purchase them on DVD a few years later. For everyone else, a prime-time berth on the nostalgia cable network was welcome news.

The network brought Andy and Don to Hollywood in January 2000 for a wave of ceremonial press coverage. TV Land also arranged for Don to receive his star finally—on the Walk of Fame. Together at the press conference, Andy and Don boasted about their forty-five-year friendship. Living now on opposite coasts, they stoked the relationship by catching up on the telephone every two or three weeks. Andy spent much of his allotted time trying to convince the reporters that Don, not he, had made *The Andy Griffith Show* so special.

"The five years we worked together," Andy said, "were the best five years of my life."

15.

Death in Mayberry

Don Knotts entered the autumn of life with newfound respect for his body, a man intent on cheating death. He had kicked sleeping pills, drinking, smoking, and bad living. He swam daily and galloped up stairs to reach his exclusive Beverly Hills gym. He dined on vegetables and fish. Sometimes, dinner was little more than a fruit plate.

And then, around his eightieth birthday, Don's doctor told him, "Your lungs scare the hell out of me."

The Knotts family seemed cursed with bad lungs. Shadow, Don's older brother and comedic muse, had died at thirty-one of asthma. Don's father had expired at fifty-five of pneumonia. Richie Ferrara, a doctor and Don's lifelong friend, believed the elder Knotts was afflicted with pulmonary fibrosis, a gradual hardening of lung tissue; perhaps Shadow had it as well. "I have a feeling there are two reasons for it," Richie said, "a genetic condition, and the coal dust." Morgantown is a mining town, and coal dust swirls in the wind.

Don fell from a pair of stilts once, during a performance in adolescence, and one of the wooden poles punctured a lung. As a young adult on *The Steve Allen Show*, Don caught a crippling case of pneumonia.

Now, at eighty, Don had contracted pulmonary fibrosis. His doctor didn't want him thinking about it, so he told Don he suffered from "scarring of the lungs" and never uttered a formal diagnosis. He urged Don to go right on swimming and climbing stairs. He assured Don the chronic condition would not slow him down.

In the new millennium, Don was Hollywood royalty. Back in Morgantown, in 1998, a stretch of University Avenue had been renamed Don Knotts Boulevard. A new generation of comedic actors worshipped his television roles and films. In 1999, Ron Howard brought Don to Universal Studios, where he was filming *How the Grinch Stole Christmas*. Ron's star, Jim Carrey, was losing it: After spending hours each day getting in and out of his green latex Grinch makeup, "he was really miserable at work," Ron recalled. Jim Carrey adored Don. When Don arrived, Jim squinted down from his perch at the mouth of his Grinch cave. Finally recognizing the visitor, Jim launched into "a really brilliant Don Knotts imitation, and I only wish the cameras were rolling, because here he was in the Grinch costume, doing Barney Fife," Ron recalled. Jim spent the rest of the day with his idol.

Andy Griffith had been mostly inactive for the

first half of the 2000s, living in secluded splendor on his Manteo estate. But he missed Don, and he admired his friend's seemingly inexhaustible work ethic. In 2004, Andy persuaded wife Cindi to relocate. They purchased a new $2.4 million home in Toluca Lake, the same place Andy had lived during the *Griffith* years.

Soon, Andy and Don were dining together once more, squiring their lovely young wives to exclusive Beverly Hills restaurants, sometimes in the company of former *Griffith* producer Aaron Ruben. Andy would tell bawdy jokes and make Francey laugh. That would make Don jealous: the simmering artistic rivalry that had rendered Andy unable to speak of Don's Emmys seemed to cut both ways. One night, when Francey noted how funny Andy had been at supper, Don snapped, "I'm the funny one!"

Andy delighted in Don's company. He would shake his head and tell Francey, "Oh, I love Don. I love him so much." Then he would laugh and say, "Ha. You'd think we were gay."

Andy and Don would send each other comedy tapes, radio performances by Garrison Keillor or Bob and Ray. They would compare notes on contemporary television and cinema. And they talked of working together again. Most of that talk came from Andy, who would call Don and fantasize about going out on the road together. But Don knew it was probably a pipe dream; Andy hadn't dared a live performance in years. Don would turn to Francey and hiss, "It's not . . . gonna . . . happen. Andy's not . . . gonna . . . do it." Then Don would turn back to the phone and say, "Oh, yes . . . Oh, yes . . ."

In his final years, Don was earning money and acclaim from the burgeoning industry of cartoon voice-overs, most notably in the role of Mayor Turkey Lurkey in the 2005 Disney feature *Chicken Little*. And he was touring the country with Tim Conway, playing the regional theater circuit.

The same month *Chicken Little* hit theaters, November 2005, Don reprised the role of lecherous landlord Ralph Furley in a brief cameo on *That '70s Show*. It would be his final on-screen performance.

As the year wore on, Don's lungs deteriorated further. He canceled a public appearance in Morgantown—something Don never did—and he started begging off gatherings with old friends. By Thanksgiving, Don was gasping for air. Within weeks, the wind seemed to have drained from his lungs. He could no longer climb stairs or even walk to the store without panting for breath.

Doctors found a tumor. Don had lung cancer.

Don asked the doctor, "Are you telling me there's no cure?" The question alarmed Francey because there is essentially no cure for lung cancer. "When we left, I felt we'd heard the worst news we could have heard, and Don seemed not to care," Francey recalled. "He said, 'I'm not going to die soon.' He was in denial. People say that's the first stage of death."

Don started chemotherapy, and for a while it seemed that he improved. His outlook remained improbably sanguine. He and Francey would lunch at Jerry's Famous Deli in Studio City, and they made regular forays to the library to borrow books on tape. Francey brought him some favorite programs to watch. Don was an Anglophile. He loved the crime writer P. D. James and old episodes of *Upstairs, Downstairs* and *Fawlty Towers*. Francey would print out columns from *The New York Times* and read them to Don.

Don told almost no one of his illness, lest news should leak to the tabloids. Don still wanted to work, and a sick actor could not get work. He didn't tell his children he was dying. He didn't tell Andy.

Late in 2005, Don dragged himself into a recording booth to lend his voice to *Air Buddies*, a direct-to-video Disney movie about talking dogs. Francey was horrified at Don's insistence on working. When she couldn't dissuade him, she appealed to Sherwin Bash, his manager, saying, "I don't think he's up for this." Sherwin couldn't stop Don. Francey tried to accept his decision with stoicism. "Don wants to die onstage," she told herself, "and that isn't any worse than dying in a hospital bed."

Air Buddies would be Don's final role.

Don and Francey went out with Andy and Cindi on Cindi's birthday, a few weeks before Christmas. They met at La Dolce Vita in Beverly Hills, a place where stars could dine unmolested. Andy noticed Don's labored breathing. When the party rose to leave, he could plainly see his friend was gasping for breath. Later, Andy telephoned. Francey answered. Andy said, "Something is wrong." Cindi joined Andy on the phone and told Francey that Don needed to see a doctor. Francey bit her tongue. "He's seen the doctor," she told them, "and he has this condition, and we're doing things for it."

Even as his lungs weakened, Don insisted on keeping up appearances. When he and Francey went out to a holiday party, Don beseeched her to hide his oxygen canister in some bushes outside the home. Later that evening, Don walked across a room and began struggling for breath. Francey told him, "I have to go out and get the oxygen." He looked at her with big, frightened eyes and hissed, "Don't do it!" Don would sooner have died than let people see him breathing canned oxygen.

The agony continued when Andy telephoned to arrange a visit on Christmas. Don replied, "It's not a good time; I don't think I can fit it in." He didn't want Andy to see him sucking oxygen from a mask. Francey feared she and Don would pass his last Christmas alone. She told Don, "I'm going to have to tell Andy. Don't worry about it, he'll understand."

Francey telephoned Andy. She told him that Don was having lung trouble, and that he was reluctant to tell anyone or be seen with his breathing aids. She said nothing of cancer.

Francey put Don on the phone. Andy told Don, "Look, I have my little scooter that I sometimes drive around the house. I don't like people to see me on my scooter. I'll have my scooter, and you'll have your oxygen." Andy laughed. Don laughed. "We're going to get through this," Andy said. After Don put down the phone, he seemed immeasurably relieved.

Andy and Don met at the Peninsula Hotel in Beverly Hills a few days before Christmas to dine at the Belvedere, a five-diamond restaurant. Andy brought Dixie, his daughter, and her children. Francey brought the dreaded oxygen canister in her purse, but Don wouldn't need it. Andy and Don told the old stories, about *No Time for Sergeants* and the *Griffith Show*. They talked of the work Don was doing, and of the work Andy wanted to do, and of working together again one day. "It was a beautiful thing to watch," Dixie recalled. "You could feel the love between the two men."

But Don looked frail. And when Dixie and her children stood to leave, Don remained seated.

"Don wanted us to leave before him so we didn't see the trouble he was having," Andy recalled later.

On Christmas Day, Don and Francey hosted the children, Karen and Tom. Don looked deathly, yet forbade Francey to tell them of his illness. When Francey protested, Don replied, "I'm not going to die anytime soon."

Shortly after the New Year, Don sank into delirium and was rushed to Cedars-Sinai hospital. "He didn't want a soul to come in," Francey recalled. But Don finally agreed to tell his children he had cancer. Karen and Tom arrived at the hospital. Francey swore them to secrecy.

During his two-week stay on the pulmonary ward, Don grew more lucid and was finally able to speak. Once, he opened his eyes, trained them on Francey and Karen, and said, "I'm waiting for the great wizard in the sky to take me away." Don was not one for spiritual pronouncements. Was he talking about God and the hereafter, or simply having a laugh? Neither listener was quite sure.

Don was sent home with a round-the-clock nurse. A few weeks later, on February 23, a sensor attached to his finger triggered an alarm, signaling that his lungs were no longer furnishing enough oxygen to his body. In the ambulance, his heart stopped, then it started again. He slipped into a coma. He had still told no one outside his family, apart from his manager, that he was dying.

From the hospital room, Francey telephoned Andy. Andy raced to the hospital. Francey called Tom Poston, Don's old friend from the *Steve Allen* days, and held the phone to Don's ear so Tom could say good-bye. She telephoned Richie Ferrara. Francey feared Don's old friends didn't grasp the finality of the moment. She told Richie, "You have to listen to me: This is it. He's not going to make it through the night." Francey held the phone to Don's ear. Richie told Don, "Keep it up. You've got things to do yet." While Richie spoke, Don's body visibly responded.

Kay, Don's first wife, was summoned to the phone, and again someone held the receiver to Don's ear so she could say a few words.

Andy arrived at the UCLA Medical Center. Francey and Karen left the room so Andy could speak to Don alone. Andy took Don's hand. He said, "Jess, breathe. You gotta make this. You gotta pull through. Breathe." Don's chest heaved. Andy said, "That's a boy. Keep breathing." Andy told Don he loved him.

Then Andy departed, leaving Karen and Francey with Don in the hospital room. "They were really just keeping him alive at that point," Francey recalled, "waiting for everybody to say good-bye," including son Tom, who was flying in from San Francisco.

Don had written in his will that he was not to be sustained artificially. Doctors unplugged the machines. Don Knotts died at 11:00 p.m. on February 24, 2006, a Friday, with Francey, Karen, and Tom embracing him.

The *Los Angeles Times* wrote that Don had, in his later years, attained the stature of "lodestar for younger comic actors. The new generation came to appreciate his highly physical brand of acting that, at its best, was in the tradition of silent-film greats such as Buster Keaton, Stan Laurel, and Harold Lloyd." *The New York Times* hailed Don as "a high-status comic who played low-status roles. Actors who worked with him almost universally deferred to him as a comedic grand-master," yet his characters inevitably found themselves the butt of jokes.

Andy appeared on the *Today* show and said, "I lost my best friend."

Later, Andy spoke by telephone to Dixie, his daughter. He said he was worried that Don, coma-tose in his hospital bed, might not have heard Andy's final words. Dixie, who worked with the dying, reassured her father: Don had heard. "I think it was really important to my dad for Don to know he was there," she recalled.

More than that, Andy yearned to know whether his best friend had accepted God and gone to heaven. He knew the Bible-thumpers back in West Virginia had spooked Don, had given him nightmares, had ultimately chased him away from organized religion. Don and Andy didn't talk much about God, but Andy sensed Don's position on faith was agnostic at best. Alas, Don had died before Andy could ask. Now he dearly hoped to see Don in the hereafter.

The funeral was set for March 6 at Pierce Brothers in Westwood, a small, storybook campus of graves and greenery set among the towers of steel and glass on Wilshire Boulevard. Don's casket, dusky-blue enamel decorated with silver dancing fish in homage to Mr. Limpet, sat before a towering rock wall. Andy, Tim Conway, and Tom Poston gathered with Don's less celebrated friends and relations inside Chapel of the Palms, a faux-Japanese pavilion.

The decidedly secular affair was led by a Unitarian minister; that all-embracing faith seemed the right choice. Though not religious himself, Don knew that other people—Andy in particular—would want a service. He had always regretted avoiding his own mother's funeral.

Andy was concerned at what the Unitarian might say. The minister called Andy and sketched out his carefully worded sermon. He asked if Andy had a problem. Andy replied, "Well, you know, I do believe that Don is going to be in heaven, and you're not going to say that."

Francey arranged for Andy himself to speak at the service. Andy stepped forward and spoke, his voice choked with emotion. "It's hard for me to say anything," he began. Andy then told the story of Jesus and the penitent thief. As Jesus hung on the cross, a condemned man beside him asked Jesus to "remember me when you come into your kingdom." Jesus replied, "I say to you today, you will be with me in paradise."

Andy's voice rose and slowed as he concluded, summoning the fire of his Preacher-and-the-Bear sermons back in North Carolina: "And I take comfort because I know that Don . . . is . . . in . . . *paradise!*" Then, his body quaking, Andy left the podium. As he exited, Andy's voice burst forth from the chapel's public address system, singing the hymn "Precious Memories" from one of his gospel albums.

Don was buried at Westwood Memorial Park, near the graves of Marilyn Monroe, Dean Martin, and Truman Capote. Frail Andy insisted on bearing Don's coffin. Francey summoned several strong men to help him.

A memorial service was held May 4 at the Writers Guild Theater in Beverly Hills, with an all-star guest list, a chocolate fountain, and an ice sculpture of Mr. Limpet. Ron Howard opened the three-hour ceremony. Andy followed. His face veritably glowed with love, and emotion no longer strangled his voice.

"I'll tell you something I believe," Andy said. "I'm Christian, but I believe there's a place for all of us in God's kingdom. I know when it comes my time, I'll see Don again with our Lord."

Joan Staley, Don's costar in *The Ghost and Mister Chicken*, heard Andy's words. "And I remember it hitting me: *He really loved him. He really loved him.*"

Andy's dream of living out his final years in the company of Don had died with his friend. Now, he told Cindi, he wanted out of LA—even though the Griffiths had barely settled into their new home. "With Don gone, I'm ready to go back to North Carolina," he told friends. By year's end, Andy and Cindi had left California.

The *Griffith* diaspora had lost its beloved Barney, and talk soon turned to the quest for a fitting tribute. Shortly after the memorial, a plan was announced. Two fans from Mount Airy, Andy's hometown, would commission a life-size bronze statue of Deputy Fife. They would donate it to the city once they had raised the necessary funds.

A statue of Andy Griffith already sat in Mount Airy, outside the Andy Griffith Playhouse. Commissioned by the cable network TV Land and installed in 2004, the monument depicted Andy and Opie holding hands and walking with their fishing poles, above the inscription A SIMPLER TIME, A SWEETER PLACE.

Don's death underscored his absence from that memorial. The statue backers thought it fitting that Barney should stand near Andy and Opie in front of the playhouse, or maybe down on Main

Street, directing traffic into eternity. "Mayberry without Barney Fife just wouldn't be the same," said Tom Hellebrand, a local restaurateur. His partner on the project, Neal Shelton, made his living restoring Ford Galaxie 500 sedans for the Mount Airy tourist circuit.

Francey, immersed in Don's memorial, knew nothing of the statue until she was blindsided one day by a call from Andy, who sounded hysterical. "They're trying to turn Don into Bob's Big Boy," he cried.

Andy said he feared the men planned the Barney statue as a glorified sandwich board to drum up sales for their respective businesses, not as a simple, altruistic tribute. Andy wanted the statue nipped in the bud. But he himself didn't dare get involved, for fear his reluctance might be read the wrong way.

Andy seemed swept up in a familiar tempest of powerful emotions: protectiveness of the Mayberry brand mixed with possessiveness of his home-town and simple egotism. For half a century, Andy had scorned Mount Airy. Now, he was fighting to protect his primacy there. Erecting a statue of Don, Andy said, "would be an absolute shot in my eye."

There seemed no basis for Andy's mistrust of the statue promoters. Yet, in early June, the two men were told they could not proceed. CBS Corp., which had granted permission for the statue, now revoked it. Company officials said the project was dead because it lacked the blessing of the Don Knotts estate—Francey. In a series of increasingly desperate phone calls, Andy had persuaded her to oppose the statue. If someone wanted to build a memorial to Don, Andy said, it should go in his own hometown of Morgantown. Mount Airy belonged to Andy.

The statue promoters were stunned. And they were broke. The fracas became a national story, and opinion quickly turned against the "big-city lawyers" and the Knotts estate for blocking the statue. No one seemed to realize the objection had come from Andy himself.

At the end of June 2006, Tom Hellebrand offered to donate the partially completed statue to anyone, anywhere, who could find it a home that appealed to the Knotts family. He suggested Morgantown, Don's birthplace. Morgantown leaders loved the idea. Andy hated it. He telephoned Francey repeatedly, frantically, begging her to shut it down. He didn't want the Barney statue going up in Morgantown, either. If there was to be a statue of Don, he told her, it should depict the man, not the deputy.

It was hard, once again, to parse Andy's reasons, or to see how a statue of Barney Fife could possibly harm Don's legacy. Andy seemed concerned that the statue would reduce his dear friend to a roadside caricature. But if a Barney Fife statue was such a bad idea, then why had

Andy permitted a statue of Andy Taylor—the character—in Mount Airy?

As he neared the end of his life, Andy seemed to be reordering his priorities. If Manteo was his home, then Mount Airy was his legacy—a living, breathing memorial to his greatest creation. Perhaps it hadn't dawned on Andy how badly he craved that tribute until he faced the prospect of sharing it with his best friend.

Francey had no objection to a statue of Don going up in Mount Airy or Morgantown. But she respected Andy, so she assented. In July, she and Andy issued a joint public statement: "No one cares more about Don's image than we do. It would be wonderful to have a statue in Morgantown, W.Va., of Don Knotts as Don Knotts. But this particular image"—Don as Barney—"does not fit with our understanding of Don's experience growing up in Morgantown."

Tom Hellebrand sold his diner and his home and severed most of his ties to Mayberry; the half-finished statue was destroyed. In the real Mayberry, a local editorial mused, no one would lose his business and his home over "this statue thing. Maybe that's just what happens when Sheriff Taylor isn't around to smooth things over." The writer didn't know the sheriff had been the one stirring things up.

Inside of a year, an effort was under way to fund a new statue in Don's birthplace. This design depicted Don in a suit, rather than a lawman's uniform, with his deputy's badge concealed coyly within a cupped palm. By the start of 2015, the project had surpassed its $50,000 fund-raising goal, and supporters had chosen a fitting location: outside the old Metropolitan Theatre, within whose seats Don had first been bitten by the acting bug.

Andy was, at seventy-six, the most famous living soul in North Carolina, the figure at the center of an $80 million tourism industry. In fall 2002, Andy prepared a triumphal return to Mount Airy for a ceremony dedicating an eleven-mile stretch of US Highway 52 in his honor. On the eve of the visit, he telephoned the Surry Arts Council.

Its director, Tanya Jones, worked inside the Andy Griffith Playhouse and had staged eleven Mayberry Days, but she had never spoken to the man. Now, Andy was on the telephone, telling Tanya he wanted to see the playhouse and meet with his old friend Emmett Forrest and stay in his old Mount Airy home.

The ceremony marked Andy's first public appearance in Mount Airy in forty-five years. "I'm proud to be from Mount Airy," Andy told the crowd. "I think of you often, and I won't be such a stranger from here out."

To that moment, Andy and his birthplace had seemed at cross-purposes. Here was an entire town laboring to define itself as the real-life Mayberry—and here was the mythical town's creator saying it wasn't so. "Now they think that I based the show on Mount Airy, and I've argued about this too long," Andy had snapped at an interviewer in 1998. "I don't care. Let them think what they want."

On this day, with the townsfolk gathered at his feet, stubborn old Andy finally, grudgingly confessed the truth. "People started saying that Mayberry was based on Mount Airy," he told the crowd with a sly grin. "It sure sounds like it, doesn't it?"

Andy lived his final years as Carolina royalty. Fans lurked at the gates to his Manteo estate. Governors courted his favor. Locals guarded his privacy with the zeal of a palace guard. Andy spent his days drinking his coffee, reading his paper, and riding his John Deere Gator around his seventy acres of forest and sand.

Don had kept working because he could not bear to turn down a job. Andy, by contrast, seemed to keep working in a ceaseless quest to prove himself—to finally earn some artistic recognition, and to undo past mistakes in a brilliant but scattershot career.

Now, like Don before him, Andy was enjoying a sort of autumnal comeback. It started with *Waitress*, an art-house project that Andy took on around the time of Don's death, inspired by his old friend's dogged work ethic. He was cast as Joe, the crotchety owner of a diner that employed Keri Russell, the film's lovelorn protagonist.

Andy's labors in *Waitress* reminded him faintly of his work five decades earlier with Elia Kazan. Adrienne Shelly, the director—later to be strangled by a construction worker in her Greenwich Village apartment—extracted a superior performance from Andy. She was a director who gave actual direction, and Andy listened. "Be firm," she would tell him, over and over, until Andy would explode, "I'm trying!" Then Adrienne would smile: "That way."

When Andy spoke his last line, Adrienne Shelly embraced him and the entire company applauded. To Andy, it felt a bit like opening night on *No Time for Sergeants*, fifty years earlier.

Waitress was released in 2007. For the first time in what seemed forever, Andy's dramatic work drew serious note. *The Wall Street Journal* opined, "This comic virtuoso is as commanding as ever, but with a new dimension of restraint."

Ron and Rance Howard telephoned separately to tell Andy how good he was. Interviewers called, too, and for once Andy answered the phone. They had no idea how he savored the attention.

Andy Griffith had earned almost no formal recognition for either his comedy or his acting. Most of the awards on his résumé were trivial, such as a 2003 Single Dad of the Year honor from

TV Land. He hadn't won even one Emmy, let alone five. Yet, in Andy's final years, Hollywood finally seemed to be coming round to the idea that he was one of the greats. "At age 81, Andy Griffith has been discovered," one reporter wrote.

In 2009, Andy starred in the independent feature *Play the Game*, cast as a lonely widower who transforms into a retirement-home lothario. Andy, ribald as ever, reveled in the sexually charged dialogue. It would be his final role.

The statue debacle seemed an ancient memory when, in September 2009, Andy's friends in Mount Airy cut the ribbon on the Andy Griffith Museum. Owned by the city and housed within the same complex as the Andy Griffith Playhouse, the twenty-five-hundred-square-foot museum gave a permanent home to Griffith memorabilia collected by Emmett Forrest, Andy's lifelong friend, who had amassed the items over the decades. Andy would sometimes show up at Emmett's door with bits of flotsam Emmett had spotted in Andy's garage months or years earlier. Andy did not attend the opening.

Andy's health was in steady decline. In summer 2000, he had survived a heart attack, quadruple bypass surgery, and the customary "Brave Last Stand" headlines in the tabloids. In the final years of Andy's life, he and Cindi pulled away from several of their old friends, and the Griffiths became progressively harder to reach. Their social circle grew steadily smaller. Few people set foot inside the Griffith home apart from those who provided goods or services to the household.

Quentin Bell had been one of Andy's closest friends in the years before he met Cindi. Quentin's property lay right next door, and the Griffith Labradors often wandered over to Quentin's yard. "So I would see Cindi and Andy," Quentin recalled. "But it was never like I came into his house for a drink or anything. Andy didn't drink at the end, I don't think." In March 2012, Andy and Cindi unexpectedly invited Quentin and his wife over for lunch. Andy gave Quentin a tour of his palatial new home, built a short distance from the older, smaller residence that Andy and Barbara had shared. The new Griffith dwelling was several years old, but Quentin had never really seen it. Andy showed Quentin his Moravian Bible and drove his old friend up and down the sand hills on his beloved Gator. Quentin would never see Andy again.

June 1, 2012, was Andy's eighty-sixth birthday. He treated himself to a glass of champagne. Francey Yarborough Knotts telephoned to wish him well and was surprised when Andy himself picked up the phone. Andy wanted to talk about Don. Francey and Andy had spoken many times since Don had died, and Andy mostly avoided discussing him, "like he felt he shouldn't be bringing up the past," Francey recalled. On this day, though, Andy held forth about Don's films, his stand-up routines, his radio voices—all the things Don was so good at. Andy kept talking, and something in his voice gave Francey the feeling that Andy might not have long to live. It occurred to her, suddenly, to tell Andy about Don's cryptic remark from his hospital bed, on that day shortly before he died, about waiting "for the great wizard in the sky to take me away."

"Wow," Andy said, then paused. "Really. *Thank you* for telling me that." His voice swelled with emotion. "That's *wonderful*. Thank you . . . thank you . . ."

It meant everything to Andy. To him, heaven was real, a place he hoped to go, and he wanted more than anything else to see Don there when he arrived. Now, he had reason for hope.

Andy telephoned his daughter, Dixie. Their conversation "was about making sure that I was at peace with certain aspects of my life, and he shared with me his peace that he had found," she recalled. "It felt very much like he was imparting to me wisdom to carry forward. Because of the nature, because of the context of the conversation, I knew, I just knew that was the last time I was going to talk to him. He told me he loved me; I told him I loved him."

Andy spoke to Jim Nabors. Jim was startled at the frailty in Andy's voice. "Goll dang," Jim told Andy, "you sound old."

Andy shot back, "Well, I'm eighty-six!"

On July 2, Andy fell suddenly, gravely ill. Tests later showed he had suffered a silent heart attack. For some reason, he elected not to go to the hospital. Instead, he summoned the small entourage of locals who remained close to the reclusive Griffiths. They included John Wilson, the former Manteo mayor who had designed Andy's new home; Billy Parker, John's partner; and Calvin Gibbs, the contractor who had built the home, and who served as a Barney Fife–styled companion to Andy in his final years. Cindi was summoned from her winter retreat in the Florida Keys and arrived after midnight.

Andy knew he was dying. He instructed Calvin on the terms of his burial and said, "Bless you, Calvin. I love you." They were his final words. Then Andy settled into a pained sleep. He awoke early the next morning, rose from bed, and sat in his wheelchair. That was where Cindi found him, unresponsive, around 7:00 a.m. She telephoned 911.

Four and a half hours later, Andy Griffith's body was in the ground.

In death, as in life, Andy shrouded himself and his loved ones in privacy. He had told Calvin to bury him immediately, before the paparazzi could storm Roanoke Island to capture his remains on film. The ever-loyal denizens of Dare County did their part: the sheriff grounded helicopters, to keep camera crews away from the Griffith estate. The hectic timetable meant that only a few of Andy's local friends could attend the makeshift service. His lone surviving child could not.

"Apparently that was his wish," Dixie recalled. "He didn't want a funeral. He didn't want a circus. He didn't want a media frenzy. And that was an unfortunate circumstance. How do I gather the girls and get on a plane and go? But I understand if that was his wish, and I have to be respectful of what he wanted."

Andy had never won an Emmy, an Oscar, or a Tony. Yet, he had attained a celebrity that transcended those honors. Like Lucille Ball or Johnny Carson, Andy had connected with American society to its core. *The Andy Griffith Show* had shaped popular culture. Those teleplays had taught America something about itself—about the virtues of friends and family and a savored life. The program had attracted devotees as disparate as J. D. Salinger, John Waters, and Dolly Parton. President Barack Obama praised Andy as "beloved by generations of fans and revered by entertainers who followed in his footsteps."

In September, Ron Howard delivered an elegant eulogy to Andy at the 2012 Emmy Awards, saying, "Andy's legacy of excellence, accessibility, and range puts him in the pantheon. But, dang, if he didn't make it look powerful easy while he was going about it. Didn't he?"

On the same broadcast, actors Bryan Cranston and Aaron Paul re-created the opening scene of *The Andy Griffith Show* in character as violent meth dealers from the celebrated television morality play *Breaking Bad*. The moment underscored the innocence and idealism of the era that had spawned the *Griffith Show*. At the close of the skit, the men pulled handguns from beneath their hazmat suits and shot Deputy Fife in the chest.

A few months later, Andy was inexplicably omitted from the "In Memoriam" tribute reel at the Oscars. An NBC affiliate in Cleveland responded by airing two hours of *Matlock* in place of its usual Thursday lineup, in protest.

In the end, whether he wanted one or not, Andy Griffith would have his memorial.

One September weekend, nearly three months after Andy's death, tens of thousands of Mayberry faithful journeyed to Mount Airy for the twenty-third annual Mayberry Days, now an ambitious three-day undertaking. At 10:00 a.m. Friday, the stage of the Blackmon Amphitheatre filled with an ensemble of Mayberry royalty: character impersonators, descendants of dead cast members, and a few frail souls who once played actual parts on Andy's show. Here was Karen Knotts, with her father's saucer eyes; and George

Lindsey Jr., who struck a passing resemblance to his father when he planted a beanie on his head; and a Don Knotts surrogate, with a few extra pounds on his frame and no magic in his eyes. No one dared impersonate Andy. Maggie Peterson Mancuso, the former Charlene Darling, offered consolation to a community in mourning. Over the past year, the town had lost not just Andy but also George "Goober" Lindsey and Doug "Darling" Dillard. "We'll always have them in our heart," Charlene Darling said, "and they're smiling down on us now."

Downtown, an entire fleet of Ford Galaxie 500s had been parked along Main Street at regular intervals. The lines at Barney's Café and Opie's Candy Store snaked out their doors. Those stores were modern Mayberry replicas; Walker's Soda Fountain was the real thing, open since 1925. Andy Griffith had worked there one summer as a bicycle delivery boy, back when it was a pharmacy.

The afternoon ended with a trivia contest: What is Thelma Lou's house number? In Episode 34, who is holding a copy of the *Press Herald* with a hole in it? What is the license number on Orville Monroe's hearse?

The eventual winner, Pat Bullins of Walnut Cove, NC, answered eighteen of the twenty questions correctly. Her son Ernie had helped her train for the contest using the freeze-frame on their VCR. Her prize: a trophy cup bearing the inscription MAYBERRY TRIVIA WORLD CHAMPION.

All day, the line outside the Andy Griffith Museum wound around the building. At the entrance, Emmett Forrest, Andy's childhood friend, held court. Many visitors were crying. Leaning in, Emmett confided, "I have people come up to me and say, 'Tell Andy I love him.' I don't know how I'm supposed to do that." A few months later, Emmett himself would be dead; perhaps he delivered the messages after all.

Saturday opened with a parade down Main Street in a chilly drizzle. The North Surry High School Band tromped past, some of the musicians dressed in hillbilly garb, just behind the float carrying Little Miss Bacon Bits. The Southern Mountain Fire Cloggers danced on a flatbed to the tune of "Goin' Down the Road Feeling Bad." Out on Haymore Street, a more sporadic parade filed past the yellow frame ranch house at 711, where Andy's family once lived, opposite a water tower.

Sunday dawned with a "Gospel Tribute" to Andy, featuring the same Moravian band that had once counted Andy as a member. Four men in black suits led the crowd in some of Andy's favorite hymns: "What a Friend We Have in Jesus," "I'll Fly Away," "Will the Circle Be Unbroken?" One of the preachers lifted his voice to sing the Lord's Prayer, and a few in the crowd raised their open palms toward heaven.

Back in town, a shopkeeper did a brisk business selling a T-shirt emblazoned with a picture of Andy in his shirt and tie, and Barney in his salt-and-pepper suit, both men kicking back on wicker chairs and laughing together above the legend HEAVEN'S FRONT PORCH.

The shirt captured the moment better than any speech, or any statue. While Andy Griffith and Don Knotts came from different towns, pursued largely separate careers, and amassed many artistic credits alone, it seemed inevitable that history would ultimately remember them together, two names to be uttered in one breath.

The Andy Griffith Show is Andy's greatest legacy, and Don's. The program endures, in the end, as a monument to their friendship. A half century on, it seems clear that the *Griffith Show* was not really about a father and his son, nor a widower and his aunt. It was about a sheriff and his deputy. The bond between Andy and Barney was the essence of Mayberry. Whenever the sheriff raced around town to clean up his deputy's messes, or to redeem his failures, we saw the comical lengths to which one friend might go to protect another. Whenever Andy gazed lovingly at his diminutive costar, or Don tortured Andy with his big bug eyes and tried a dozen different ways to crack him up, we saw the depth of the friendship that lay so plainly behind the performance.

We can only hope Andy and Don are together now, beneath the setting sun, lazily plotting a walk into town to fetch a bottle of pop.

Acknowledgments

I first met Don Knotts at Walt Disney World. The year was probably 1992, and Don was in Florida for a promotional tour. (Forgive me: I was there as a brother-in-law, not a reporter, and I took no notes.) Don was in a relationship with Francey, beloved sister of my wife, Sophie. We were there mainly so the sisters could reconnect, and I don't suppose it had occurred to either Sophie or me what it meant to visit Disney World with Don Knotts.

Don, you see, was like Elvis. People mobbed him whenever he and Francey set forth from their penthouse suite at the Disney hotel. Grandparents from Phoenix, young couples from Atlanta, teenagers from Fort Lauderdale—everyone recognized him, everyone approached him, everyone wanted a piece of him. Thousands of smiles greeted us at every turn, along with seemingly endless requests for an autograph, or a conversation, or a hug. Tiny children would stop and point and cry, "Mr. Limpet!" The dimensions of his celebrity were staggering. How could this man get from one end of a room to the other?

Later that year, we moved to California, and Don became a fixture at holiday gatherings, sitting quietly in the corner of my mother-in-law's living room, smiling benignly as the family pageant played out around him. Here, oddly, Don was invisible, and Sophie would periodically prod me to walk over and talk to him. I would approach Don sheepishly and invoke my interview skills. "I'd love to hear the story of how you created the Nervous Man," I would say, although I had heard it before; or, "Tell me again how you broke into radio." Then Don would straighten up, clear his throat, and raise his raspy but instantly recognizable voice.

He still sounded a bit like Barney Fife, but an entirely different brain labored behind those eyes: serious, intelligent, contemplative, calm. Don was Barney at his most relaxed, chuckling with Andy on the front porch and sharing some serene meditation on the day's events.

I met Andy Griffith just once, at Don's funeral, in 2006. Andy was old and frail, but his face still shone with that unmistakable glow of celebrity. When his time came to speak, Andy didn't just speak: he testified. Andy's body shook as he summoned that big, booming voice. "And ah take comfort," he quaked, "because ah know that Don . . . is . . . in . . . *paradise!*" At that moment, Andy's love for Don all but knocked us out of our chairs.

In fall 2012, shortly after Andy's death, I set out to write something about their historic friendship. I took my family down to Mount Airy, North

Carolina, for the annual Mayberry Days festival, and I brought two yellow legal pads. I filled them up with all the sights and sounds of an event that felt like a big memorial service for Andy. We returned home, and I set about interviewing everyone I could find who had ever been close to Andy or Don. The project quickly grew too big for an article, and I pitched it as a book.

This manuscript came together between fall 2012 and spring 2014, and I continued to collect interviews and ephemera through the end of the year. I amassed a cubic foot of articles about my subjects from newspapers, magazines, and wire services, purchased and read every significant book on Andy or Don or *The Andy Griffith Show*, scanned dozens of memoirs for pertinent chapters, and tracked down every lengthy interview I could find, including the impressive collection at the Archive of American Television. My main subjects were dead, but I found and interviewed every living soul who would talk to me about their lives: *Griffith Show* costars Ron Howard, Jim Nabors, Betty Lynn, Elinor Donahue, and Maggie Peterson Mancuso; Don's manager, Sherwin Bash; Andy's manager, Dick Linke; Don's children, Karen and Tom Knotts; Andy's daughter, Dixie; Don's former wives, Kay and Loralee, and his widow, Francey; Don's friends, including Al Checco, John Pyles, Mary Lopez, and the late Richie Ferrara; Andy's friends and old classmates, including the late Emmett Forrest, Garnett Steele, J. B. Childress, Robert Merritt, Barbara Folger Chatham, Betsy Mills McCraw, Ed Sutphin, Robert Hurley, George Vassos, the late Carl Perry, Quentin Bell, Edward Greene, Craig Fincannon, and William Ivey Long. I also spoke to many of Andy's and Don's professional peers, some of whom had become dear friends. That group includes actors Clive Rice, Ivan Cury, Lee Grant, Earle Hyman, Tim Conway, Pat Harrington, Rance Howard, Ken Berry, Ronnie Schell, Elaine Joyce, Frank Welker, Claudette Nevins, Joan Staley, Barbara Rhoades, Lee Meriwether, Michael Brandon, Joyce DeWitt, Richard Kline, Dodie Brown, Stella Berrier, Sharon Spelman, Jamie Smith-Jackson, Billy Bob Thornton, and Nancy Stafford; producers Dean Hargrove and Joel Steiger; directors Bruce Bilson and Peter Baldwin; and writer Sam Bobrick. I spoke to surviving relatives of key characters who had died, including Robert and Mike King, Barbara Griffith's nephews; Bridget Sweeney, daughter of director Bob Sweeney; Kit McNear, son of actor Howard McNear; George Lindsey Jr.; and Jesse Corsaut and Jennifer Scarlott, brother and niece, respectively, of actress Aneta Corsaut. I interviewed *Griffith Show* scholars Neal Brower and Richard Kelly. I am deeply indebted to all of them for their help.

Many others provided inspiration and counsel:

Karyn Marcus, Sydney Tanigawa, and Molly Lindley, my wonderful editors at Simon & Schuster; Geri Thoma, my terrific agent at Writers House; John Cuthbert, director of the West Virginia and Regional History Center at West Virginia University; the Reverend Dr. Arvid Straube, who led Don's funeral service; Pat Bullins, queen of *Griffith Show* trivia; Marjorie Harrington, whose memories helped me set the scene; Charisse Gines, who put me in touch with Jim Nabors, and Jacqueline Beatty, who helped me connect with Tim Conway; Tom Hellebrand, whose statue dream may finally become reality; Jeff Gossett and Ivan Shreve, who helped me track down long-lost episodes; Beth Lancaster at Converse College, Barbara's alma mater; Troy Valos at the Norfolk Public Library; David Bushman at the Paley Center for Media; David Lombard at the CBS Photo Archive; Amy Snyder at the Mount Airy Museum of Regional History; and numerous helpful souls at the vast Library of Congress and the University of Maryland Libraries.

My reporting efforts did not always succeed. I could not reach Andy's second wife, Solica; Andy's widow, Cindi, politely declined interview requests. Some sources died before I could speak to them. Others, including the wonderful Richie Ferrara and the loyal Emmett Forrest, died before we could finish our conversations.

I heard contradictory accounts of some stories and incomplete accounts of others, leaving unanswered questions that I have attempted to flag in the manuscript. Who really conceived "The Pickle Story"? Who persuaded Don to take his Nervous Man to Steve Allen? We may never know.

Many excellent books have explored *The Andy Griffith Show* and its legacy; I must single out four titles that I reduced to tatters through repeated consultation: *The Andy Griffith Story*, by Terry Collins; *Barney Fife and Other Characters I Have Known*, by Don Knotts with Robert Metz; *The Andy Griffith Show*, by Richard Kelly; and *Mayberry 101*, by Neal Brower.

Deepest thanks to everyone at Simon & Schuster, including Jonathan Karp, who believed in this book; Megan Hogan, who guided me through the final months; and Maureen Cole, a superb publicist. And thank you to the friends and loved ones who tendered advice when I needed it, including Betty de Visé, my mother; and Paul Dickson and John Grogan, my dear friends and fellow authors.

Twenty Great Episodes of
The Andy Griffith Show

1.2. "The Manhunt." Written by Charles Stewart and Jack Elinson, broadcast October 10, 1960. This story, which would win a Writers Guild Award for comedy writing, established Don as the comedic center of *The Andy Griffith Show.* State police arrive in town to hunt an escaped prisoner. Barney cannot bear to be left out and promptly finds himself captured by the criminal. Andy hatches a plan to recapture the crook and vindicate Barney, setting a template for many more *Griffith* episodes to come.

1.11. "The Christmas Story." Written by Frank Tarloff, broadcast December 19, 1960. This was the first of eighty episodes directed by the great Bob Sweeney, and his ear for pathos is immediately evident. The script pays artful homage to Dickens and Seuss. Hard-hearted merchant Ben arrests a local moonshiner on Christmas and insists that he go to jail over Andy's protests. So, Andy transforms the jail into a joyous Christmas party, enlisting Barney as an anemic Santa Claus. Repentant Ben is reduced to standing outside the jailhouse window, clinging to the bars, tears pooling in his eyes as he wordlessly joins Andy and Ellie in a refrain of "Away in a Manger."

2.11. "The Pickle Story." Written by Harvey Bullock, broadcast December 18, 1961. No one seemed to like this script when Bullock first presented it. Today it stands as perhaps the quintessential *Griffith* episode. "The Pickle Story" celebrates the Mayberry virtue of going to comic lengths to protect people's feelings. Aunt Bee presents Andy and Barney a batch of her ghastly homemade pickles. The boys can't bear to eat them; to protect Bee's feelings, they secretly swap her pickles for store-bought surrogates. But their plan implodes when Bee elects to enter her pickles in the county fair. Now, Andy and Barney must choose between hurting Bee's pride and perpetrating fraud.

2.20. "Barney and the Choir." Written by Charles Stewart and Jack Elinson, broadcast February 19, 1962. Andy revisited his childhood choral memories in this story, a sweet lesson in human frailty. Andy labors to protect Barney from hurt when he joins the town choir and it becomes painfully obvious that he cannot sing. The choir director wants Barney out. But Andy refuses to fire him, searching instead for some means to coax him away. Several ploys fail. As a concert draws near, it becomes increasingly plain that Andy is not merely concerned for Barney's welfare; he is reluctant to deliver the bad news—a gentle reminder that Andy, too, is only human.

2.29. "Andy on Trial." Written by Jack Elinson and Charles Stewart, broadcast April 23, 1962. Andy confronts a big-city businessman over a neglected speeding ticket. The executive manipulates Barney to gather dirt on the sheriff and publishes a hit piece in his newspaper. A state prosecutor comes after Andy, and Barney is called to the stand to defend him. He testifies that Andy "is more than just a sheriff. He's a friend." Barney delivers his speech with striking conviction, reflecting Don's powerful real-life friendship with Andy.

3.1. "Mr. McBeevee." Written by Ray Saffian Allen and Harvey Bullock, broadcast October 1, 1962. Season three of *The Andy Griffith Show* opened with this meditation on fatherhood and faith. Opie appears at the sheriff's office with tales of Mr. McBeevee, a man who lives in the trees. It sounds fanciful—until the boy begins to show up bearing gifts from his imaginary friend. Andy fears Opie has stolen the items. Opie insists his friend is real, but he can produce no evidence. This is agony for viewers, who know Mr. McBeevee is a man from the power company, up in the "trees" to work on the lines. In the end, Andy decides to trust in his son.

3.11. "Convicts at Large." Written by Jim Fritzell and Everett Greenbaum, broadcast December 10, 1962. *The Andy Griffith Show* never got weirder than in this gender-bending parody of the escaped-convict drama *The Desperate Hours*. Mayberry milquetoasts Barney and Floyd visit the old O'Malley cabin and stumble upon three escaped convicts, a trio of tough broads led by lantern-jawed Maude Tyler. The women force Barney to dance at gunpoint, and Floyd succumbs to Stockholm syndrome. The story ends with a slapstick scene worthy of Buster Keaton, Andy laboring to slap a cuff on Big Maude as she and Barney tango in and out of the cabin door.

3.13. "The Bank Job." Written by Jim Fritzell and Everett Greenbaum, broadcast December 24, 1962. This story showcases Barney and his delusions of law-enforcement grandeur; it also marks the on-screen *Griffith* debut of Jim Nabors. Barney frets that Mayberry is ripe for a crime wave. He decides to teach the town a lesson, sneaking into the bank to stage a theft. Caught by the manager, he panics and closes himself in the vault, whence he must be rescued. Barney's charade catches the attention of real bank robbers, who stage a real robbery; Andy thwarts it, and Barney is vindicated.

3.16. "Man in a Hurry." Written by Everett Greenbaum and Jim Fritzell, broadcast January 14, 1963. Surely the finest *Griffith* episode, "Man in a Hurry" stands as the ultimate expression of the Mayberry maxim that life is to be savored. An out-of-town businessman wanders into Mayberry on a Sunday morning after his car breaks down. Mayberry is closed for business, a scenario Malcolm Tucker cannot accept. He is trapped in the Mayberry Twilight Zone. Andy takes him in, and Tucker paces across the front porch as Andy and Barney hum a spiritual. In time, Tucker lifts his voice and joins them in song.

3.27. "Barney's First Car." Written by Jim Fritzell and Everett Greenbaum, broadcast April 1, 1963. This story, which earned the *Griffith Show* its second Writers Guild Award, tells a father-son story about life's lessons learned, but with Barney cast as the son. Barney buys his first car, handing his life savings to a little old lady who spots an easy mark. Barney packs the gang into his new car for a ceremonial first ride, bobbing his head with smug pride. Tragedy descends in a hilarious sequence of taps and clanks. This episode includes the classic Andy-Barney septic-tank skit.

3.31. "Mountain Wedding." Written by Jim Fritzell and Everett Greenbaum, broadcast April 29, 1963. This late-season entry introduces Ernest

T. Bass, an unvarnished hillbilly set loose like a Tasmanian devil among the gentle souls of Mayberry. Ernest T. scampers through the brush and hurls rocks through windows, intent on romancing a fellow rustic named Charlene Darling. He charges into Charlene's wedding ceremony and drags off the bride—who turns out to be Barney in drag, planted as a decoy. Then Barney comes crashing out of the woods in his dress, fleeing unknown horrors and crying out for Andy, one of the odder scenes on prime-time television in 1963.

3.32. "The Big House." Written by Harvey Bullock, broadcast May 6, 1963. The season-three finale displayed all the talents of three *Griffith* funnymen and showcased an ascendant partnership between Don and Jim Nabors to complement the interplay between Don and Andy. The sheriff is charged with holding two hardened cons for a few hours. He begs Barney not to intervene, but of course Barney cannot resist. Barney deputizes Gomer and sets about finding new and inventive ways to enable the convicts' escape. The highlight is Barney delivering his "Here at the Rock" speech to the bewildered cons, while Andy tries his best not to crack up.

4.1. "Opie the Birdman." Written by Harvey Bullock, broadcast September 30, 1963. The season-four opener was the best among many *Griffith* episodes to explore the relationship between Andy and Opie. It was a daring broadcast because Harvey Bullock's script wasn't really a work of comedy. Opie inadvertently kills a bird with his slingshot. When Andy learns what has happened, he punishes Opie by throwing open his bedroom window, so Opie can hear the plaintive tweets of three baby birds that have lost their mother. By morning, Opie has decided to raise the baby birds himself. This is Andy at his most Lincolnesque.

4.2. "The Haunted House." Written by Harvey Bullock, broadcast October 7, 1963. This classic episode displays Andy's impish side. Opie hits a baseball through a window in an abandoned house. Opie fears the house is haunted. When Barney lectures Opie on childish fears, Andy teasingly goads Barney into entering the house himself. Now terrified, Barney enlists Gomer and Andy to join him. Andy quickly traces the ghostly happenings to a mundane source. Don later parlayed this story into *The Ghost and Mr. Chicken.*

4.10. "Up in Barney's Room." Written by Jim Fritzell and Everett Greenbaum, broadcast December 2, 1963. Viewers had never been afforded a glimpse inside Barney's inner sanctum:

a simple room on the upper floor of a boarding-house, with a hot plate and a jug of sweet cider. When Barney defies the house rules, his landlady, the gentle Mrs. Mendelbright, asks him to leave. With Barney gone, Mrs. Mendelbright swiftly falls prey to a con man, who woos her and plots to take her money. Andy and Barney arrive in the nick of time to apprehend the villain. The story affirms the quiet power of friendship.

4.11. "Citizen's Arrest." Written by Everett Greenbaum and Jim Fritzell, broadcast December 16, 1963. This story explores the fragility of Barney's worldview and the stark emptiness of his life outside the sheriff's office. Barney catches Gomer making a U-turn and insists on writing him a ticket. When Gomer protests, inflexible Barney warns, "It's from little misdemeanors that major felonies grow." Gomer takes this lesson to heart: when Barney executes a U-turn of his own, Gomer cries, "Citizen's ar-ray-yest!" Now, Barney must write himself a ticket. Seething, he chooses jail over a five-dollar fine. Only the next morning does he realize he might lose his prized job and his best friend.

4.16. "Barney's Sidecar." Written by Jim Fritzell and Everett Greenbaum, broadcast January 27, 1964. This episode is built from a single sight gag—one purloined from the Marx

Brothers, to boot. But Don makes the most of a fine script, a comic expedition into Barney's puerile soul. The deputy returns from an army-surplus auction with a World War I motorcycle and sidecar, with which he intends to police the state highway. His menacing helmet, black leather jacket, and reptilian goggles induce peals of laughter everywhere Barney goes, even as they impel the deputy toward fascist extremes. Andy confides to Aunt Bee, "I wish we had a psychiatrist in town. I bet Barney'd be a real study."

4.21. "The Shoplifters." Written by Bill Idelson and Sam Bobrick, broadcast March 2, 1964. This story won the *Griffith Show* its third and final Writers Guild Award. Working from a one-line concept—What if Barney posed as a mannequin to catch a shoplifter?—the writers built a story populated with quirky characters from previous episodes: Ben Weaver, the impatient department-store manager; and Asa Breeney, the doddering night watchman. The episode climaxes with a farcical midnight stakeout inside Weaver's store.

5.25. "The Case of the Punch in the Nose." Written by Bill Idelson and Sam Bobrick, broadcast March 15, 1965. Most viewers didn't know it, but this would be the last great *Griffith* episode to feature Barney as a regular. Barney stumbles upon a minor scuffle from years before, utterly trivial—but unsolved. Over Andy's strenuous objections, Barney reopens the case. His interrogations set off a fresh outbreak of nose punching. By the end, Andy seems genuinely angry at Barney for his meddling, perhaps reflecting real-life strain as Don prepared to exit.

6.17. "The Return of Barney Fife." Written by Sam Bobrick and Bill Idelson, broadcast January 10, 1966. This is the first, and probably the best, of five reunion episodes filmed in the three years after Don left the *Griffith Show.* (All are worth watching; they earned Don two of his five Emmys.) Barney has decamped to Raleigh for big-city police work, but he returns to Mayberry for a stirring visit with Andy. They attend the Mayberry High School reunion, where Don has a poignant encounter with Thelma Lou, his old girlfriend, who now has a husband. Barney is devastated, and Thelma's revelation stands as perhaps the saddest moment in the series.

Andy and Don:
A Selective Filmography

A Face in the Crowd, 1957, directed by Elia Kazan. Andy Griffith's finest single performance.

No Time for Sergeants, 1958, directed by Mervyn LeRoy. A fitting memorial to the first collaboration between Andy and Don.

The Ghost and Mr. Chicken, 1966, directed by Alan Rafkin. Don's first and best Universal feature.

Angel in My Pocket, 1969, directed by Alan Rafkin. Andy's cinematic comeback, a well-written, well-acted flop.

The Love God?, 1969, directed by Nat Hiken. Don's most ambitious Universal film.

Pray for the Wildcats, 1974, directed by Robert Michael Lewis. Andy bikes through Baja. A midnight-movie classic.

Three's Company, 1979–84. Don's television comeback.

The Private Eyes, 1980, directed by Lang Elliott. Don's best film collaboration with Tim Conway.

Murder in Coweta County, 1983, directed by Gary Nelson. Andy's finest moment in a long run of television bad-guy roles.

Return to Mayberry, 1986, directed by Bob Sweeney. The long-awaited *Griffith Show* reunion.

Matlock, 1986–95. Andy Griffith's television comeback, and a touching reunion with Don.

Notes

In compiling the sources listed below, I have sought to avoid duplicate or unenlightening citations. Generally speaking, I have supplied endnotes wherever I cite material from a previously published work and do not identify the publication in the text. I have provided a single citation for any passage, no matter its length, that draws from a single interview. I mostly avoid notes for brief or inconsequential quotes from my own interviews, for conversations reconstructed from multiple sources, for things said at public events, and for material taken from sources who wished not to be identified.

Prologue: The Call

2 *"the wheels in my brain"*: Don Knotts, undated audio recording created in preparation of the book *Barney Fife and Other Characters I Have Known* (New York: Berkley Boulevard, 1999), accessed at the West Virginia and Regional History Collection of the West Virginia University Libraries.

1. Don's Demons

4 *"I did not come into the world"*: Don Knotts, undated handwritten notes provided by the Don Knotts estate.

5 *"one of the truly good people"*: Knotts, *Barney Fife* audio.

5 *When Don's older brother:* Ibid.

6 *"My mother took me":* Don Knotts, interview by Gary Rutkowski for the Archive of American Television, July 22, 1999.

6 *"The clowning would begin"*: Knotts, *Barney Fife* audio.

7 *"Sid was a real hick":* Richie Ferrara, interview by author, October 24, 2012.

8 *"I think my mother"*: Knotts, undated handwritten notes.

10 *"But when he got"*: Knotts, *Barney Fife* audio.

10 *"We were supposed":* Richie Ferrara, interview by author, October 5, 2012.

11 *"They had a little bit":* Ferrara, interview by author, October 24, 2012.

11 *"the happiest and most fertile":* Knotts, *Barney Fife* audio.

11 *"His father employed":* Ferrara, interview by author, October 24, 2012.

12 *"He'd do* 'Ave Maria' *":* Knotts, *Barney Fife* audio.

12 *"We called ourselves":* Ferrara, interview by author, October 24, 2012.

12 *"We always had":* Remarks by Richie Ferrara at Don Knotts memorial service, May 4, 2006.

12 *"I had walked"*: Don Knotts with Robert Metz, *Barney Fife and Other Characters I Have Known* (New York: Berkley Boulevard, 1999), 29.

13 *"I was a terrible president"*: Dick Hobson, "The Wages of Fear," *TV Guide*, October 21, 1967.

13 *"We told everyone"*: Ray Gosovich, uncredited interview, June 19, 2008, provided by the Don Knotts estate.

13 *"Remember, Donald"*: Knotts, *Barney Fife* audio.

14 *"You seem like"*: Ibid.

14 *"Most of us in our teens"*: Knotts with Metz, *Barney Fife*, 36.

16 *"It was an experimental thing"*: Al Checco, interview by author, February 1, 2013.

16 *"Before I knew it"*: Knotts, *Barney Fife* audio.

17 *"We performed on whatever"*: Remarks by Al Checco at Don Knotts memorial service, May 4, 2006.

17 *"If you wonder why"*: Knotts, *Barney Fife* audio.

17 *"The Japanese kept bombing"*: Checco, remarks at Don Knotts memorial.

17 *"The constant rain"*: Knotts, *Barney Fife* audio.

18 *"Out of the clear"*: Checco, remarks at the Don Knotts memorial.

19 *"Everybody was in stitches":* Jim Allen, uncredited interview, June 26, 2008, provided by the Don Knotts estate.

20 *"And she died laughing":* Ferrara, interview by author, October 5, 2012.

20 *"In most cases":* Knotts, undated handwritten notes.

20 *"When we got back":* Ferrara, interview by author, October 5, 2012.

21 *"He was very charismatic":* Kay Knotts, interview by author, November 5, 2012.

22 *"Guess what?":* Knotts, *Barney Fife* audio.

2. Laugh, Lest Ye Cry

23 *"Mama wasn't quite":* James Brady, "In Step with Andy Griffith," Parade, June 2, 1996.

23 *Young Andy had a shock of blond hair:* Some facts in this passage were taken from Terry Collins, *The Andy Griffith Story: An Illustrated Biography* (Mount Airy, NC: Explorer Press, 1995).

24 *"It seemed like he had":* J. B. Childress, interview by author, April 19, 2013.

24 *"She didn't really care":* Garnett Steele, interview by author, April 18, 2013.

24 *"We picked on him":* Childress, interview by author.

24 *"The other fellas":* Tricia Jones,

"Everybody Was Laughing—but Me!," *TV Radio Mirror*, December 1963.

25 *"I don't know why I didn't"*: Andy Griffith, interview by Michael Rosen for the Archive of American Television, May 5, 1998.

25 *"I don't know to this day"*: Jones, "Everybody Was Laughing."

26 *"I did it as a matter"*: Griffith, interview by Rosen.

26 *"He was a person"*: Steele, interview by author.

27 *"If something really"*: Dotson Rader, "Why I Listened to My Father," *Parade*, February 4, 1990.

27 *"He simply adored"*: Dixie Nann Griffith, interview by author, April 29, 2013.

27 *"A lot of the men"*: Childress, interview by author.

27 *"This'll tell you"*: Griffith, interview by Rosen.

29 *"Sitting astride his bicycle"*: Edward T. Mickey, "The Andy Griffith I Know," *Wachovia Magazine*, February 1968.

29 *"was the turning point"*: Griffith, interview by Rosen.

30 *"was the kind they used to"*: Lillian and Helen Ross, *The Player* (New York: Simon and Schuster, 1962), 217.

30 *"All the younger students"*: Eleanor Powell, "Andy Griffith Left Imprint on 'Mayberry'

Residents," *Mount Airy News*, undated.

30 *"And what I remember":* Robert Merritt, interview by author, April 19, 2013.

31 *"He stood on":* Steele, interview by author.

31 *"My major was sociology":* Griffith, interview by Rosen.

31 *"Some people thought":* Robert Merritt, interview by author, April 24, 2013.

32 *"I had a wonderful time":* Andy Griffith, remarks to the North Carolina Literary & Historical Association, November 1982.

32 *"I didn't even know who":* Griffith, interview by Rosen.

32 *"tell what you know":* William Ivey Long, interview by author, May 17, 2013.

32 *"breakfast and eight dollars":* Griffith, remarks to the North Carolina Literary & Historical Association.

33 *"Have you heard":* Freda Balling, "Hillbilly Hero," *TV Radio Mirror*, October 1957.

33 *"They were a genteel":* Robert Edwards King, interview by author, April 22, 2013.

34 *"Barbara Edwards was a sweetheart":* Carl Perry, interview by author, May 3, 2013.

34 *"They were doing the Haydn":* Barbara Griffith, interview by Edward R. Murrow, June 14, 1957.

34 *He asked her:* Jody Andrews, "The Secret Life of a Married Man," *TV Radio Mirror*, September 1963.

34 *"They paid only twenty-five"*: Griffith, interview by Rosen.

35 *"My dad started out"*: Dixie Nann Griffith, interview by author, April 29, 2013.

35 *Barbara remained, to this point:* Lawrence Maddry, "Old Lost Colonist Seeks Self," *The Virginian-Pilot*, August 27, 1972.

35 *"would play popular songs"*: Robert Hurley, interview by author, May 7, 2013.

36 *"I remember helping pick"*: Long, interview by author.

36 *"They only had six hundred students"*: Griffith, interview by Rosen.

37 *"I don't know how"*: Andy Griffith, interview by Edward R. Murrow, June 14, 1957.

37 *"Every night after the show"*: George Vassos, interview by author, May 22, 2013.

37 *"Singing had always"*: Griffith, interview by Rosen.

39 *"He talked just like"*: Edwards King, interview by author.

39 *"I really think our families"*: Barbara Griffith, interview by Murrow.

40 *"She'd sing"*: Griffith, interview by Rosen.

40 *"We figured that at least"*: Ross and Ross, *Player*, 220.

40 *"They were like a"*: Mike King, interview by author, October 30, 2014.

40 *"I'm trying to gain"*: Childress, interview by author.

41 *"And I didn't have but one"*: Andy Griffith, interview by Fred Griffith, *The Morning Exchange*, WEWS-TV, 1972.

41 *"so blue Andy wouldn't tell"*: Marjory Adams, "4,000,000 People in the United States Know Andy Griffin [sic]," *Daily Boston Globe*, October 9, 1955.

41 *"could have held the stage"*: History of the Raleigh Little Theatre, http://raleighlittle theatre.org/about/history/index.html.

41 *"We've got to make"*: "Andrew Samuel Griffith (1926–2012)," http://blogs.lib.unc .edu/morton/index.php/2012/07/andrew-samuel-griffith-1926-2012/.

3. The Bumpkins Take Broadway

43 *"We would go to a place"*: Kay Knotts, interview by author, November 10, 2012.

44 *"He introduced me all around"*: Knotts, *Barney Fife* audio.

45 *"I walked onstage"*: Ibid.

47 *"There was quite a technique"*: Ibid.

48 *"There were hundreds"*: Ivan Cury, interview by author, February 6, 2013.

49 *"He had quite a collection"*: Clive Rice, interview by author, February 2, 2013.

49 *"everything was up for grabs"*: Knotts with Metz, *Barney Fife*, 67–68.

50 *"He played a nebbish"*: Lee Grant,

interview by author, March 18, 2015.

50 *"He didn't have to speak"*: Kay Knotts, interview by author.

51 *"the most boring thing"*: Don Knotts, interview by Gary Rutkowski, July 22, 1999.

51 *"My day went something like this"*: Knotts, *Barney Fife* audio.

52 *"Have you looked into"*: Ibid.

53 *"I'm sorry"*: Ibid.

54 *"I was determined"*: Knotts, undated handwritten notes.

54 *"I was learning"*: Knotts, *Barney Fife* audio.

54 *"My name is Maurice"*: Knotts with Metz, *Barney Fife*, 78–79.

55 *"His teeth"*: Donald Freeman, "I Think I'm Gaining on Myself," *The Saturday Evening Post*, January 25, 1964

55 *"And we went over"*: Dick Linke, interview by author, October 6, 2012.

56 *"I have found"*: Gayle White, "Behind the Badge," *The Atlanta Journal-Constitution*, July 14, 1996.

56 *"I 'preciate it"*: Joan Barthel, "How to Merchandise an Actor on TV," *The New York Times*, October 25, 1970.

56 *"They put on my"*: Griffith, interview by Rosen.

57 *"Now, I want you"*: Andy Griffith, interview by Larry King, June 1, 1996.

57 *"He needed a lot"*: Linke, interview by author, October 6, 2012.

58 *"And I scored"*: Griffith, interview by Rosen.

58 *"The effect on the audience"*: Lawrence Laurent, "Andy Hit It 'Right Nice,' " *The Washington Post*, December 11, 1960.

58 *"an old man"*: Andy Griffith, remarks at Don Knotts memorial service, May 4, 2006.

59 *"If there's ever anything"*: Griffith, interview by Larry King, June 1, 1996.

59 *"Andy, you have to know"*: Andy Griffith, interview by Larry King, November 27, 2003.

59 *"I didn't read well"*: Griffith, interview by Rosen.

60 *"I have Will Stockdale"*: Hedda Hopper, "Cotton-Pickin' Talk Dandy for Andy," *Los Angeles Times*, August 13, 1961.

60 *"as nervous as a cat"*: Knotts, *Barney Fife* audio.

60 *"this thin little man"*: Griffith, remarks at the Don Knotts memorial.

4. Nervous Men

62 *"Sheee-it, yes"*: Knotts, undated handwritten notes.

63 *"Mr. DaCosta?"*: Knotts, *Barney Fife* audio.

64 *"It's there or it's not"*: Griffith, interview by King.

64 *"You can't win"*: Knotts, *Barney Fife* audio.

64 *"He played Stockdale"*: Collins, *Andy Griffith Story*, 45.

64 *"Everyone was there"*: Dick Linke, interview by author, November 17, 2014.

65 *"We had similar backgrounds"*: Bill King, "25 Years Later, Mayberry's Never Looked So Good," *The Atlanta Journal-Constitution*, October 3, 1985.

65 *"They talked about everybody"*: Kay Knotts, interview by author.

65 *"One thing we've talked"*: "TV-Radio," *Newsweek*, October 23, 1961.

66 *"she was the big girl"*: Kay Knotts, interview by author.

67 *"from prominent families"*: Powell, "Andy Griffith Left Imprint."

67 *"I had finally gotten"*: Knotts, *Barney Fife* audio.

67 *"I didn't feel he"*: Earle Hyman, interview by author, January 25, 2013.

68 *"Griffith could give us"*: Collins, *Andy Griffith Story*, 47.

68 *"I knew I had to do"*: Griffith, interview by Rosen.

69 *"Remember all those people"*: Gilbert Millstein, "Strange Chronicle of Andy Griffith," *The New York Times*, June 2, 1957.

69 *"He became the part"*: "Andy Griffith Biography," http://www.biography.com /people/andy-griffith-9542091.

70 *"I did a lot of things"*: Millstein, "Strange Chronicle of Andy Griffith."

70 *"This was more like it"*: Knotts, *Barney Fife* audio.

70 *"Is it funny?"*: Griffith, remarks at the Don Knotts memorial.

71 *"they brought out two stools"*: Lee Pfeiffer, *The Official Andy Griffith Show Scrapbook* (New York: Citadel, 1994), 18.

71 *"monologues of [Don's] own"*: Steve Allen, *Hi-Ho Steverino!: My Adventures in the Wonderful Wacky World of TV* (Fort Lee, NJ: Barricade, 1992), 150.

72 *"His habit would be"*: Kay Knotts, interview by author.

73 *"Not Don"*: Richard Gehman, "A Mouse of a Different Color," *TV Guide*, May 12, 1962.

73 *"My mind went"*: Knotts with Metz, *Barney Fife*, 99.

74 *"Where are you going"*: Tom Poston, remarks at Don Knotts memorial service, May 4, 2006.

74 *"Most of the people"*: Sherwin Bash, interview by author, October 19, 2012.

74 *"I remember him telling"*: Kay Knotts, interview by author.

75 *"I would see Kay"*: Bash, interview by author, October 19, 2012.

75 *"When I questioned"*: Knotts, *Barney Fife* audio.

76 *"There were a few people"*: Merritt, interview by author, April 19, 2013.

76 *"He was just taking"*: Mike King, interview by author, November 5, 2014.

77 *"Dick, you have a"*: Linke, interview by author, November 17, 2014.

78 *"Now, no matter what happens"*: Collins, *Andy Griffith Story*, 52.

78 *"She'd just stand there"*: Martha Sherrill, "Mayberry for a Day," *The Washington Post*, October 1, 1990.

79 *"Well, we was sittin' "*: Uncredited, "Doin' What Comes Natural," *TV Guide*, October 1, 1960.

79 *"that's fine"*: Hal Humphrey, "Andy Griffith's Shadow Speaks," *Los Angeles Times*, October 4, 1966.

79 *"half a hit"*: Sheldon Leonard, *And the Show Goes On* (New York: Limelight, 1995), vii.

5. Andy Takes a Deputy

80 *"I'd always been afraid"*: Richard Kelly, *The Andy Griffith Show* (Winston-Salem, NC: John F. Blair, 1981), 15.

80 *"Mr. Lastfogel"*: Griffith, interview by Rosen.

80 *"Yeah, he did a record"*: Sheldon Leonard, interview by Sam Denoff for the Archive of

American Television, July 11, 1996.

81 *"I was told"*: Leonard, *And the Show Goes On*, vii.

81 *"We went to his"*: Leonard, interview by Denoff.

81 *"Why all this advance"*: Lee Edson, "Cornball with the Steel-Trap Mind," *TV Guide*, February 3, 1961.

82 *"I didn't realize it"*: Leonard, interview by Denoff.

82 *"What is this magic"*: Kelly, *Andy Griffith Show*, 16.

83 *"The first day"*: Griffith, interview by Rosen.

84 *"That's a hell of"*: Griffith, interview by King, June 1, 1996.

85 *"prodded me with questions"*: Knotts, *Barney Fife* audio.

85 *"Backstage, Jean would have"*: Rance Howard, interview by author, October 25, 2012.

86 *"I'm a graduate"*: Uncredited, "Frances Bavier at Home," *TV Guide*, January 11, 1964.

87 *"I worked out"*: Bash, interview by author, October 19, 2012.

88 *"Television isn't a director's"*: Aaron Ruben, interview by Morrie Gelman for the Archive of American Television, February 25, 1999.

89 *"I hate those three-camera"*: Griffith, interview by Rosen.

89 *"Don and I used to do"*: Kelly, *Andy Griffith Show*, 27.

89 *"beating our brains out"*: Earle Hagen, interview by Jon Burlingame, November 17, 1997.

90 *"one of the most"*: Knotts, *Barney Fife* audio.

90 *"They came walking"*: Bruce Bilson, remarks at Mayberry Days festival, Mount Airy, NC, September 24, 2011.

91 *"Andy and this man"*: Ron Howard, remarks at the Don Knotts memorial service, May 4, 2006.

92 *"There was such an electricity"*: *Thirty Years of Andy: A Mayberry Reunion*, aired October 3, 1990, on TBS.

92 *"We liked it"*: Bruce Bilson, interview by author, November 29, 2012.

93 *"You'll be in the top ten"*: Griffith, interview by King, June 1, 1996.

93 *"By that episode"*: Griffith, interview by Rosen.

94 *"To be a straight man"*: Bill King, "Memories of Mayberry," *The Atlanta Journal-Constitution*, January 24, 1982.

94 *"Our timing was alike"*: Knotts, interview by Rutkowski.

94 *"Hey, Andy"*: Bruce Bilson, interview by author, October 31, 2012.

6. A Hollywood Friendship

96 *"Ah want you":* Bash, interview by author, October 19, 2012.

97 *"I said, 'Boy' ":* Bilson, interview by author, October 31, 2012.

97 *"He had never directed":* Bridget Sweeney, interview by author, December 16, 2013.

97 *"were feeling around":* Bilson, remarks at Mayberry Days.

98 *"Hal, this might":* Uncredited, "Mayberry's Bon Vivant," *TV Guide*, December 29, 1962.

98 *"It was sort of":* Elinor Donahue, interview by Jennifer Howard, April 6, 2006.

98 *"There's things ah can":* Charles Denton, "Andy Griffith Knows His Limitations!," *Hartford Courant*, August 14, 1960.

99 *"Andy would say":* Elinor Donahue, interview by Jennifer Howard, April 25, 2006.

100 *"We spent every day":* Griffith, remarks at the Don Knotts memorial.

100 *"You know, you're the":* Dan Harrison and Bill Habeeb, *Inside Mayberry* (New York: HarperPerennial, 1994), 7.

101 *"You never knew":* Knotts with Metz, *Barney Fife*, 125.

101 *"We never ate":* Bilson, remarks at the Mayberry Days.

102 *"kind of like Ed"*: Ron Howard, interview by author, March 15, 2014.

103 *"Barney ran around"*: *The Andy Griffith Show Reunion*, aired February 10, 1993, on CBS.

103 *"I remember my dad"*: Dixie Nann Griffith, interview by author, November 29, 2012.

103 *"All these characters"*: White, "Behind the Badge."

104 *"Barbara's life changed"*: Edwards King, interview by author.

104 *"He worked very long"*: Karen Knotts, interview by author, October 17, 2012.

105 *"I'm convinced my dad"*: Tom Knotts, interview by author, November 10, 2014.

105 *"We had a very"*: Kay Knotts, interview by author.

105 *"Listen to me"*: Betty Lynn, interview by author, October 26, 2012.

107 *"Barney was such a"*: Betty Lynn, interview by Neal Brower, September 29, 2012.

107 *"After Elinor left"*: Lynn, interview by author.

107 *"I got tears"*: Elinor Donahue, interview by author, November 1, 2012.

108 *"a script came in"*: Rance Howard, interview by author, October 25, 2012.

109 *"Anywhere you are"*: Ken Beck and Jim Clark, *Mayberry Memories* (Nashville: Rutledge Hill, 2000), 60.

110 *"I was visiting"*: Karen Knotts, interview by author.
110 *"The never-ending maw"*: Kelly, *Andy Griffith Show*, 109.
110 *"We'd sit around"*: Ruben, interview by Gelman.
111 *"from the imaginations"*: Pfeiffer, *Official Andy Griffith Show Scrapbook*, 22.
111 *"Andy took him"*: Sweeney, interview by author.
113 *"When do I get"*: Lynn, interview by author.

7. A Slight Thread of Insanity

115 *"Somewhere in the genes"*: Kelly, *Andy Griffith Show*, 108.
116 *"What is it?"*: Ron Howard, interview by author.
116 *"It was pretty funny"*: Stephen J. Spignesi, *Mayberry: My Hometown: The Ultimate Guidebook to America's Favorite TV Small Town* (Ann Arbor, MI: Popular Culture Ink, 1991), 227.
116 *"You wouldn't know"*: Howard, remarks at the Don Knotts memorial.
118 *"a community can be"*: Ron Howard, interview by Gary Rutkowski, October 18, 2006.
119 *"His and Barbara's"*: Sweeney, interview by author.

121 *"Hey, Reggie"*: Kelly, *Andy Griffith Show*, 37.

122 *"I frankly prefer"*: Don Quigg, "Knotts Sold on California," *Chicago Tribune*, May 13, 1962.

122 *"played like he was"*: Stephen Cox and Kevin Marhanka, *The Incredible Mr. Don Knotts* (Nashville, TN: Cumberland House, 2008), 51.

123 *"You've got a funny"*: Knotts with Metz, *Barney Fife*, 137.

123 *"I never worked with"*: Bilson, interview by author, November 29, 2012.

123 *"It was way off"*: Mike King, interview by author, April 25, 2013.

124 *"For writers to listen"*: Kelly, *Andy Griffith Show*, 110.

8. Men in a Hurry

126 *"order a cup of coffee"*: Griffith, interview by King, June 1, 1996.

126 *"Waal, you see"*: Uncredited, "The Sylacauga Flash," *TV Guide*, March 21, 1964.

127 *"this strange-looking man"*: Griffith, interview by King, November 27, 2003.

127 *"He read for me"*: Ruben, interview by Gelman.

127 *"Is this really"*: Jim Nabors, interview by author, December 27, 2012.

128 *"Heck, a lot of the boys"*: *Andy Griffith Show Reunion.*

128 *"the typical well-fed"*: Neal Brower, *Mayberry 101: Behind the Scenes of a TV Classic* (Winston-Salem, NC: John F. Blair, 1998), 91.

131 *"She had more dates"*: Leslie Raddatz, "Aneta Corsaut," *TV Guide*, May 20, 1967.

131 *"[They] admitted that they"*: Spignesi, *Mayberry, My Hometown*, 201.

131 *"I think he respected"*: Harrison and Habeeb, *Inside Mayberry*, 90.

132 *"that feminism that comes"*: Jennifer Scarlott, interview by author, October 24, 2013.

132 *"I know that our house"*: "Frances Bavier at Home," *TV Guide.*

133 *"And I remember we"*: Rance Howard, interview by author, October 8, 2013.

133 *"Absolutely not"*: Jim Nabors, interview by author, June 28, 2013.

9. A Date for Gomer

138 *"Three things made Andy"*: Linke, interview by author, November 17, 2014.

138 *"You play golf"*: Freeman, "I Think I'm Gaining on Myself."

139 *"Jim, has anybody"*: Nabors, interview by author, December 27, 2012.

139 *"I've always been out"*: Nabors, interview by author, June 28, 2013.

139 *"We kept quiet"*: Linke, interview by author, November 17, 2014.

140 *"You're shittin' me"*: Nabors, interview by author, December 27, 2012.

140 *"Well, Jim"*: Harrison and Habeeb, *Inside Mayberry*, 81.

140 *"You need some experience"*: Nabors, interview by author, December 27, 2012.

141 *"When one episode"*: Donahue, interview by author.

143 *"Warner Bros. released"*: Knotts, *Barney Fife* audio.

143 *"Jim and I"*: George Lindsey, *Goober in a Nutshell* (New York: Avon, 1995), 4.

144 *"He was paralyzed"*: Kelly, *Andy Griffith Show*, 49.

144 *"Andy Griffith had a big"*: Kit McNear, interview by author, September 25, 2013.

145 *"Gomer'll be back"*: Leslie Raddatz, "Dear Frayands," *TV Guide*, November 21, 1964.

10. Andy and Barney, Phfftt

147 *"was coming over"*: Jesse Corsaut, interview by author, January 17–18, 2013.

148 *"They were trying to"*: Sweeney, interview by author.

148 *"was always a horrible"*: Corsaut, interview by author.

148 *"That was true love":* Ronnie Schell, interview by author, January 18, 2014.

149 *"I have an idea how":* Linke, interview by author, November 17, 2014.

150 *"some pretty attractive":* Knotts with Metz, *Barney Fife*, 139.

150 *"We've got a new deal":* Kelly, *Andy Griffith Show*, 58.

151 *"When it got down":* Bash, interview by author, October 9, 2013.

152 *"Andy, if you'll be":* Griffith, interview by King, June 1, 1996.

152 *"If they'd been":* Ron Howard, interview by author.

153 *"I was really stunned":* Lynn, interview by author.

153 *"There was no rancor":* Ron Howard, interview by author.

153 *"Andy would get":* Peter Baldwin, interview by author, November 8, 2013.

154 *"So I never saw":* Tom Knotts, interview by author, February 20, 2014.

157 *"They're gone":* Collins, *Andy Griffith Story*, 80.

11. The Color Years

159 *"It worried Andy":* Brower, *Mayberry 101*, 456.

161 *"This is the last time":* Collins, *Andy Griffith Story*, 81.

162 *"cluttered with old"*: Raddatz, "Aneta Corsaut."

164 *"I think The Andy Griffith"*: Sam Bobrick, interview by author, September 25, 2013.

164 *"But there was also"*: Baldwin, interview by author.

165 *"I thought to myself"*: Knotts with Metz, *Barney Fife*, 141.

165 *"No, that's not"*: Griffith, interview by Rosen.

166 *"He was a master"*: Joan Staley, interview by author, February 4, 2013.

166 *"would come to work"*: Cox and Marhanka, *Incredible Mr. Don Knotts*, 76.

167 *"Have they told him"*: Schell, interview by author.

167 *"The three of us"*: Knotts with Metz, *Barney Fife*, 149–50.

169 *"I made up this"*: Lynn, interview by author.

170 *When he came home:* John Pyles, interview by author, January 6, 2015.

170 *"We talked about it"*: Kay Knotts, interview by author.

170 *"He would take us"*: Tom Knotts, interview by author, February 20, 2014.

171 *"Don and I would just"*: Griffith, remarks at the Don Knotts memorial.

171 *"I think, for Andy"*: Ron Howard, interview by author.

172 *"Most of us were":* Lindsey, *Goober in a Nutshell*, 9.

172 *They brought only:* Collins, *Andy Griffith Story*, 83.

173 *"just raved about it":* Harrison and Habeeb, *Inside Mayberry*, 100-101.

176 *"People kept coming up":* Cox and Marhanka, *Incredible Mr. Don Knotts*, 85.

176 *"Are you still going":* Nabors, interview by author, December 27, 2012.

177 *"to some nonsense":* "Griffith Determined to Leave 'Matlock,' " *Chicago Sun-Times*, November 12, 1990.

178 *"come to work without":* Bob Longino, "Griffith: Mayberry Set Was No Bed of Roses," *The Atlanta Journal-Constitution*, November 26, 1996.

180 *"They were well into":* Mike King, interview by author, April 25, 2013.

180 *"We did the* Joey*":* Schell, interview by author.

181 *"He had two personalities":* Linke, interview by author, November 17, 2014.

181 *"I felt strange":* Don Page, "Sheriff Dies in Boots," *Los Angeles Times*, March 14, 1968.

181 *That night, 251 guests:* Richard Warren Lewis, "The Wheels Keep Turning," *TV Guide*, July 20, 1968.

182 *"When we got":* Ron Howard, interview by author.

182 *"Well, it's been"*: Lewis, "Wheels Keep Turning."

12. The Death of Andy Taylor

183 *"wrote an entirely"*: Knotts with Metz, *Barney Fife*, 165.

183 *"The first night he"*: Barbara Rhoades, interview by author, January 25, 2013.

185 *"It was sort of"*: Sherwin Bash, interview by author, October 9, 2013.

185 *"Ooh, you're so cute"*: Karen Knotts, *Tied Up in Knotts*, performed September 28, 2012, in Mount Airy, NC.

185 *"Frank and I"*: Dorothy Manners, "Don Knotts a 'Womanizer!,' " *Los Angeles Herald-Examiner*, May 26, 1970.

185 *"I came out of"*: Maggie Peterson Mancuso, interview by author, February 5, 2013.

186 *"Who wants to"*: Barthel, "How to Merchandise an Actor."

186 *"I remember him crying"*: Schell, interview by author.

187 *"He was parked"*: Lee Meriwether, interview by author, December 19, 2013.

188 *"I talked to [Leticia"*: Ken Berry, interview by author, December 5, 2013.

189 *"We saw a lot of"*: Tom Knotts, interview by author, February 20, 2014.

190 *"Each of us had"*: Lindsey, *Goober in a Nutshell*, 109–10.

190 *"We'd go out to"*: Ken Berry, interview by author, December 6, 2012.

191 *"Here's the gal"*: Kerry L. Black, "Don Knotts Credits Mother with Launching TV Career," *Dominion-News* (Morgantown, WV), January 23, 1969.

192 *"Even though the sexual"*: Knotts with Metz, *Barney Fife*, 178.

192 *"I went to the theater"*: Tom Knotts, interview by author, February 20, 2014.

193 *"I just had this scene"*: Elaine Joyce, interview by author, January 27, 2014.

194 *"picked his male friends"*: Loralee Knotts, interview by author, April 14, 2014.

194 *"I spent six months"*: Knotts with Metz, *Barney Fife*, 182.

194 *"Nobody knows Andy"*: Barthel, "How to Merchandise an Actor."

194 *"were so enthralled"*: Bill Davidson, "Andy Griffith's $3,500,000 Misunderstanding," *TV Guide*, January 9, 1971.

195 *Dick conveyed the offer*: Carol Kramer, "Film Hopes Dashed, Andy Griffith Set for New TV Series," *Chicago Tribune*, February 9, 1970.

195 *"Andy was interested"*: Claudette Nevins, interview by author, January 8, 2014.

196 *"Griffith seems none too"*: Clarence Petersen, "Andy, CBS at Odds on Comic Line?," *Chicago Tribune*, July 7, 1970.

196 *"Print it"*: Davidson, "Andy Griffith's $3,500,000 Misunderstanding."

197 *"The truth, plain and simple"*: Ibid.

198 *Andy was furious*: Collins, *Andy Griffith Story*, 98.

199 *"For the first time"*: Knotts with Metz, *Barney Fife*, 182.

199 *"That's the hardest"*: Tom Knotts, interview by author, February 20, 2014.

200 *"He suffered so much"*: Joyce, interview by author.

201 *"CBS canceled all three"*: Kelly, *Andy Griffith Show*, 69.

201 *"you could have shot"*: Barbara Holsopple, " 'I Need This Series,' Desperate Andy Griffith Says," *Pittsburgh Press*, January 30, 1979.

202 *"Say, didn't you"*: Vernon Scott, "Andy Griffith Misses His Show," *The Palm Beach Post*, May 13, 1972.

202 *"had put my name"*: Knotts with Metz, *Barney Fife*, 184–85.

203 *"Barbara wasn't thick-skinned"*: Mal Vincent, "The Real Andy Griffith Lives among Us, Quietly," *The Virginian-Pilot*, February 17, 2008.

204 *"and that's when she dried"*: Mike King, interview by author, November 5, 2014.

204 *"It was an idyllic"*: Craig Fincannon, interview by author, February 26, 2014.

205 *"had a big pontoon"*: Quentin Bell, interview by author, February 23, 2014.

206 *"I don't think anybody"*: Griffith, interview by Griffith.

206 *"Andy and I are making"*: Genie Campbell, "He's a Red Hot Lover," *Elk Grove Herald*, June 23, 1972.

207 *"was a big deal"*: Jamie Smith-Jackson, interview by author, January 20, 2014.

207 *"I dreamed I hit"*: Bill King, "Andy Griffith Changes His Image," *The Atlanta Journal-Constitution*, February 13, 1983.

13. Second Chances, Second Wives

209 *"I had always thought"*: Knotts with Metz, *Barney Fife*, 195.

210 *"If I'm in the business"*: Tim Conway, interview by Karen Herman, April 20, 2004.

210 *"His career had just gone"*: Loralee Knotts, interview by author.

212 *"And it's up in"*: Tim Conway, interview by author, February 6, 2013.

212 *"Don would get in"*: Tim Conway, remarks at the Don Knotts memorial, May 4, 2006.

213 *"He was real close"*: Bell, interview by author.

213 *"She was funny"*: Berry, interview by author, December 5, 2013.

214 *"It was beautiful"*: Loralee Knotts, interview by author.

215 *"But it was all"*: Sharon Spelman, interview by author via e-mail, February 2014.

215 *"I need this series"*: Holsopple, " 'I Need This Series.' "

216 *"I did five pilots"*: Kent Demaret, "What It Is, Is the Tough Game of TV Ratings That Veteran Andy Griffith Is Playing Again," *People*, February 19, 1979.

217 *"Every day there would"*: Kim Weiskopf, interview included on DVD *Three's Company: Season 5* (Anchor Bay Entertainment, 2005).

217 *"He was a legend"*: Joyce DeWitt, interview by author, April 15, 2014.

217 *"I was totally aware"*: Richard Kline, interview by author, January 29, 2014.

217 *"Everybody was good"*: Don Knotts, interview included on DVD *Three's Company: Season 4* (Anchor Bay Entertainment, 2005).

217 *"what seemed to be"*: Chris Mann, *Come and Knock on Our Door: A Hers and Hers and His Guide to* Three's Company (St. Martin's Griffin, 1998), 119.

218 *"I was doing falls"*: Ibid., 122.

218 *"And God forbid"*: DeWitt, interview by author.

219 *"They started writing"*: Mann, *Come and Knock*, 163.

219 *"I've got a pad"*: Tom Knotts, interview by author, February 20, 2014.

219 *"a much smaller life"*: Loralee Knotts, interview by author.

220 *"He never said a kind"*: Bell, interview by author.

220 *"Then, I started"*: Roy Lakeman, "Andy's Long Road to Success," *Sunday Mail* (Queensland, Australia), October 11, 1987.

221 *"rough death"*: Edwards King, interview by author.

221 *"She had some problems"*: Frank Lovece, "Good Ol' Boy, 'Matlock's' Andy Griffith Has Aged Well," *Indiana (PA) Gazette*, December 18, 1991.

222 *"terrible, searing pain"*: Andy Griffith, "What Faith, Family Meant to Andy Griffith," *Guideposts*, November 1996.

14. The Gentleman Lawyer

223 *"Maybe it's a good"*: Griffith, "What Faith, Family Meant to Andy Griffith."

224 *"Andy was a remarkable"*: Dean Hargrove, interview by author, February 25, 2014.

226 *"they both agreed"*: Loralee Knotts, interview by author.

227 *"I will not say underwear"*: Harrison and Habeeb, *Inside Mayberry*, 49.

227 *"weren't all that unhappy"*: Dean Hargrove, e-mail interview by author, March 10, 2014.

227 *"When I got to"*: Lindsey, *Goober in a Nutshell*, 105.

228 *"how personal the show"*: Ron Howard,
interview by author.

228 *Mayberry fans flocked*: Collins, *Andy
Griffith Story*, 122.

228 *"Return to Mayberry was the nicest"*: Beck
and Clark, *Mayberry Memories*, 213.

229 *"The whole set was"*: Nancy Stafford,
interview by author, March 6, 2014.

230 *"There are those people"*: Joel Steiger,
interview by author, February 26, 2014.

230 *"He was enormously"*: Hargrove, interview
by author.

230 *"They squeaked, and"*: Jerry Buck, untitled
article, The Associated Press, April 12, 1987.

230 *"He was always"*: Stafford, interview by
author.

231 *"When I was doing"*: Griffith, interview by
Rosen.

231 *"His ideas of comedy"*: Hargrove, interview
by author.

232 *"He loved to invent"*: Stafford, interview by
author.

232 *"Andy was very fond"*: Hargrove, interview
by author.

232 *"I'd like to put"*: Steiger, interview by
author.

233 *"We had an instant"*: Francey Yarborough
Knotts, interview by author, March 6, 2014.

234 *"And I realized"*: Jerry Buck, untitled article,
The Associated Press, January 31, 1989.

234 *"He wanted to put Don"*: Steiger, interview by author.

235 *"We always gave Andy"*: Edward Greene, interview by author, February 22, 2014.

236 *"I'm sorry we didn't get"*: Longino, "Griffith: Mayberry Set Was No Bed of Roses."

236 *"I said that we absolutely"*: Tanya Jones, interview by author, March 10, 2014.

238 *Cindi clipped the article:* Jefferson Graham, "Court Resumes for Griffith's 'Matlock,' " *USA Today*, October 17, 1991.

238 *"She was his greatest"*: Stafford, interview by author.

239 *"Don's eyesight"*: Hargrove, interview by author.

239 *"crackle of excitement"*: Stafford, interview by author.

240 *"It didn't work"*: Griffith, interview by Rosen.

240 *"I told him that"*: Francey Yarborough Knotts, interview by author, March 19, 2014.

240 *"It was the same guy"*: Stella Berrier, interview by author, March 6, 2014.

241 *"I don't think Warren"*: Mark Mayfield, "Griffith's Winning Case," *USA Today*, January 13, 1993.

241 *"Andy, let me tell you"*: Linke, interview by author, November 17, 2014.

242 *"That's why he drank"*: King, interview by author, November 5, 2014.

242 *"falling out"*: Hargrove, interview by author.

243 *"I saw Andy walk"*: Fincannon, interview by author.

244 *"He came into my"*: Griffith, interview by Rosen.

244 *"He sang and sang"*: Francey Yarborough Knotts, interview by author, March 19, 2014.

245 *"They would line up"*: Dodie Brown, interview by author, February 28, 2014.

245 *"It's Don Knotts"*: Francey Yarborough Knotts, interview by author, March 13, 2013.

246 *"Then, he started calling me"*: Billy Bob Thornton, interview by author, May 25, 2015.

247 *"I had a little"*: Don Knotts, interview by Bill Dana and Jenni Matz, March 9, 2005.

247 *"The five years we"*: Mark Dawidziak, " 'Andy Griffith Show' Actors Still Have That Chemistry," Newhouse News Service, January 25, 2000.

15. Death in Mayberry

248 *"I have a feeling"*: Ferrara, interview by author, October 24, 2012.

249 *"he was really miserable"*: Ron Howard, interview by author.

249 *"a really brilliant"*: Ron Howard, interview by Larry King, March 1, 2006.

249 *"Oh, I love Don"*: Francey Yarborough Knotts, interview by author, November 21, 2012.

250 *"When we left"*: Francey Yarborough Knotts, interview by author, October 11, 2012.

251 *"He's seen the doctor"*: Ibid.

252 *"It was a beautiful"*: Dixie Nann Griffith, interview by author, November 29, 2012.

252 *"Don wanted us to"*: Griffith, remarks at Don Knotts memorial.

252 *"I'm not going to"*: Francey Yarborough Knotts, interview by author, October 11, 2012.

253 *"Jess, breathe"*: Andy Griffith, interview by Larry King, March 1, 2006.

254 *"I think it was really"*: Dixie Nann Griffith, interview by author, November 29, 2012.

254 *"Well, you know"*: Arvid Straube, interview by author, March 3, 2014.

255 *"And I remember it"*: Staley, interview by author.

256 *"Mayberry without Barney"*: Uncredited, "Fans Commission Don Knotts Statue," The Associated Press via Fox News, May 17, 2006.

257 *"this statue thing"*: Unsigned editorial, " 'Mayberry' Blues," *Winston-Salem Journal*, July 27, 2006.

258 *"Now they think that"*: Griffith, interview by Rosen.

259 *"Be firm"*: Martha Waggoner, "Sheriff Andy Steals Show in 'Waitress,' " The Associated Press, June 2007.

259 *"At age 81"*: Ibid.

260 *"So I would see Cindi"*: Bell, interview by author.

260 *"like he felt he"*: Francey Yarborough Knotts, interview by author, December 3, 2012.

261 *"was about making sure"*: Dixie Nann Griffith, interview by author, November 29, 2012.

261 *"Goll dang"*: Nabors, interview by author, December 27, 2012.

262 *"Apparently that was his"*: Dixie Nann Griffith, interview by author, November 29, 2012.

Photo Credits

30: © ImageCollect.com/Robert Dominguez/Globe Photos, Inc.
31: Paul Drinkwater/NBCU Photo Bank/Getty Images
32: © ImageCollect.com/Tammie Arroyo/ipol/Globe Photos, Inc.
34: Meribona
35: Bisse Bowman

About the Author

Daniel de Visé is an author and journalist. His first book, *I Forgot To Remember* (with Su Meck), began as a front-page article de Visé wrote for *The Washington Post*, part of a twenty-three-year career spent at the *Post*, *The Miami Herald*, and three other newspapers. De Visé has won more than two dozen national, regional, and local journalism awards, including a shared 2001 Pulitzer Prize for deadline reporting. His investigative reporting twice led to the release of wrongly convicted men from life terms in Florida prisons. De Visé's second book, *Andy and Don*, began as a journalistic exploration into the storied career of his late brother-in-law, Don Knotts. De Visé lives with his wife and children in Garrett Park, Maryland, where he can sometimes be found managing his son's youth baseball team or playing with the Stepping Stones, a Monkees cover band.

Center Point Large Print
600 Brooks Road / PO Box 1
Thorndike, ME 04986-0001 USA

(207) 568-3717

US & Canada:
1 800 929-9108
www.centerpointlargeprint.com